Alfred Ernest Daniell

London Riverside Churches

Alfred Ernest Daniell

London Riverside Churches

ISBN/EAN: 9783744791311

Printed in Europe, USA, Canada, Australia, Japan

Cover: Foto ©ninafisch / pixelio.de

More available books at **www.hansebooks.com**

LONDON RIVERSIDE CHURCHES

BY
A. E. DANIELL
AUTHOR OF "LONDON
CITY CHURCHES"

WITH 84 ILLUSTRATIONS
BY ALEXANDER ANSTED

WESTMINSTER
ARCHIBALD CONSTABLE & CO
2 WHITEHALL GARDENS
1897

BUTLER & TANNER,
THE SELWOOD PRINTING WORKS,
FROME, AND LONDON.

CONTENTS

	PAGE
INTRODUCTION	xi
ALL SAINTS, KINGSTON-UPON-THAMES	1
ST. PETER, PETERSHAM	9
ST. MARY MAGDALENE, RICHMOND	17
ST. MARY, TWICKENHAM	28
ALL SAINTS, ISLEWORTH	44
ST. ANNE, KEW	49
ST. MARY, MORTLAKE	56
ST. NICHOLAS, CHISWICK	63
ST. MARY, BARNES	74
ST. PAUL, HAMMERSMITH	79
ALL SAINTS, FULHAM	87
ST. MARY, PUTNEY	99
ALL SAINTS, WANDSWORTH	106
ST. MARY, BATTERSEA	113
ST. LUKE, CHELSEA	122
ST. MARY, LAMBETH	140
ST. JOHN THE EVANGELIST, WESTMINSTER	151
ST. MARGARET, WESTMINSTER	157
ST. MARTIN-IN-THE-FIELDS	181
ST. MARY-LE-STRAND	189
ST. CLEMENT DANES	195
ST. SAVIOUR, SOUTHWARK	207
ST. GEORGE THE MARTYR, SOUTHWARK	224
ST. OLAVE, SOUTHWARK	230
ST. MARY MAGDALENE, BERMONDSEY	234
ST. MARY, ROTHERHITHE	240

CONTENTS

	PAGE
St. George-in-the-East	250
St. Dunstan, Stepney	257
St. Anne, Limehouse	272
Poplar	278
St. Alfege, Greenwich	288
St. Paul, Deptford	299
St. Nicholas, Deptford	304

ILLUSTRATIONS

	PAGE
The Huguenot Graveyard, Wandsworth	*Frontispiece*
The Coronation Stone, Kingston-upon-Thames	1
Kingston Church	
Petersham Church	11
Ham House	15
Kean Memorial, Richmond Church	17
Richmond Church	19
Richmond Bridge	26
Twickenham Church	28
Twickenham, from the River	31
Isleworth, from Above	42
Isleworth, from Below	43
Kew Palace	50
Kew Church	51
Kew Church, West Front	53
Tombs of Gainsborough, Gardiner, Kirby, and Meyer	54
Mortlake Church	57
Mortlake View from Chiswick	59
Chiswick Old Church	65
Chiswick, from the River	69
A Street in Chiswick, with East End of Church	72
Barnes Church, from the South	74
Barnes Church, from the East	75
Barnes Bridge	76
Hammersmith Old Church (demolished)	80
Hammersmith New Church	81
Fulham Church and Putney Bridge	89

ILLUSTRATIONS

	PAGE
Fulham Church and the Bishops' Walk	91
Fulham and Putney Churches, from the River	95
Putney Church—the Sundial	99
Putney Church	101
Putney Church and Bridge	103
Wandsworth and the Wandle	106
Wandsworth Church	109
Battersea Church, West Front	113
Battersea Church	114
Battersea Church, Window in West Front	115
Chelsea, from the River	122
The Bray Tomb	123
The More Chapel	128
Chained Books	129
Lawrence Chapel	133
Lambeth Palace Gateway and Lambeth Church	140
Lambeth Church	143
Lambeth and Westminster, from the River	145
St. John's, Westminster—Main Front	151
St. John's, Westminster—View from River	152
St. Margaret's Church and the Abbey at Westminster	159
St. Margaret's, Westminster—West End	161
St. Margaret's, Westminster—Interior	163
St. Martin-in-the-Fields	183
St. Mary-le-Strand	191
St. Clement Danes—Holywell Street	196
St. Clement Danes	197
St. Saviour's, Southwark—South Aspect	206
St. Saviour's, Southwark—one Bay of Nave	207
St. Saviour's, Southwark—Nave and Transept	209
London Bridge, with St. Saviour's and St. Olave's Church, Southwark	211
St. George's Church, Southwark, from the North-east	225
St. George, Southwark—View from Borough High Street	227
St. George, Southwark—the Great Tomb	228
St. Olave's, Southwark—the Tower	230
St. Olave's Church	231
St. Mary Magdalene, Bermondsey—South View	234
St. Mary Magdalene, Bermondsey—West Front	237

ILLUSTRATIONS

	PAGE
Rotherhithe Church	240
Tomb of Captain Anthony Wood	241
Rotherhithe Churchyard	243
St. George-in-the-East—West Front	250
St. George-in-the-East—Interior	253
St. Dunstan's Church, Stepney	259
St. Dunstan, Stepney—South Porch	261
St. Anne's Church, Limehouse	272
St. Anne, Limehouse—the Tower	275
All Saints, Poplar	278
All Saints, Poplar—East End and Pulpit	281
St. Matthias, Poplar	283
St. Matthias, Poplar—Interior	285
St. Alfege, Greenwich	288
St. Alfege, Greenwich—Interior	293
St. Paul, Deptford	301
St. Nicholas, Deptford	304
St. Nicholas, Deptford—one of the Gateposts	305
St. Nicholas, Deptford—the Tower	307

INTRODUCTION

IN the following pages I have attempted to describe the most noteworthy churches situated on or near the banks of the Thames, between Kingston on the west and Greenwich on the east, omitting those within the City boundaries, with which I have already dealt in a former volume.

The edifices which I have thus grouped together are rich in interest, and that of a very varied kind. They claim the attention alike of the student of architecture and of the student of our history and literature. The former will view with delight the noble Early English work which he will find in St. Saviour's, Southwark, and will admiringly contemplate the fine examples of the Perpendicular period presented to him in the churches of St. Margaret, Westminster, Stepney and Kingston. In the church of St. Clement Danes he will do homage to the genius of Wren, and in its steeple he will observe the delicate art of Gibbs. Hard by are Gibbs's two greatest achievements, the churches of St. Mary-le-Strand and St. Martin-in-the-Fields. Lower down the river the peculiarities of the bolder, though less refined, Hawksmoor may be studied at St. George's-in-the-East, at Limehouse, and at Greenwich; while Archer's stately church of St. Paul, Deptford, cannot fail to be admired. Among edifices of recent construction, the rebuilt parish churches of Fulham and Chiswick—more especially the latter—must evoke warm commendation, and the new nave of St. Saviour's, Southwark, will be acknowledged to be worthy of the grand mediæval work with which it combines in forming so magnificent a whole.

INTRODUCTION

The man of letters will venerate St. Saviour's, Southwark, as the last resting-place of John Gower, Edmund Shakespeare, Fletcher, Massinger, and Bishop Andrewes. In Chelsea Old Church, he will mark the chapel and monument of Sir Thomas More, and the monument of the Duchess of Northumberland, Lady Jane Grey's mother-in-law. He will love to linger in St. Margaret's, Westminster, which will appeal to him both from its long connection with the House of Commons and as the place of interment of Caxton, Raleigh, Blake, and Milton's second wife. In St. John's, Westminster, he will remember that Churchill once ministered there. At St. Nicholas, Deptford, he will think of John Evelyn, and at Rotherhithe, of Gulliver. At St. Clement Danes, he will be reminded of Dr. Johnson; at St. George's, Southwark, of Charles Dickens. Twickenham is the burial-place of Pope; Richmond, of Thomson; Battersea, of Bolingbroke; Greenwich, of General Wolfe; Chiswick, of Hogarth; Kew, of Gainsborough; Mortlake, of Sir Philip Francis. Lambeth has tombs of Archbishops of Canterbury; Fulham, of Bishops of London; and Theodore Hook lies in Fulham Churchyard. In Hammersmith Church may be seen the bust of Charles I. and the urn beneath it, which constitute a lasting memorial of the devoted loyalty of Sir Nicholas Crispe.

Thus, there is here no want of matter to engage the inquirer, whether his tastes be artistic or literary. In conclusion, I would express the hope that I may be successful in imparting to others some portion at least of the very great pleasure which I have myself derived from the study of these sacred buildings.

THE CORONATION STONE

ALL SAINTS
KINGSTON-UPON-THAMES

KINGSTON-UPON-THAMES is a town of great antiquity. There is a strong probability that the Romans had a settlement here, and it was certainly a place of great importance in Saxon times. This seems to have been due to the fact that it was the next ford above London. Even as late as the middle of the sixteenth century, there was no bridge across the Thames between those of London and Kingston. Several of the Saxon kings were crowned here, and the chapel of St. Mary, which adjoined the church on the south side, was said to have been the scene of some of these ceremonies. Aubrey, in his *Antiquities of the County of Surrey*, describes the chapel as containing pictures of Kings Athelstane, Edred, Edwy, Edward the Martyr, and Ethelred, and also a picture of King John, who gave the town its first charter in 1200. In 1730 the chapel fell down, the pillars having been undermined by the incautious grave-digging of the sexton, who was himself buried in the ruins.

The stone on which the kings are reputed to have been crowned has, however, been preserved. It was removed from the church to the market-place. In 1850 it was placed in its present position in front of the Court House, and, for its better protection, mounted on a granite base, which is surmounted by an iron railing in the Early English style. The stone itself is a rugged boulder of no particular shape. The granite base is heptagonal, and its sides are inscribed with the names and dates of the following Saxon kings, said to have been crowned on the stone: Edward, 901; Athelstane, 924; Edmund, 943; Edred, 946; Edwy, 955; Edward, 975; Ethelred, 978. A silver penny of each of these monarchs has been inserted above his name. The design was furnished by Mr. C. E. Davis of Bath, and the total cost of the work was £140: £50 was granted by the Corporation, and the remainder was raised by subscription.

The church of All Saints, Kingston, is situated close to the market-place and bridge. It was appropriated by Henry II. to the Abbey of Merton, to which it continued to belong till the suppression by Henry VIII. In 1344 the church was polluted with blood, and a commission was issued to reconcile it. In 1367 the inhabitants were cited to repair their chancel, which had become very ruinous. In 1445, when "On Candlemas Even in divers places of England was great weathering of wind, hayle, snow, rayne, thunders with lightning," and many churches were damaged by the storm, and the steeple of Old St. Paul's was set on fire, "The steeple of Kingston in Surrey," Stow records in his *Annals*, "was also fired by the same lightnings." William of Worcester tells us further, that "One in the church died through fear of a spirit which he saw there." In 1505 the steeple was

KINGSTON CHURCH

extensively repaired, and as the name of Robert Somersby, "sometime vicar of Kyngston," who had died in 1502, was inscribed on the tower, it seems probable that he bequeathed money towards the reparation. In Aubrey's time there was a leaded steeple, but this was severely injured in the memorable storm of November 27, 1703. The upper part of the tower was rebuilt of brick in 1708; the parishioners were also desirous of re-erecting the spire, but, as their resources were scanty, and an appeal which they made for assistance to the House of Commons met with an unfavourable response, they were compelled to relinquish their design. In 1721 the aisles were rebuilt of brick.

The church is cruciform, and is remarkable as possessing three chancels; but an organ has been erected at the north of the middle chancel, and the north chancel has been turned into a vestry. The south chancel appears to date from the close of the fourteenth century, and this and the lower part of the tower are probably the oldest existing portions of the church. The north chancel is decidedly less ancient, and may be ascribed to the conclusion of the fifteenth or the commencement of the sixteenth century. The nave belongs to the Perpendicular period, and is separated from the aisles by octangular columns and pointed arches. The tower is central, rising from between the nave and chancels. It is of massive proportions, and the lower and ancient portion is of flint and stone. The brick upper part is completed by a pineapple at each corner, and a long flagstaff, surmounted by a vane, crowns the centre. In consequence of the spire never having been rebuilt, the tower, which is 81 feet in height, appears somewhat short in proportion to the size of the church. It contains ten bells. Kingston Church is one of the largest in Surrey, measuring 155 feet in length by 97 feet 6 inches in breadth at the widest part, and it presents an aspect of stately dignity not often met with in a parish church. It was restored in 1862, and the western portion underwent a further reparation a few years ago. The eighteenth century galleries have been taken away, and a new open timber roof has been erected. A new organ has been set up as a memorial of a late vicar, the Rev. H. P. Measor. Further repairing operations are contemplated for the chancel and tower.

There are finely executed figures in brass, about three feet high, and in very good preservation, of Robert Skern, who died in 1437, and his wife, Joan. They were formerly attached to the floor in front of the communion table, but are now, for fear of injury from their being trodden on, fastened to one of the pillars of the chancel. Skern, who was a lawyer, is represented in a gown. He lived in Kingston parish in a house called Downe Hall. His wife was a daughter of Alice Perrers, Edward III.'s mistress. Another of this family, William Skern, founded a chantry at Kingston during the reign of Henry VI. There is another fifteenth century brass, which is affixed to one of the pillars beneath the tower. This is on a much smaller scale than Skern's, and displays figures of John Hertcombe, who died in 1488, and his wife, Katherine, who died in 1477, in an attitude of devotion. John, who is attired in the dress of a merchant, is in perfect condition, but Katherine has unluckily lost her head.

Against the south chancel wall is an altar tomb, on which is a recumbent effigy in alabaster of Sir Anthony Benn. Sir Anthony, who died in his fiftieth year on September 29, 1618, had been Recorder of Kingston, and was at the period of his death Recorder of London. He is represented in gown and ruff. The gown was originally painted scarlet, but only a few slight traces of the colouring are now discernible. His widow, Jane, by whom the monument was erected, was a daughter of John Evelyn of Godstone, the Diarist's uncle. Near Benn's monument, on the same wall, is a tablet to Colonel Anthony Fane, a son of the Earl of Westmoreland, who married his daughter, Amabel. He died at Kingston in December, 1642, from the results of a wound which he had received at the siege of Farnham. Beneath Fane's memorial is an old altar tomb, surmounted by a canopy, with no inscription or figure or coat of arms remaining. It has been—somewhat indecently, it must be confessed—made use of for the accommodation of a monument to Lieutenant Colonel George Jenkinson, a brother of the first Earl of Liverpool, who died in 1823. The remains of two other Gothic monuments, of which the history has been utterly lost, may be observed, one against the east and the other against the north wall of the vestry at the north of the chancel. In the south chancel is a statue of Louisa Theodosia, first wife of the second Earl of Liverpool, the Prime Minister. She was the third daughter of Frederick Augustus Hervey, fourth Earl of Bristol, who as Bishop of Derry had played a very prominent part in Irish politics. Her statue, which is of white marble, shows her in a sitting position: it is by Chantrey, and is a very fine piece of work. The inscription is as follows:—

> "Louisa Theodosia, Countess of Liverpool, born February, 1767, died June, 1821. She visited the fatherless and widows in their affliction, and kept herself unspotted from the world."

Further west, against the south wall, is a statue by Chantrey's pupil, Ternough, of Henry Davidson, who is also displayed seated. This, too, is very well executed. The inscription is brief: "Hic jacet in expectatione diei supremi Henricus Davidson, ob. vii Jan., 1827, aet 56. Qualis erat iste dies indicabit." Close by is a monument, ornamented with a weeping female figure, to Henry Davidson, of Tulloch, N.B., who died in 1781: his son Duncan, who died in 1799: and Lucy, the wife of Duncan, who died in 1777.

Among the remaining monuments two brass plates are noticeable. One is to Mark Snellinge, who was nine times bailiff of Kingston, and a great benefactor to the town, and died in 1633.

The other was placed in the church in the time of the Commonwealth in memory of the ten children of Edmund Staunton, D.D., who had been vicar of Kingston, but was then President of Corpus Christi College, Oxford: a piece of preferment which he obtained as a reward for his zealous advocacy of the Puritan cause. The children have a quaint rhyming epitaph, one line of which describes them as:—

"Seven sons and daughters three, Job's number right."

The mural monuments are numerous, but the inscriptions are rather difficult to decipher. They include those of Dr. George Bate, physician successively to Charles I., Cromwell, and Charles II., who died in 1668, and Captain Francis Wilkinson, who beautified the whole body of the church at his own charge, and died in 1681. William Cleave, Alderman of London, the founder of the picturesque almshouses in the London Road, was buried beneath the south chancel in 1667. At the east end of the nave hang the colours of the old 3rd Royal Surrey Militia, which now forms the 4th Battalion of the East Surrey Regiment.

The patronage of the benefice of Kingston, after passing through a good many hands, came into the possession of the Hardinges. On the wall of the north aisle is a tablet to the memory of Nicholas Hardinge. He was the elder son of Gideon Hardinge, vicar of Kingston, and was born in 1699. He was distinguished as a scholar and antiquary, and held the offices of Recorder of Kingston and Chief Clerk in the House of Commons. The latter post he disposed of in 1747 to Jeremiah Dyson, the generous friend of the poet Akenside. He died in April, 1758. His son, George Hardinge, who became Senior Justice of the counties of Brecon, Glamorgan, and Radnor, and to whom we are indebted for some anecdotes of Akenside, with whom he and his father became acquainted through the latter's business with Dyson, parted with the advowson in 1786 to the Provost and Fellows of King's College, Cambridge, who have ever since remained patrons.

In the central chancel, within the rails, is a large altar monument to Mr. Williams, the late vicar. There are several memorial windows. That at the east end of the south chancel commemorates the Rev. Samuel Whitlock Gundy, who died on Christmas Day, 1851, having been vicar of Kingston for thirty-five years. The one at the west end of the south aisle is in memory of Mr. Henry Shrubsole, thrice in succession—1877, 1878, and 1879—chosen Mayor of Kingston. The south transept window is to the memory of his brother, Mr. John Shrubsole, and there is a monument in the form of a scroll to his parents against one of the pillars of the south aisle. A fountain has been erected in the market-place as a public memorial to Mr. Henry Shrubsole; it is stated in the inscription that he "died suddenly in the third year of his office, whilst presiding on an occasion of public charity," January 18, 1880.

ST PETER
PETERSHAM

THE village of Petersham obtained its name, and the church its dedication, from the manor having been a possession of the Abbey of St. Peter at Chertsey, to which it belonged as far back as the time of the Conquest. When Henry II. appropriated the church of Kingston-upon-Thames to Merton Abbey, he annexed to it the chapel of Petersham amongst others; and Petersham continued a chapel of ease to Kingston till 1769, when it was united with Kew, and the two were made one vicarage. It is now a separate vicarage, in the gift of the Crown.

A church existed at Petersham at the period of the Conquest, for mention is made of it in Domesday. In 1505 the church is stated to have been rebuilt; but the chancel, the walls of which are rough-cast, and which possesses a decorated window, would appear to have been originally a portion of the previous building. The remainder of the church is of red brick. It was repaired and enlarged in 1790, and again in 1820. At the west end is a short tower surmounted by a small cupola-shaped turret, and beneath it is a porch through which the main entrance is reached. Long transepts having been built out on the north and south, the church has become cruciform. The old fittings have been retained. The pulpit stands on the north side of the entrance to the chancel, and on the south side is a high reading desk with clerk's desk below. The pews are high and roomy.

RIVERSIDE CHURCHES

There are galleries on the north, west, and south, in the last of which the organ is placed. Above the entrance to the chancel the royal arms are affixed. There are three hatchments against the east wall of the transepts. The old-fashioned appearance of the church would have a decidedly picturesque effect, if only the woodwork were of a better class; unfortunately it is but commonplace. The font, which stands at the west, was presented as a memorial of an infant, as appears by the inscription upon it: " Georgina Ellen Hussey, born February 11, died September 5, 1874."

On the north side of the chancel is a fine monument to George Cole, who died in 1624, and Frances, his wife, who died in 1633. Two Corinthian columns of black marble support an elaborate canopy, culminating in a pediment broken to allow room for a coat of arms. Beneath are reclining effigies of the husband and wife. He is represented clothed in a black gown, has a ruff round his neck and a cap on his head; his right hand supports his head, and his left holds a roll. She is shown in the usual costume of the time, with a ruff and head-dress; she rests on her right elbow with the hand hanging down, and in her left hand she clasps a book. George Cole, who was a member of the Middle Temple, was granted a lease of the manor of Petersham by James I. His son, Gregory Cole, sold the family mansion—Petersham Lodge—to Charles I. It was destroyed by fire in 1721, and rebuilt by the Earl of Burlington for its then possessor the Earl of Harrington, whose second title was Viscount Petersham. Thomson, in his description, in *Summer*, of the landscape from Richmond Hill, mentions—

> " The pendant woods
> That nodding hang o'er Harrington's retreat."

From the Harrington family it passed to Lord Camelford, who

PETERSHAM CHURCH.

in 1784 purchased the fee-simple from the Crown, and in 1790 sold the property to the Duke of Clarence. The house was pulled down about sixty years ago, and the grounds were incorporated with Richmond Park.

On the opposite site of the chancel is an ornate monument to Sir Thomas Jenner, who was appointed Recorder of London in 1683, and at the commencement of 1686 was made a Baron of the Exchequer, and a few months later a Justice of the Common Pleas. He died, in his sixty-ninth year, on January 7, 1707.

On the north of the chancel, to the west of Cole's monument, is a tablet to Thomas Gilbert, who died in 1766, aged fifty-four. The inscription tells us that he was educated at Eton, and subsequently studied at both Universities, and that he was inspired in these seats of learning with a fondness for composing Greek and Latin verses which accompanied him through life, for nothing could tear him away from the cultivation of this art, which he practised with no ordinary knowledge and eloquence. His moral qualities also receive a glowing eulogium. His epitaph is written in Latin, and a Greek couplet is appended at the conclusion, surely a highly appropriate method of commemorating so enthusiastic a classical scholar. On the other side of the chancel, west of Jenner's monument, is a tablet erected by the inhabitants in memory of the Rev. Robert Mark Delafosse, who died in 1819, after ministering at Petersham for nearly forty years. Underneath is a tablet to a grandson and granddaughter of his, children of his son, the Rev. D. C. Delafosse, who was vicar of Wandsworth, and afterwards of Shere in Surrey. His second son, John Robert Delafosse, who died at Boulogne in 1856, has a monument in the churchyard.

On the east wall of the north transept is an urn with an inscription to Jane Long, daughter of James Long of Draycott in Wiltshire, who died at the early age of eleven, in December, 1651. On the west wall of the north transept is a tablet to the memory of Captain Vancouver, the maritime discoverer. The inscription is as follows :—

> "In the cemetery adjoining this church were interred in the year 1798, the Mortal Remains of Captain George Vancouver, R.N., whose valuable and enterprising voyage of Discovery to the North Pacific Ocean, and round the World during five years of laborious survey, added greatly to the geographical knowledge of his countrymen.
>
> "To the Memory of that celebrated Navigator this monumental Tablet is erected by the Hudson's Bay Company."

Next to Vancouver's memorial, on the south side, is a tablet to Caroline Maria, Duchess Dowager of Montrose, widow of James, third Duke of Montrose, and daughter of George, fourth Duke of Manchester. She died in 1847 in her seventy-seventh year, and lies buried in a vault beneath the church. Close to the entrance from the vestibule into the nave are tablets to Lieutenant-General the Honourable Sir Charles Stuart, Governor of Minorca, and his son, Captain John Stuart, R.N., of whom the former died in 1801 and the latter in 1811. They were respectively son and grandson to the celebrated John, Earl of Bute, George III.'s unpopular minister. On the south wall are tablets to Lieutenant-General Sir William Moore, who died in 1862, and the Rev. Richard Burch Byam, who died in 1867, aged eighty-two. Mr. Byam had been for thirty-eight years vicar of Kew and Petersham, and this memorial was erected by his parishioners and friends.

On the east wall of the south transept is a tablet to a lady whose father and husband were both Deans of Hereford. This was Elizabeth Jane Mellish, who died at the age of seventy-six in February, 1862. She was the daughter of the Very Rev. William Leigh, and the wife of the Very Rev. Edward Mellish. On the same wall is a monument to Vice-Admiral Sir George Scott, who died in 1841. Some naval imagery is introduced at the conclusion of this sailor's epitaph.

> "Trusting to that Hope which is as an Anchor to the soul, both sure and stedfast, he now rests in the Haven where he would be, the Bosom of his Saviour and his God."

On a tomb above his grave in the churchyard the same sentiment is expressed with some slight verbal differences.

In the churchyard are monuments to several members of the nobility. Here, too, were interred Mary and Agnes Berry, in whose society Horace Walpole took such great delight, and for whose benefit he wrote his *Reminiscences of the Courts of George I. and II.* Both sisters died in 1852, Mary in her ninetieth and Agnes in her eighty-eighth year. The inscription on the stone which covers the vault where their bodies rest was written by the Earl of Carlisle. Hard by is the tomb of Isabella Harrott, who was "for nearly sixty years" their "faithful and devoted housekeeper." She survived them, and had attained the age of ninety, when she died towards the close of 1854. On a handsome coffer-shaped tomb of red and grey granite is an inscription to Albert Harry Scott, student of Exeter College, Oxford, third son of George Gilbert and Caroline Scott, who died January 30, 1865, in his twenty-first year. This was a son of Sir Gilbert Scott, the architect, who then resided at the Manor House at Ham.

The churchyard, which extends to the east and north-east of the church, is a pleasant spot, and excellently kept; and the situation of the church between the Richmond Road and the river is a very agreeable one. With its quaint little turret and its north front shrouded with ivy, it is a most picturesque object when viewed from the meadows of the waterside.

In the parish register is the following noteworthy entry:—

> "The ryght honourable John Earl of Lauderdale was married to the ryght honourable Elizabeth Countess Desart, by the Reverend Father in God Walter Lord Bishop of Worcester, in the church at Petersham, on the 17th day of Februarie, 1671-2, publiquely in the time of reading the common-prayer; and gave the carpet, pulpit cloth, and cushion."

HAM HOUSE

This Earl of Lauderdale was the minister of Charles II. whose initial supplied the final letter of the "cabal." He was subsequently created Duke of Lauderdale in the Scottish peerage, and Baron Petersham and Earl of Guildford in England. The Countess of Dysart, whom he thus married in Petersham Church, had inherited Ham House from her father, the first Earl. She was buried at Petersham in June, 1696, but has no memorial.

By Lauderdale, who was her second husband, she had no children; but through her daughter by her first husband, Sir Lionel Tollemache, the earldom of Dysart was perpetuated, and Ham House has ever since continued the property of this family.

ST MARY MAGDALENE RICHMOND

KEAN MEMORIAL, RICHMOND CHURCH

THE church of St. Mary Magdalene, Richmond, is situated at the end of Church Court, a narrow passage which branches off on the left-hand side as one ascends the hill, a little above the London road. The old battlemented tower of flint and stone, which contains eight bells, presents a pleasing appearance; but the body of the church, which is of brick and has been several times altered, is not particularly attractive. It includes nave, chancel, and two aisles. But though the fabric is commonplace, its associations and numerous monuments render Richmond Church one of the most interesting in the neighbourhood of the metropolis.

The earliest monument is a brass tablet, with kneeling effigies, in the chancel to "Mr. Robert Cotton, gentleman, some time Officer of the removing Wardroppe of Bedds to Queene Marie, whoe by her Ma^{ts} speciale choice was taken from the Wardroppe to serve her Ma{ti} as a groom in her Privie Chamber al her lyfe time, and after her decease again he became an Officer of the Wardroppe where he served her Ma{tie} that now is Queen Elizabeth many yeres, and died Yeoman of the same Office." The date of his death is not stated. Walter Hickman of Kew, who died in 1617, has a monument in the chancel with kneeling effigy and some moral lines on the transitoriness of human life. Near this is a memorial to "the Lady Margaret Chudleigh, Daughter of Sir William Coortney of Powderham, Knight, by Elizabeth his wife, daughter to Henry Earl of Rutland—first wife to Sir Warwick Hele, Knight, and afterwards to Sir John Chudleigh of the same order." She died in 1628. There are kneeling figures of her and Sir John. Another monument with kneeling figures commemorates Dame Dorothy Wright, who was the widow of Sir George Wright, and died in 1631. Sir George, who predeceased her by nearly eight years, had founded in 1600 some almshouses at Richmond for eight poor women, which he named in honour of his sovereign, "Queen Elizabeth's Almshouses." They were originally erected under the hill, but in 1767 they were rebuilt, on an enlarged plan, in their present situation in the Vineyard.

A small brass tablet recalls the stirring scenes of the great rebellion. It is to the memory of Margaret Jay. She was the wife of Thomas Jay, "in these unhappy wars his Ma'tties Commissiary Generall for p'visions, for all his armyes of Horse," and the mother of Thomas Jay, "Captn. of Horse, whose short life was beautifyed with many graces of nature and rare pieces of arte, and his end exprest his loyalty and courage." High on the south wall is the monument of a gentleman who, though he lived in those warlike times, was of an eminently pacific disposition. This was Robert Lewis, a Welshman and a barrister-at-law, who died in 1649. He was, according to his epitaph, so great a lover

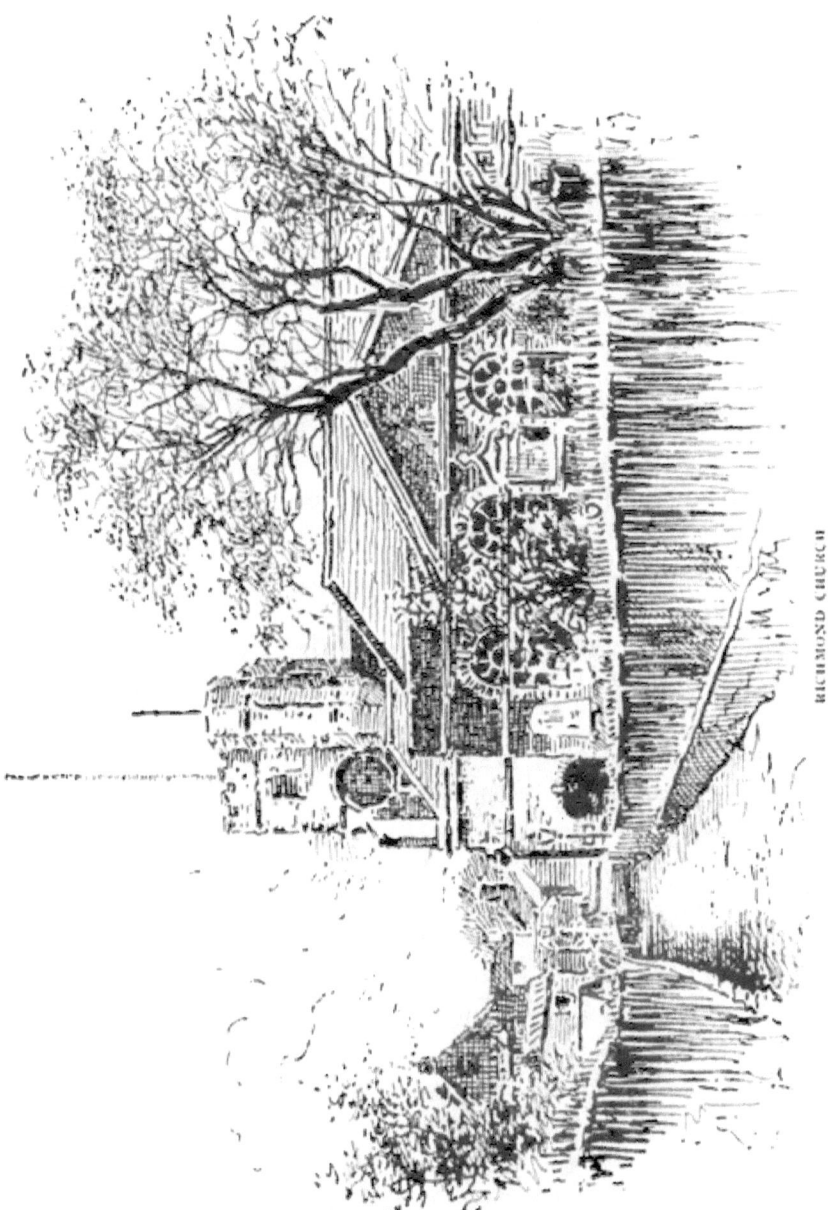

RICHMOND CHURCH.

of peace that, when a contention began to arise between life and death, he immediately yielded up the ghost to end the dispute.

There is a monument in the chancel to Henry, Lord Viscount Brouncker, of the kingdom of Ireland, cofferer to King Charles II. He was younger brother of William, the scientific lord, who was, from its incorporation in 1662 till 1677, President of the Royal Society, and in 1684 he succeeded to the title, which on his death, in 1688, became extinct. Pepys was assured by his friend Captain Cocke "that Henry Brouncker is one of the shrewdest fellows for parts in England, and a dangerous man." The diarist expresses a very unfavourable opinion of him: "He was a pestilent rogue, an atheist, that would have sold his king and country for sixpence almost, so corrupt and wicked a rogue he is by all men's report."

Beneath the chancel floor was interred another member of the nobility, Charles, the last Lord Howard of Escrick, who died in 1715, and in the following year his mother was laid beside him. She was the widow of that William, Lord Howard of Escrick, Dryden's "canting Nadab," who was implicated in the Ryehouse Plot, and, as Sir Walter Scott puts it, "did not hesitate to contaminate the noblest name in England" by turning informer against Russell and Sidney.

But the most memorable person buried at Richmond is James Thomson, the poet of the *Seasons*, who here sleeps amongst the scenes which he so deeply loved and so beautifully celebrated. He died at his house in the lane between the Green and the Kew Road, on August 27, 1748, and was buried on the 29th. A monument was erected to his memory in Westminster Abbey in 1762, but the "Druid's" "sylvan grave" remained for many years unmarked. At length, in 1792, a brass plate was placed on the west wall at the end of the north aisle, by Thomson's fellow-countryman and enthusiastic admirer, the Earl of Buchan.

ST MARY MAGDALENE, RICHMOND

The inscription, which concludes with a well-known passage from *Winter*, is as follows:—

> "In the earth, below this tablet,
> are the remains of
> James Thomson,
> Author of the beautiful poems entituled
> 'The Seasons,' the 'Castle of Indolence,' &c.,
> who died at Richmond
> on the 27th of August
> and was buried
> on the 29th O — S — 1748.
> The Earl of Buchan,
> unwilling that
> so good a Man, and sweet a Poet
> should be without a memorial,
> has denoted the place of his interment
> for the satisfaction of his Admirers
> in the year of our Lord
> M.DCC.XCII.
>
> 'Father of Light and life, Thou Good Supreme!
> O teach me what is good, teach me Thyself·
> Save me from folly, vanity, and vice,
> From every low pursuit, and feed my soul
> With knowledge, conscious peace, and virtue pure,
> Sacred, substantial, never-fading bliss!'"

The tablet, which is not large, is placed rather high on the wall, and, as it sadly needs cleaning, the inscription is somewhat difficult to read. But the poet has a more prominent memorial. Few of those who

> "Ascend,
> While radiant summer opens all its pride,
> Thy hill, delightful Shene!"

fail to observe on the very summit within the Park, the board bearing "Lines on James Thomson, the Poet of Nature."

In the chancel is a monument to William Rowan, King's

Counsel, and Fellow of Trinity College, Dublin, who died in
1767, with a bust, the workmanship of which was very highly
commended by Chantrey. To the north of the chancel is an
elaborate monument, erected long subsequent to their decease
in memory of two theatrical celebrities, Richard and Mary Ann
Yates, the former of whom died in 1796, the latter in 1787.
Their histrionic abilities are criticised by Churchill in the *Rosciad*.
Yates' qualifications he considered as restricted to the representation of the meaner sort of characters :—

"In characters of low and vulgar mould,
Where nature's coarsest features we behold ;
Where, destitute of every decent grace,
Unmannered jests are blurted in your face ;
There, Yates with justice strict attention draws,
Acts truly from himself, and gains applause :
But when, to please himself or charm his wife,
He aims at something in politer life,
When, blindly thwarting nature's stubborn plan,
He treads the stage by way of gentleman,
The clown, who no one touch of breeding knows,
Looks like Tom Errand dressed in Clincher's clothes,
Fond of his dress, fond of his person grown,
Laughed at by all, and to himself unknown,
From side to side he struts, he smiles, he prates,
And seems to wonder what's become of Yates."

He admired the beauty of Mrs. Yates, but did not rate her
talents as an actress highly :—

"Might figure give a title unto fame,
What rival should with Yates dispute her claim ?
But justice may not partial trophies raise,
Nor sink the actress in the woman's praise.
Still hand in hand her words and actions go,
And the heart feels more than the features show ;
For, through the regions of that beauteous face,
We no variety of passions trace ;

> Dead to the soft emotions of the heart,
> No kindred softness can those eyes impart ;
> The brow, still fixed in sorrow's sullen frame,
> Void of distinction, marks all parts the same."

At the east end of the south aisle is a tablet to Gilbert Wakefield with this inscription :—

> "In the adjoining churchyard, at the east end of the chancel, lie the remains of Gilbert Wakefield, A.B. formerly Fellow of Jesus College, Cambridge, third son of George Wakefield, A.M. late vicar of Kingston and Minister of this parish ; he died September 9, 1801, aged forty-five.
>
> "Simplicity of manners and benevolence of temper, united with eminent intellectual accomplishments, greatly endeared him in private life. To the public he was known by high attainments in biblical and classical literature, and the honesty and intrepidity of his endeavours to promote the cause of truth and liberty. Sustained by the affection of numerous and estimable friends, as well as by the testimony of conscience, he endured with fortitude a State prosecution, and two years' imprisonment, for his 'Reply to the Address of the Bishop of Landaff to the people of Great Britain.' Returning from the County prison of Dorchester, with an unbroken spirit but impaired strength, and resuming his accustomed exertions, he sunk under them fourteen weeks after his enlargement. The expectation of immortality by the Christian covenant, and the remembrance of his conscientious life, enabled him to meet death with complacency. His loss, irreparable to his wife and children, was deeply regretted by all his friends and relations.
>
> "Thomas Wakefield, B.A. the Minister of this parish, erects this memorial of his brother's desert and his own affection."

Thomas Wakefield, after officiating at Richmond for thirty years, died in November, 1806. There is a tablet to his memory, near that to his brother. Their father, George Wakefield, who preceded Thomas in the curacy of Richmond, has also a memorial. He died in February, 1776, having been for eighteen years rector of St. Nicholas, Nottingham, and Claypole, Lincolnshire, and for nine years vicar of Kingston and minister of Richmond.

On the south wall is an exceedingly graceful monument by Flaxman to Barbara Lowther (died 1805), sister of the first Earl of Lonsdale, and of the last Duchess of Bolton, by the latter of whom it was erected. This Duchess was the lady to whom, as Katherine Lowther, General Wolfe was engaged; whose portrait he always wore, till the night before his final victory, when, having a presentiment that he should fall, he entrusted it to his sailor friend, John Jervis, afterwards Lord St. Vincent. She died in 1809. At the east end of the south aisle is another of Flaxman's works—a memorial to the Rev. Robert Mark Delafosse, whose tablet in Petersham Church has been already noticed. It includes a medallion portrait, and was set up, as we learn from the Latin inscription, by his former pupils. In the chancel is an elaborate monument by the younger Bacon, commemorating Major George Bean, who fell at Waterloo.

Affixed to the north wall, on the outside, is a large monument to Sir Matthew Decker; his widow; his daughter Catherine, Viscountess Fitzwilliam; and his grandson Richard, the seventh Viscount Fitzwilliam. Sir Matthew Decker, who died in 1749, was a very charitable man and a benefactor to the parish. He resided at Wentworth House, on the north side of the Green, which was subsequently occupied by his grandson. It was here that Lord Fitzwilliam kept that magnificent collection of books, pictures, etc., which he bequeathed to the University of Cambridge, of which he was a graduate, together with £100.000 for the erection of a museum to contain it. Lord Fitzwilliam died, aged seventy-one, on February 5, 1816.

On the west front of the church, to the south of the tower, is a tablet to Edmund Kean, who died in a room adjoining the Richmond Theatre, of which he was lessee. Beneath a medallion portrait of the great tragedian is this simple inscription:

> "Edmund Kean
> Died May 1833
> Aged 48
> A memorial erected by his son
> Charles John Kean
> 1839."

Close to this, at the west end of the south wall, is a monument by Wyon to Barbara Hofland, "Relict of Thomas Christopher Hofland, Artist, Authoress of 'The Son of a Genius,' etc., etc." She was a prolific writer of tales for the young, and died at Richmond on November 9, 1844, aged seventy-four.

Richmond is fertile in memories of the stage. In addition to Kean and the Yateses, it is the last resting-place of James Fearon, an actor of some repute in his day, who died in 1789. He was buried in the churchyard, with an epitaph stating that "in dramatic life he held the mirror up to nature; in private life he fulfilled the duties relative and social, and as he lived respected he died lamented." And another and earlier player is said to have been interred here. This was Joseph Taylor, who is reported to have been instructed by Shakespeare to play Hamlet, and to have played it "incomparably well." He was appointed Yeoman of the Revels to Charles I., and died about 1653. The parish register does not extend so far back, but Wright, in the *Historia Histrionica*, states that he was buried at Richmond.

Amongst those interred in the newer burying ground are Dr. John Moore, the author of *Zeluco*, and editor and biographer of

RIVERSIDE CHURCHES

Smollett, and father of the Hero of Corunna, who died in 1802; and Lady Diana Beauclerk, widow of Johnson's friend Topham Beauclerk, who died in 1808.

When Thomson lived at Richmond, he was frequently visited there by his friend George Lyttelton, afterwards Lord Lyttelton, to whose constant kindness he was indebted for considerable benefits, and whose sterling worth he has immortalized in *Spring* and the *Castle of Indolence*. It was at Thomson's house that

RICHMOND BRIDGE

Lyttelton wrote his *Observations on the Conversion and Apostleship of St. Paul*. But this is not the only connection of the family with Richmond. Sir Thomas Lyttelton, the father of Thomson's friend, was baptized here on December 20, 1685. He was the son of Sir Charles Lyttelton. Sir Charles was Lord Brouncker's executor, as appears by that nobleman's epitaph, and resided at West Sheen before he inherited the estate at Hagley. Another interesting name in the register is that of Hester

Johnson, Swift's Stella, baptized at Richmond on March 20, 1681.

The church of Richmond was originally a chapel of ease to Kingston, by the vicar of which the curate was appointed. Among the curates was Nicholas Brady, remembered from the metrical version of the Psalms which he and Nahum Tate produced. He was an Irishman, and, having come over to England, was in 1691 appointed curate of St. Katherine Cree, in the city of London. In 1696 he left St. Katherine Cree, and became curate of Richmond. In 1702 he also obtained the rectory of Stratford-on-Avon. This he resigned on receiving the rectory of Clapham in 1706, but he continued to hold the curacy of Richmond, where he resided, and kept a school, for the remainder of his life. He died at Richmond in 1726, and was buried in the church, but there is no memorial to him.

In 1769 Richmond was made a perpetual curacy. The living is now a vicarage in the gift of King's College, Cambridge.

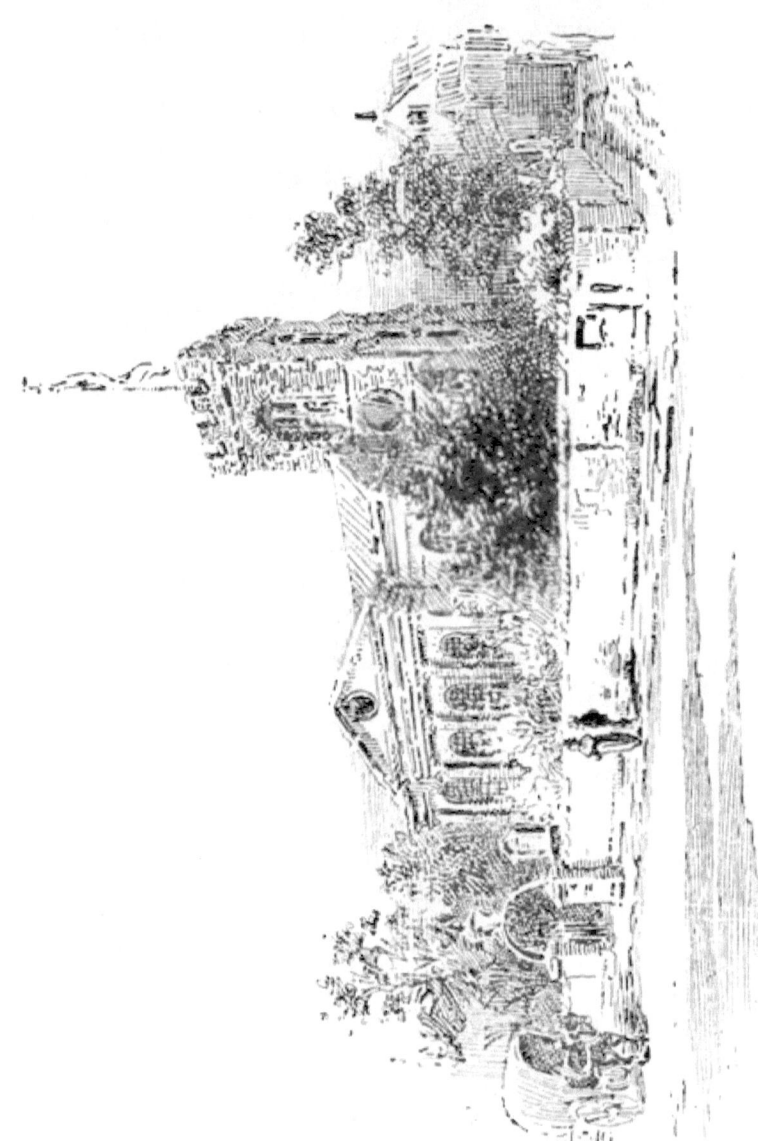

TWICKENHAM CHURCH

ST MARY
TWICKENHAM

THE church of St. Mary, Twickenham, stands on the south side of the road between the bridge and the railway station. It has a tower of the Perpendicular period, built of flint and stone, and about sixty feet high. There are eight bells. The body of the old church fell down in April, 1713, and the present red brick edifice, a classical building of the Tuscan order, was thereupon erected from a design of John James. It has stone quoins, cornices, and pediments. The interior was repaired and altered in 1859 and 1871. The chancel was rearranged, and the organ placed on the north of it; benches were substituted for the old high pews, but the galleries, north, south, and west, have been retained.

The monuments are numerous, and are much more interesting than the church which contains them. By far the most ancient is a stone slab on the south wall near the vestry door, on which is a brass plate with a Latin inscription to Richard Burton, who died in 1443, and his wife, Agnes. On the south wall of the chancel is a slab with a quaint Latin inscription commemorating Bridget, widow of Sir Anthony Markham, who died in 1609. She was first cousin to Lucy, Countess of Bedford, the generous patroness of the poets of her time, and died at Twickenham Park, which was then the Countess's residence. On the east wall at the south side is a monument, ornamented with terra-cotta busts, to Francis Poulton, a Bencher of Lincoln's Inn, who died in 1642.

RIVERSIDE CHURCHES

On the east wall over the south gallery is the monument of a famous cavalier, John, Lord Berkeley of Stratton, whose epitaph is as follows:—

"Under this marble lye the renowned ashes of the Right Honourable the Lord John Berkeley, Baron of Stratton, youngest son of Sir Maurice Berkeley, of Bruton in Somersetshire. In the civil warres in the dayes of Charles the First (for his singular valour and conduct in recoveringe the city of Exeter out of the hands of the rebells) he was made Governor thereof, and one of his Majesty's Generals in the West. Those unhappy warres ended, he served many campaigns in Flanders, both in the French and Spanish armies, according as their alliances with England engaged him. After the happy Restoration of Charles II. he was made Privy Counsellour, Governor of Connaught, and after Lord Lieutenant of Ireland; sent twice Extraordinary Embassador, first into France, secondly to the treaty of Nimeguen. His other felicities were crowned by his happy marriage of Christina, daughter of Sir Andrew Riccard; a young lady of a large dowry, and yet larger graces and virtues, who also enricht him with a most hopefull progeny. He deceased Aug. the 26. 1678, in the 72 year of his age.

> Though sprung from Danish Kings of brightest fame,
> Whose blood and high exploits exalt their name,
> Berkeley's own virtues most his tombe do grace,
> Adde glory to, not borrow from his race.

"N.B. The ancient name of the Berkeleys was Fitzhardinge; they descending from Fitzhardinge, a younger son of the King of Denmark."

Sir John Berkeley, who was one of the most distinguished of Charles II.'s commanders in the west of England, was created

TWICKENHAM FROM THE RIVER

Lord Berkeley of Stratton by Charles II. in honour of his victory over the Parliamentary forces at that place. He died at his country seat, Twickenham Park, which had once been the habitation of Francis Bacon. His name, birthplace, and victory are commemorated in Berkeley Square, Bruton Street, and Stratton Street, built on the gardens belonging to his great town mansion, Berkeley House, which occupied the site of the present Devonshire House.

Christina, the "young lady of a large dowry and yet larger graces and virtues," survived her lord twenty years, and was buried at Twickenham on September 1, 1698. His brother, Sir William Berkeley, had been interred here in July, 1677. He was Governor of Virginia under Charles I., remained there in a private capacity during the Commonwealth, and resumed the government at the Restoration. After having spent thirty years in America, he returned to his native country about a year before his death. The second and third Lords Berkeley of Stratton, both sons of the first Lord, and both naval officers, were also buried at Twickenham, but there is no memorial either to them or to their uncle, Sir William. With the fifth Lord, who was laid in the family vault in 1773, the title became extinct.

At the sides of the altar are monuments to Sir Joseph Ashe and Sir William Humble, both of whom died in 1686. Sir Joseph had a house at Twickenham, which afterwards became the property of Richard Owen Cambridge, the author of the *Scribleriad*, to whom Thomas Edwards addressed a sonnet, and whom Johnson and Boswell visited. Cambridge died at Twickenham in 1802 at the advanced age of eighty-five, and a monument was erected to him in the church.

Lady Frances Whitmore, who died in 1690, has for her memorial an urn of veined marble, from which a flame is represented as issuing; on the pedestal is engraved the following epitaph by Dryden:—

> "Fair, kind, and true! a treasure each alone;
> A wife, a mistress, and a friend in one;
> Rest in this tomb, raised at thy husband's cost,
> Here sadly summing what he had and lost.
> Come, virgins, ere in equal bands you join,
> Come first, and offer at her sacred shrine;
> Pray but for half the virtues of this wife,
> Compound for all the rest with longer life;
> And wish your vows, like hers, may be returned,
> So loved when living, and when dead so mourned."

The urn was originally placed in the north-east corner of the chancel, but at the reparation of the church was relegated to the top of the staircase leading to the north gallery. One cannot but feel grieved to see it thus thrust aside into unworthy seclusion. Its removal from its original place may have been necessitated by the alterations, but surely some more prominent and dignified position might have been found for a monument which bears the "full resounding lines" of "glorious John."

But it is Dryden's successor on the poetical throne who has made both the town and church of Twickenham illustrious. Pope and his mother removed from Chiswick to the celebrated villa at Twickenham (long since, alas! demolished) soon after his father's death. He erected in the church a marble monument to the memory of that "good man" who "walked innoxious through his age," and when "the tender office" which had "long engaged" him —

> "To rock the cradle of reposing age,
> With lenient arts extend a mother's breath,
> Make languor smile, and smooth the bed of death,
> Explore the thought, explain the asking eye,
> And keep awhile one parent from the sky"

was at last finished, her remains were interred at Twickenham, and her name was added to her husband's on the monument. Eleven years afterwards the poet followed her; he had left instructions—

> "As to my body, my will is, that it be buried near the monument of my dear parents at Twickenham, with the addition, after the words 'filius fecit,' of these only, 'et sibi; qui obiit anno 17 — aetatis.'"

His wishes were duly carried out. He was buried in a vault beneath the middle aisle, and a circle marked in the floor, slightly west of where the lectern stands, still points out the site of his grave. The inscription on the monument, thus completed, is as follows:—

> "D — O — M
> Alexandro Pope
> Viro innocuo, probo, pio —
> Qui vixit annos 75; obiit anno, 1717:
> Et Edithae, conjugi inculpabili, pientissimae,
> Quae vixit annos 93, obiit 1733:
> Parentibus bene merentibus
> Filius fecit:
> Et sibi,
> Qui obiit anno 1744, aetatis 57."

Unfortunately this most interesting monument is no longer visible. It is affixed to the east wall over the north gallery, corresponding with Lord Berkeley of Stratton's monument on the other side. The organ, in its altered position, has entirely hidden it.

Bishop Warburton, Pope's vigorous champion and literary executor, was not content that the poet should be only commemorated in the simple, touching way which he had himself desired. He set up a large monument of blue marble, with a medallion portrait of his friend in white marble, over the north gallery. It is inscribed :—

> "Alexandro Pope
> M — H
> Gulielmus Episcopus Glocestriensis
> Amicitiae causa fac-cur.
> MDCCLXI."

At the base are Pope's lines :—

> "Poeta Loquitur
> For one who would not be buried
> in Westminster Abbey —
> Heroes and Kings, your distance keep,
> In peace let one poor poet sleep,
> Who never flattered folks like you ;
> Let Horace blush and Virgil too !"

On the outside of the church, against the east wall of the north aisle, is a tablet to Pope's nurse, thus inscribed :—

> "To the Memory of Mary Beach, who died Nov. 5, 1725, aged 78. Alexander Pope, whom she nursed in his infancy, and constantly attended for thirty-eight years, in gratitude to a faithful old servant, erected this stone."

Over the south gallery is a monument to Nathaniel Pigott, one of Pope's Roman Catholic friends, with an epitaph written by the poet :—

> "To the Memory of Nathaniel Pigott, Barrister at Law ; possessed of the highest character by his learning, judgment, experience, integrity ; deprived of the highest stations only by his conscience and religion. Many he assisted in the law ; more he kept from it. A friend to peace, a guardian to the poor, a lover of his country. He died July 5, 1737, aged 76 years."

Over the north gallery, to the east of Pope's monument, is a large memorial, embellished with naval trophies, to Admiral Sir Chaloner Ogle, a gallant officer, who rose to be Commander-in-Chief of the Fleet. He died, in his seventieth year, in 1750. Over the south gallery is a monument with weeping female figure, by Bacon, to George Gostling, who died in 1782, and his wife, Anne, who died in 1799. On the same wall is a tablet to Sir Richard Perryn, for twenty-three years a Baron of the Exchequer, who died in 1803. On the wall of the north aisle, are the memorials of Lucia, Viscountess Clifden, who died, aged seventy, in 1802, and of the Hon. Caroline Anne Agar-Ellis, daughter of Henry, Viscount Clifden, who passed away in 1814, before she had completed her twentieth year. On the south wall is a tablet to Laetitia Matilda Hawkins, who died in 1835. She was the daughter of Sir John Hawkins, author of a *History of Music* and Dr. Johnson's executor and biographer.

On the outside of the church, against the north wall of the chancel, is a tablet to Mrs. Catherine Clive, the great actress, who died on December 7, 1785, aged seventy-five. She has an epitaph in verse :—

> "Clive's blameless life this tablet shall proclaim,
> Her moral virtues and her well-earned fame.
> In comic scenes the stage she early trod,
> Nor sought the critic's praise, nor feared his rod.
> In real life was equal praise her due,
> Open to pity, and to friendship true :
> In wit still pleasing, as in converse free
> From aught that could afflict humanity :
> Her gracious heart to all her friends was known,
> And e'en the stranger's sorrows were her own.
> Content with fame, e'en affluence she waved,
> To share with others what by toil she saved ;
> And nobly bounteous from her splendid store,
> She bade two dear relations not be poor.
> Such deeds on life's short scenes true glory shed,
> And heavenly plaudits hail the glorious dead."

ST. MARY, TWICKENHAM

These lines were written by Miss Pope, who had been trained by Mrs. Clive, and whom Churchill had heartily praised in the *Rosciad*:—

> "Not without art, but yet to nature true,
> She charms the town with humour just yet new:
> Cheered by her promise, we the less deplore
> The fatal time when Clive shall be no more."

The fourth line of the epitaph is borrowed from Churchill's description of Mrs. Clive:—

> "In spite of outward blemishes, she shone,
> For humour famed, and humour all her own:
> Easy, as if at home, the stage she trod,
> Nor sought the critic's praise, nor feared his rod:
> Original in spirit and in ease,
> She pleased by hiding all attempts to please:
> No comic actress ever yet could raise,
> On humour's base, more merit or more praise."

The "two dear relations" whom she assisted "from her splendid store" were her brother and sister. "She nobly retrenched," says Lysons, "from the luxuries which it might have afforded her, to administer to the comforts of a brother and sister whose means of subsistence were but slender." She retired from the stage about sixteen years before her death, and her last years were spent at Twickenham, in a house called "Little Strawberry," the use of which was given her by Horace Walpole, who greatly admired her talents.

On the east wall of the chancel is a tablet to Thomas Twining, who died in 1741. There are memorials in the south gallery to other members of this family, who have been great benefactors to the church and parish.

Sir Godfrey Kneller, the painter, resided at Whitton, a hamlet of Twickenham. He was a justice of the peace, and his unconventional method of adjudicating on the cases brought before him is referred to by Pope :—

> "I think Sir Godfrey should decide the suit,
> Who sent the thief that stole the cash away,
> And punished him that put it in his way."

He also served the office of churchwarden at Twickenham, and he was there buried on November 7, 1723. His widow wanted Pope to take down his father's monument, in order to make room for a large one to her husband, asserting that he had promised Sir Godfrey before his death so to do. This Pope denied, and after duly considering the matter, refused to comply with her request. She then brought an action against him, but in this she was defeated, and as she apparently could not find any other position to her liking in Twickenham Church, she erected no memorial to her husband in the place of his burial. His monument was, however, set up in Westminster Abbey, and Pope contributed the epitaph :—

> "Kneller, by Heaven, and not a master, taught,
> Whose art was nature, and whose pictures thought;
> Now, for two ages having snatched from fate
> Whate'er was beauteous, or whate'er was great,
> Lies crowned with prince's honours, poet's lays,
> Due to his merit and brave thirst of praise.
> Living, great Nature feared he might outvie
> Her works; and, dying, fears herself may die."

Nicholas Amherst, the editor and principal writer of the *Craftsman*, the leading organ of the Opposition against the administration of Sir Robert Walpole, was buried at Twickenham in May, 1742. In the family vault of the Berkeleys was interred, on September 21, 1757, Frances, Lady Byron, daughter of the fourth Lord Berkeley of Stratton, and sister of the fifth and last Lord. She was the widow of the fourth Lord Byron, and mother of the eccentric fifth Lord, the poet's great-uncle and predecessor in the title, and of Admiral John Byron, the poet's grandfather, whose " Narrative " " of the great distresses suffered by himself and his companions on the coast of Patagonia from the year 1740 till their arrival in England 1746," afforded some hints for the shipwreck in *Don Juan*, and is alluded to in the second canto of that poem :—

> " His hardships were comparative
> To those related in my grand-dad's ' Narrative.' "

The Admiral was buried at Twickenham on April 10, 1786.

Another stout seaman here interred was Sir George Pocock, who had commanded the British Fleet both in the East and West Indies. He died in 1792, at the advanced age of eighty-six. There is a tablet on the west wall of the south gallery to a descendant of his, also a sailor, Edward Osborn Pocock, a promising young officer, who perished at sea in 1813, aged nineteen.

There are also several interesting entries in the register among the baptisms and marriages. Sir John Suckling, the poet, who was the son of Sir John Suckling, Comptroller of the Household and a resident at Whitton, was baptized here on February 10, 1609. A daughter of the Earl of Manchester, who played a prominent part on the Parliamentary side during the Civil War, was baptized at Twickenham in 1655, and his third wife's death is recorded on October 28, 1658. Here was celebrated on April 6, 1703, the marriage of John, Earl of Mar, who subsequently commanded the Jacobite army in Scotland during the insurrection of 1715, with Margaret Hay, daughter of the Earl of Errol; and here on February 21, 1712, his daughter, Lady Jane Erskine, was married to Sir Hugh Paterson of Bannockburn. The marriage is also noted on May 9, 1737, of Richard Grenville and Anna Chambers. He became Earl Temple in 1752, and was for many years a leading statesman. Lord Chatham married his sister. His Countess was something of a poetess, and her productions were among the works printed at Strawberry Hill. William, eldest son of Henry Fielding by his second wife, was baptized at Twickenham, on February 25, 1748; and Chantrey, the sculptor, was married here on November 23, 1809.

The benefice of Twickenham has had the same history as that of the neighbouring parish of Isleworth. It was anciently appropriated to the Abbey of St. Walerick in Picardy; was given by Richard II. to William of Wykeham, who made it a part of the endowment of his College at Winchester; was obtained by means of an exchange from the Warden and Fellows by Henry VIII.; and was bestowed by Edward VI. on the Dean and Chapter of Windsor, who have ever since continued patrons.

Among the vicars of Twickenham are numbered Dr. Daniel Waterland, the distinguished theological writer, who held the living from 1730 till his death ten years later; Richard Terrick, who was instituted in 1749, and being made Bishop of Peterborough in 1757, still continued to hold the living, but resigned it on his translation to London in 1764; and George Costard, a man of great learning in the Oriental languages and an able and enthusiastic astronomer, who succeeded Terrick and remained at Twickenham till his death in 1782. He was buried on the south side of the churchyard, close to the chancel wall; but, by his own wish, no monument was erected to mark the site of his grave.

ALL SAINTS
ISLEWORTH

THE church of All Saints, Isleworth, stands on the river bank, just to the west of the grounds of Syon House. Being mantled with ivy, it presents a picturesque appearance when viewed from the opposite side of the Thames; but on nearer inspection, excepting the stone tower at the west, which is of the Perpendicular period, and contains eight bells, it reveals itself to be a decidedly ugly building. The body of the old church had become ruinous at the opening of the 18th century; it was accordingly rebuilt of brick in the years 1705, 1706. The parochial authorities had obtained a design from Sir Christopher Wren, but it proved too expensive for them to adopt in its entirety. They therefore altered it to suit their convenience, and in consequence spoiled it. About thirty years ago a new chancel was appended, and other alterations were made; but, as far as we can judge from views of the church in its original condition, it has been by no means improved by these innovations.

A conspicuous feature of the exterior is the large sundial on the south wall. The interior includes two aisles, and there are galleries on the north and south. The roof of the nave, which is coved, is painted a lightish blue and ornamented. The ceilings of the aisles are flat. The walls are coloured, but the effect produced is not a very happy one. The east window is filled with stained glass, as are also those of the aisles, which are memorials to parishioners. On the window at the east end of the north gallery, and on that at the west end of the south gallery, is a head of our Lord. The organ, which was originally built by Father Smith, is placed on the south of the chancel. Above the tower arch at the west end is a fresco, which an inscription states was executed at the expense of the parishioners in memory of the Rev. H. W. P. Richards, vicar of Isleworth from 1855 to 1888.

The monuments are numerous and interesting. There are three brasses on the floor of the nave at the north-east. The

ISLEWORTH FROM ABOVE.

finest of these is that of William Chase, which displays a figure of the deceased in armour. He died in 1544, and is described as "Serjeant to King Henry VIII. and of his honourable household of the hall and woodyard." Another, on which appears a female effigy, has an inscription to Frances, daughter of Edward Holland, a gentleman of Lancashire, but the date is lost. The third shows two figures of female children; beneath it is an inscription

to Katherine, wife of Richard Cox, merchant-taylor, who died in
1598; but the figures seem to be of an earlier date, and they
probably belonged to some brass which has been destroyed, and
have merely been pieced on to this plate. To the wall at the east
end of the south aisle has been affixed a brass with a small effigy
of a nun, inscribed to "Margaret Dely, a Syster professed yn Syon
who decessed the 7 of October anno. 1561." The convent of Syon,
was suppressed by Henry VIII., but Queen Mary revived it;
it had, however, been finally suppressed by Queen Elizabeth
before the death of Margaret Dely, who seems to have remained

ISLEWORTH FROM BELOW.

in the neighbourhood of her old home, while most of her sisters
migrated to the Continent. On the floor at the east end of the
south aisle the impression of this brass is plainly visible; it was
removed to its present position to avoid the risk of its being injured.
Beneath it is fastened on the wall a brass plate of very modern
date, on which is a kneeling figure in clerical attire. It is inscribed
to the memory of the Rev. Henry Glossop, who was for thirty-three
years vicar of Isleworth, and died in 1869, and Charlotte, his wife,
who expired in the following year.

Within the tower on the north wall is a large and elaborate

monument by Halfpenny to Mrs. Anne Dash. Her history is fully recorded in her epitaph, and is a somewhat remarkable one. She was the daughter of a Derbyshire gentleman named Newton, and married first Henry Sisson, and secondly John Tolson. After the death of her second husband, she became very poor, and was obliged to keep a school in order to support herself; but after a time the failure of her sight compelled her to relinquish this occupation, and being utterly destitute she had to be maintained by charity. But on May 2, 1741, died Dr. Caleb Cotesworth, a physician, leaving to his wife upwards of £120,000. She died a few hours after him, and Mrs. Tolson, being one of her nearest of kin, inherited a large share of this fortune. She testified her thankfulness for "this signal deliverance" by allotting £5,000 for the erection of almshouses at Isleworth for six poor men and six women. She afterwards married a third husband, Joseph Dash, a merchant, and died, at the age of eighty-nine, in 1750. On her monument, which is said to have cost £500, appears her bust in white marble, and there are likewise medallion portraits of Dr. and Mrs. Cotesworth, who were also buried at Isleworth.

On the opposite wall of the tower is the monument of Sir Orlando Gee, of whom there is a half-length effigy in white marble. He is represented wearing a flowing peruke. Sir Orlando, who had been steward to two Earls of Northumberland and Registrar of the Court of Admiralty, died in 1705, at the age of eighty-six. It was by the timely aid of a legacy from him of £500 that the parishioners were enabled to set about the rebuilding of their church.

At the west end of the north aisle is a tablet to Margaret, wife of Henry Scardevile, Dean of Cloyne, who died in 1698. On the north wall is a large slab to the memory of Richard Downton, who died in 1672, and Sir Richard Downton, his son, who died in

1711. On the south wall is a monument to several of the Baron and Daw families, of whom the earliest recorded, Edward Baron, died in 1640; and there are also monuments to Simon Basill, Clerk of the Works to Charles I. for Greenwich and Eltham, and to Charles II. for Hampton Court, who died in 1663; and to John Bedingfield, who died in 1692.

In the north gallery is a very handsome, but now, unhappily, somewhat dilapidated monument to Sir Francis Darcy, who died in 1641, and his wife Catherine, who died in 1625. Under a canopy supported by Corinthian columns are their kneeling effigies, Sir Francis being represented in armour. On the same wall is a monument by Nollekens to George Keate, F.R.S., F.S.A., who was the author of some poems, and in 1788 published an account of the adventures of Captain Wilson, commander of the *Antelope*, a vessel belonging to the East India Company, who had been shipwrecked at the Pelew Islands five years before. Keate died in 1797, and his widow, Jane Catherine Keate, who was likewise here interred, in 1800.

In the south gallery is a monument with kneeling figures to Richard Wiatt, a benefactor to the parish, who died in 1619; and, a little to the west of it, is a large and ornate memorial to Sir Theodore De Vaux, physician to Charles II. and Catherine of Braganza, who died in 1694. There are also here tablets to John Land, who died in 1697, and Thomas Musgrave, who died in 1756, and his three sisters.

Against the west wall of the churchyard is a rather large monument, which bears no name or date, only an owl as a crest, and this inscription:—

> "Si Christicola es, siste, viator, et aeternos annos meditare."

Margaret, daughter of Theophilus, Earl of Suffolk, and widow of Roger, Earl of Orrery, whose marriage was celebrated by

Suckling in his famous "Ballad upon a Wedding," was buried at Isleworth in 1689. Here was baptized, on October 5, 1617, Dorothy, daughter of Sir Robert Sidney, afterwards Earl of Leicester, and Lady Dorothy, his wife, daughter of Henry, Earl of Northumberland, the first owner of Syon of the Percy family, who was then enduring a long imprisonment in the Tower, on a suspicion that he had been privy to the Gunpowder Plot. Dorothy Sidney, who was Algernon Sidney's elder sister, grew to be Waller's "Sacharissa," and married the Earl of Sunderland, who fell in 1643 at the battle of Newbury, as Clarendon records:—

"Here fell the Earl of Sunderland, a lord of a great fortune, tender years (being not above three and twenty years of age) and an early judgment; who, having no command in the army, attended upon the King's person under the obligation of honour; and putting himself that day into the King's troop a volunteer, before they came to charge, was taken away by a cannon bullet."

The Countess was residing at Isleworth in 1655, as her name appears in the parish accounts for that year. The register also records the baptism, on June 22, 1676, of Anthony Collins, the deistical writer.

In Isleworth Church, on March 27, 1679, Lady Elizabeth Percy, daughter and sole heiress of Joceline, eleventh Earl of Northumberland, was married, while yet quite a child, to the Earl of Ogle. He died on November 1, 1680; and the heiress was speedily again married to Thomas Thynne of Longleat, "wise Issachar," as Dryden calls him, the Duke of Monmouth's "wealthy western friend," whose great riches won for him the nickname of "Tom of Ten Thousand." Thynne was shot in his coach on the night of September 12, 1682, by the emissaries of his rival, Count Königsmarck; and on May 30 following Lady Elizabeth was married to the sixth Duke of Somerset, who was known as "the proud Duke," and who, by entering the Council Chamber unannounced, together with the Duke of Argyle, two days before the death of Queen Anne, did much to facilitate the peaceable accession of the House of Hanover. The Duchess was zealous in the same cause as her husband, and her influence over Queen Anne as Mistress of the Robes was much dreaded by the Tories. Hence Swift, in his "Windsor Prophecy," alluding to the Duchess's red hair, exhorted England to

"Beware of Carrots from Northumberland."

Her son, Algernon, the seventh Duke of Somerset, was created Earl of Northumberland, with remainder to Sir Hugh Smithson, who married his daughter, Lady Elizabeth Seymour. Sir Hugh was, in 1766, created Duke of Northumberland, and from him is descended the present Duke of Northumberland and owner of Syon House.

The benefice of Isleworth is a vicarage. The rectory was anciently given, and was confirmed by Henry III., to the Abbey of St. Walerick in Picardy, and the vicar was appointed on behalf of that Abbey by the Prior of Takeley. But Richard II. having seized it as being a possession of a priory alien, it was obtained from that king by William of Wykeham, who bestowed it on the College which he had founded at Winchester. Henry VIII. procured it from the Warden and Fellows by an exchange, and his son and successor gave the rectory to the Dean and Chapter of Windsor. The advowson of the vicarage remained a few years longer in the hands of the Crown; but the Dean and Chapter presented a vicar in 1562, and have ever since continued patrons.

Three of the vicars of Isleworth—John Hall, Nicholas Byfield, and William Cave—ought not to be passed over unmentioned.

Hall, who was instituted in 1521, was, together with Richard Reginalds, a monk of Syon, and three other ecclesiastics, hanged and quartered at Tyburn for denying the King's supremacy on May 4, 1535. Byfield, who was an ardent Puritan, was vicar from 1615 till his death in 1622. "He was great," says Newcourt, "in the opinion of the zealots, and his writings and works shew him to have been a person of great parts, industry, and readiness. He left behind him a son named Adoniram Byfield, a most zealous and forward brother for the cause in the late rebellious times." The zeal of Adoniram is noticed by Butler in the third part of *Hudibras* :—

> "Their dispensations had been stifled,
> But for our Adoniram Byfield."

Cave was a Doctor of Divinity and a man of great learning. He was educated at St. John's College, Cambridge, and in 1662 was presented to the vicarage of Islington; he was Rector of All Hallows the Great in the city of London from 1679 to 1689; and was admitted to the vicarage of Isleworth on November 19, 1690. He was a Canon of Windsor, and died there on August 4, 1713, in his seventy-sixth year. He was buried at Islington. He was the author of several erudite works dealing with the early history of the Christian Church.

ST ANNE
KEW

KEW was originally a hamlet to Kingston. In 1769 it was united with Petersham, as has been already noted. It is now a separate parish: the vicarage is in the gift of the Crown. The church was built in 1714, the last year of Queen Anne, and in her honour St. Anne was selected as its patron saint. It stands on the Green in a pleasant situation, and the ivy which crowns its brick walls gives it a picturesque appearance. At the west end projects a Doric portico, which gives access to the main entrance; above is an octagonal turret, which contains the clock, and is completed by a small lead-covered cupola supporting a ball and vane. On the south a porch, through which the side door is approached, juts out into the churchyard. A sepulchral chamber, shaped somewhat in the fashion of an apse, has been appended at the east, and gives this end of the church a very strange, though not unpleasing aspect. The interior includes two aisles. In a recess at the west is the Royal Gallery, which was built by George III. The chancel has three eastern windows, but also obtains light from above by means of windows in the dome. It was considerably altered some twelve years ago. The organ now on the north of the chancel was set up about the same period; it replaced an instrument, which was said to have belonged to Handel, was long in the possession of George III., and was given to the church by George IV.

RIVERSIDE CHURCHES

On the south wall is an elaborate monument to the memory of Dorothy, Lady Capel. She was the daughter and heiress of Richard Bennet, of Kew House, and married Sir Henry Capel, who was in 1692 created Lord Capel of Tewkesbury, and who died in Ireland, being Lord Deputy of that kingdom, in 1696. Lady Capel spent her widowhood of a quarter of a century at Kew, and at her death in 1721 left charitable bequests for the education of poor children to this and several adjacent parishes.

KEW PALACE

From the Capel family, Frederick, Prince of Wales, procured a long lease of Kew House, and the estate was afterwards purchased by his son, George III., who resided much at Kew.

There is a monument to Elizabeth, Countess of Derby, who died in 1717, and bequeathed £1,000 to the poor of Kew and Brentford. She was not, however, buried here, but in Westminster Abbey. General William Douglas, who died in Holland in 1747, has likewise a memorial. A tablet, surmounted by a bust,

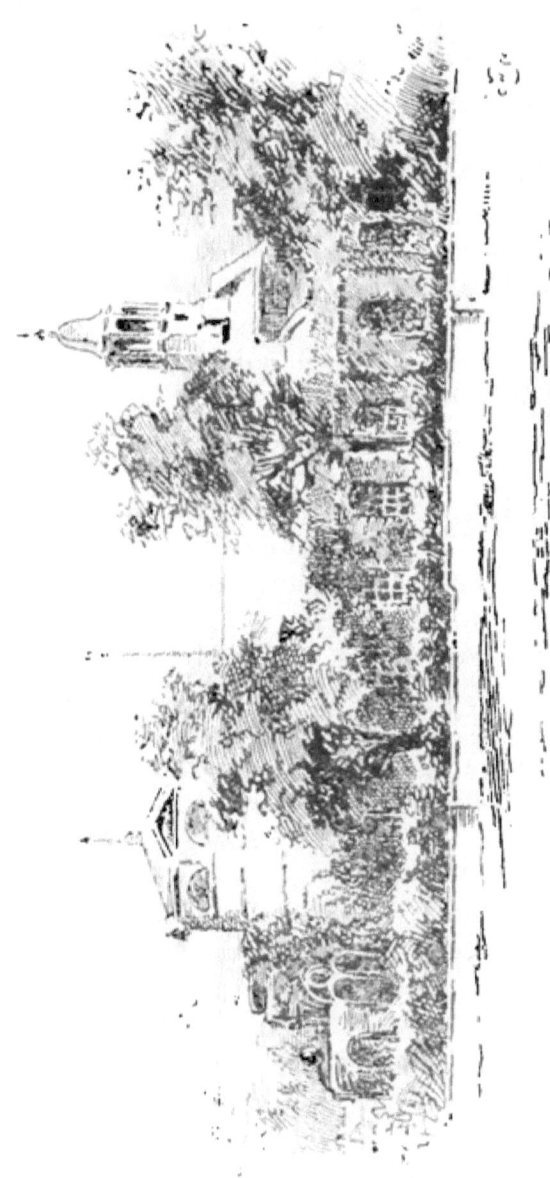

KEW CHURCH

commemorates Jeremiah Meyer, R.A., painter in miniature and enamel to George III. He was a native of Wurtemburg, but came over to England in his boyhood. He died in 1789, at the age of sixty-one. On the tablet are inscribed some lines by Hayley, in which warm praise is bestowed on his virtuous and amiable character as well as on his artistic talents. There is another poetical epitaph by Hayley in Kew Church. It appears on a tablet, on the south wall, erected to the memory of William Aiton and his son, William Townsend Aiton, who were successively Directors of Kew Gardens. William Aiton was born in Scotland, and came at an early age to England. He was the author of *Hortus Kewensis*, an elaborate botanical work in five volumes. He died in 1793. William Townsend Aiton died in 1849.

On the north wall is a tablet with medallion bust to Sir William Jackson Hooker, who was Director of Kew Gardens from 1841, when he succeeded the younger Aiton, to 1865. He died on August 12 of the latter year, aged eighty. On the same wall is a monument, with a medallion bust at the summit and emblems of the art of painting at the base, to Francis Bauer, Botanic Painter to Her Majesty, who died in 1840. Bauer furnished the drawings for Hooker's *Genera Filicum ; or, Illustrations of the Ferns and other Allied Genera*. John Tyrrell, a barrister of Lincoln's Inn, who died in 1840, has at the extreme south-east what may be termed a professional monument; for beneath his epitaph are carved representations of law books and legal documents. There is a tablet on the south wall, "erected as a token of their respect by the Parishioners of Kew," to the Rev. Richard Burch Byam, whose memorial in Petersham Church has been already mentioned.

The Duke of Cambridge, George III.'s youngest son, who died in 1850, and the Duchess, who died in 1889, are buried at Kew. Their coffins are in the sepulchral chamber. The central window of the chancel was given by the present Duke in memory of his mother. Four of the windows in the dome also constitute

KEW CHURCH, WEST FRONT.

a memorial to the Duchess. The north window of the chancel is to the memory of the late vicar, the Rev. Wemyss Percy Nott.

The most illustrious person buried in the churchyard is the great painter, Thomas Gainsborough, who died on August 2, 1788,

TOMBS OF GAINSBOROUGH, GARDINER, KIRBY, AND MEYER

aged sixty-one. He lies on the south side of the churchyard, not far from the church wall, under a plain flat slab. It bears an inscription stating it to have been restored and enclosed with rails in September, 1865, by E. M. Ward, R.A., as a mark of respect to Gainsborough's memory. At the same time, Mr. Ward set up a tablet in the church, against the south wall, calling attention to the fact that Gainsborough was buried in the adjoining churchyard. Gainsborough desired to be interred in Kew Churchyard, in order that his bones might rest beside those of his friend, Joshua Kirby, who had been buried there fourteen years before. Kirby was an architect and the author of two treatises on Perspective; he was the father of Mrs. Trimmer, the well-known writer for the young. His stone is next to Gainsborough's. Close by is that of Meyer. There is another painter buried in the churchyard, Johan Zoffany, R.A., who died in 1810. He has a large monument to the east of the church.

Here was interred Sir Charles Eyre, Governor of Fort William, Bengal, who died in 1729. At the south-east corner of the churchyard is an enormous and hideous monument, surmounted by an urn. It bears an inscription to Thomas Gardiner, Esq., of Bedford Row, who died in 1738, and "whose integrity and early knowledge in polite learning rendered him acceptable to all his acquaintance."

ST MARY
MORTLAKE

THE church of St. Mary, Mortlake, stands to the south of High Street. Mortlake was originally part of the parish of Wimbledon, but for the convenience of the inhabitants a church was built here in 1348. It was rebuilt in 1543. In the lowest story of the tower is the principal entrance doorway; in the next stage is a window, and above the window are inscribed the date of the erection of the church and the initials of the then reigning monarch :—

"Vivat R   H   S
1543."

Upon the tower, which contains eight bells, has been imposed a cupola, above which is a ball and vane. Both the tower and church are thickly encircled with ivy. The church, which is of considerable size, includes two aisles. Against the north aisle is a two-storied brick building, the lower portion of which serves as a vestry. The church has been much altered since its first erection. The south aisle was rebuilt in 1725, and not many years back—in 1885—a new chancel was made. This has been within the last few months fitted with choir stalls of oak. There are galleries on the north, south, and west. The pulpit, which is lofty, is placed at the south-east of the nave. The organ is located on the north of the chancel. A window at the north side of the chancel was fitted with stained glass in commemoration of Her Majesty's Jubilee. One of the windows of the north aisle contains a representation of the Supper at Emmaus, and is

ST MARY, MORTLAKE

inscribed: "To the glory of God, and in memory of W. Harman Nicholls, M.A. Clerk. Died July 13th, 1867."

The font, which is placed at the west end of the nave, bears the arms of Archbishop Bourchier. Thomas Bourchier was Archbishop of Canterbury from 1454 to 1486. He was a Cardinal, and figures in *Richard III*. The Manor of Mortlake belonged to the Archiepiscopal See, until it was given to

MORTLAKE CHURCH

Henry VIII. in exchange for other lands by Archbishop Cranmer. The Church of Mortlake was also in the peculiar jurisdiction of the Primate. This connection of Mortlake with the Archbishops would account for the church having been thus favoured by Bourchier, for the presence of his arms on the font seems to show that he was the donor.

Affixed to the north wall, to the east of the side entrance door, is a brass plate with the following quaint and pretty inscription: —

> "In Obitum D⁻ — Abigail
> Rashleygh 5 Ann
> Defunct XX⁰ Die
> July 1616.
>
> For yeares a childe, for
> Sparkles of God's Grace
> A Jewell Rich, Intombde
> Lies in this Place
> Her ashes (onelie) here; all ells
> Is gone to Rest
> God takes them youngest, who
> He loveth best."

On the same wall, to the west of the door, are two small brass plates. The upper is inscribed thus:—

> "Here lyeth buried ye body of Edward Myles, Servant to Prince Henry and Prince Charles, who deceased ye 20 of May, A' 1618."

The inscription on the lower plate runs as follows:—

> "Here lyeth the body of Ann Jeames, the daughter of Lewis Jeames, Gent. who departed this life ye first daye of April, An. 1608, beinge of the age of 6 yeres."

On the south wall above the gallery is a tablet to Richard Byfield, Rector of Long Ditton, who had been a member of the Assembly of Divines. He died at the close of 1664. On the south-east wall is a very large and profusely decorated monument, commemorating the Hon. Francis Coventry, second son of Thomas, Lord Coventry, "Lord Keeper of the Great Seal of England in the reign of King Charles I." He died in 1699 in his eighty-seventh year. He is described in his epitaph as inferior to no member of his family in either moral or intellectual qualities, but as a man ardently devoted to a quiet life. Beneath is a tablet setting forth the particulars of a charity to the poor of Mortlake, given by his widow Margaret. This was, it is recorded, "repaired at the sole expense of William, Earl of Coventry, 1811."

At the east end of the south gallery are the monuments of Henry Addington, who was Prime Minister from 1801 till 1804, and was subsequently created Viscount Sidmouth, and of Viscountess Sidmouth. When Addington took office, George III., who was very fond of him, gave him the occupation of the White Lodge in Richmond Park. He retained this residence till his death, which occurred on February 15, 1844. The White Lodge is in Mortlake parish, and he had thus been a parishioner for forty-three years. His Viscountess, Ursula, died long before him (June 23, 1811). Lord Sidmouth has a weighty sarco-

MORTLAKE VIEW FROM CHISWICK

phagus of white marble. Lady Sidmouth appears on her memorial at the point of death with attendant figures, and has for her epitaph a panegyric in verse. Another political celebrity buried at Mortlake was Sir Philip Francis, to whom the authorship of the *Letters of Junius* is generally attributed. There are three tablets: the first to Sir Philip's daughters Harriet and Elizabeth, of whom the former died in 1803, and the latter in 1804; the second to Sir Philip himself, who died on December 22, 1818, and was here buried "in fulfilment of the earnest wish expressed in his will that he might be interred in the same grave with his dearest and most lamented daughter, Elizabeth"; the last tablet is to another daughter, Catherine, wife of George James Cholmondeley, who died in 1823. These memorials were originally erected in the chancel; but when that portion of the church was rebuilt, they were removed to the vestry-room beyond the north aisle.

In this chamber may also now be seen a painting of the Entombment by Gerard Zeghers, a Flemish artist (1589-1651), formerly used as an altarpiece. It was presented by Benjamin Vandergucht, an engraver and picture dealer, who was an inhabitant of the parish, and was buried in the church in 1794. Conspicuous among the contents of the vestry-room are two massive old oak chests, the lid of one of which is beautifully veneered on the inside. There are numerous monumental tablets on the walls of the church besides those already mentioned, some of them dating from the seventeenth century; but the persons whose names they display are of no particular celebrity. Over the north gallery are four hatchments.

In the chancel of Mortlake Church was buried Alderman Sir John Barnard, Lord Mayor 1737-8, and a representative of the City of London in the last Parliament of George I. and all the Parliaments of George II.—a period of nearly forty years. He was very highly esteemed by his fellow-citizens for the sterling integrity of his character, and was complimented by Pope in his " Epistle to Bolingbroke " :—

> " Barnard in spirit, sense, and truth abounds ; "

and again, in the second of the two poetical Dialogues which he published in the year of Barnard's mayoralty :—

> " Yet think not, friendship only prompts my lays ;
> I follow virtue ; where she shines, I praise ;
> Point she to priest or elder, Whig or Tory,
> Or round a Quaker's beaver cast a glory.
> I never (to my sorrow I declare)
> Dined with the Man of Ross, or my Lord Mayor.

ST MARY, MORTLAKE

> "Some in their choice of friends (nay, look not grave)
> Have still a secret bias to a knave;
> To find an honest man, I beat about;
> And love him, court him, praise him, in or out."

Barnard's parents were Quakers, and he was educated in the tenets of the Society of Friends. But as he neared man's estate he became dissatisfied with this mode of religion, and attached himself to the Church of England, being baptized at the age of eighteen by Bishop Compton in Fulham Church. He died in his eightieth year on August 29, 1764.

Another notable Alderman, John Barber, who died on January 2, 1741, lies buried at Mortlake. The epitaph on his tomb in the churchyard says of him that he was "a constant benefactor to the poor, true to his principles in church and state. He preserved his integrity and discharged the duty of an upright magistrate in the most corrupt times. Zealous for the rights of his fellow-citizens, he opposed all attempts against them: and being Lord Mayor in the year 1733, was greatly instrumental in defeating a scheme of a general excise which (had it succeeded) would have put an end to the liberties of his country." His name is likewise mentioned by Pope, but in a very different manner from Barnard's:—

> "Thus Britain loved me, and preserved my fame,
> Pure from a Barber's or a Benson's name."

Pope suggested this couplet for the scroll under Shakespeare's bust in Westminster Abbey, alluding to the monuments there set up to Butler by Barber, and to Milton by Benson. But Barber hardly deserved this censure. Unlike Benson, who, as Dr. Johnson remarks, "has in the inscription bestowed more words upon himself than upon Milton," Barber merely recorded, and that in no immodest language, that he was the person by whom the monument had been erected. But, whatever Pope may have thought of Barber, the Alderman seems to have esteemed Pope, for he left him a legacy of £100. He also left £200 to Swift, and £300 to Bolingbroke. In 1725 he subscribed £50 towards the enlargement of Mortlake Churchyard. He had an estate at East Sheen, which afterwards belonged to Sir Philip Francis.

Under a flat stone in the churchyard lies John Partridge, the almanac-maker, who was so ridiculed by Swift. In his Latin epitaph it is stated that he was born at East Sheen on January 8, 1644, and died in London on June 24, 1715.

An earlier astrologer, the famous Dr. John Dee, resided at Mortlake in a house near the church, and was often visited there by Queen Elizabeth. He died at Mortlake in 1608, and was buried in the chancel, but his tomb has long perished.

Sir John Temple, Master of the Rolls in Ireland, was buried at Mortlake in 1704, but has no memorial. He was brother to Sir William Temple, and grandfather to the first Viscount Palmerston. Augustine Phillips, a fellow-actor with Shakespeare, lived at Mortlake. In his will he bequeathed Shakespeare "a thirty-shilling piece in gold," and also gave directions that he should be buried in the chancel of Mortlake Church. But whether his remains were actually there deposited cannot be ascertained, as the register for 1605, the year of his death, is not in existence. The burial is recorded, on January 16, 1629, of Everard, an infant son of Sir Kenelm Digby.

The benefice of Mortlake is a vicarage, and is in the patronage of the Dean and Chapter of Worcester.

ST NICHOLAS
CHISWICK

THE church of St. Nicholas, Chiswick, is beautifully situated by the river-side. The tower dates from the early part of the fifteenth century, as is recorded by a tablet on its inner wall, thus inscribed:—

"Mr. William Bordale, principal Vicar of this churche of Chiswicke, was founder of ye steeple of ye same. He died ye 15th day of October, in ye year of our Lord MCCCCXXV. Both wh appeare in the brass on his tombstone in this church, which monument of this worthy benefactor, being by William Walker, his successor, happily preserved, is now in this stone comended to the lasting memorie of posteritie by ye Right Honorable and truly noble Lorde, Francis Lorde Russell Earle of Bedford, anno Domini MDCXXXI."

Bordale's brass has since then been lost; but Weever, who has given a copy of the inscription, in which he was designated "principalis vicarius huius Ecclesie et fundator Campanilis eiusdem," makes the year of his death 1435, which is probably the correct date.

Bordale's tower has been extensively repaired, but it still remains. It is built of flint and stone, and is about sixty-five feet high. In it are six bells. The rest of the church was rebuilt between the years 1882-1884, under the direction of Mr. J. L. Pearson, R.A.

RIVERSIDE CHURCHES

St. Nicholas, Chiswick, is one of the handsomest modern churches in the neighbourhood of the metropolis. It is mostly in the Perpendicular style, and its total measurements are 110 feet in length by about 75 feet in width. The fittings are worthy of their position, all the woodwork being of oak, and well designed. The easternmost window of the south wall contains painted glass which was originally in Cologne Cathedral. In the old church this glass occupied the east window. The other windows are by Powell and Clayton & Bell. The south porch, which gives access to the church from the churchyard, is surmounted by a figure of the patron saint; it has a beautiful fan-groined ceiling.

On the outside of the east wall of the churchyard is this inscription :

> "This wall was made at ye charges of ye Right Honorable and trulie pious Lorde Francis Russell Earle of Bedford, out of true zeale and care for ye keeping of this Church yard and ye Wardrobe of Godd's Saints whose bodies lay theirin Buryed from violateing of swine and other prophanation. So Witnesseth William Walker —V— A.D.— 1623."

Beneath has been added : "Rebuilt 1831—Refixed 1884."

The wife of this Vicar, Mary Walker, who died on February 21, 1619, has a monument in the church, which is now placed to the north of the chancel between the organ and the inner wall of the vestry. She was, says her epitaph, "daughter of ye venerable divine Mr. Robert Kay, who honoured his pfession and profited ye people of Ware in Hertfordshire with his faithfull preaching and holy life for above LX yeares."

The eastern portion of the south aisle has been formed into a side chapel for week-day services. On the wall is a splendid monument to Sir Thomas Chaloner. The Knight and his lady are represented kneeling under a sort of tent, on each side of

CHISWICK OLD CHURCH

which stands the figure of a soldier in the military costume of the period. Sir Thomas was Chamberlain to Henry, Prince of Wales, and a man of much learning. He was the first person to work alum mines in England, applying the knowledge of the preparation of alum which he had acquired in Italy to some mines which he discovered at Guisborough in Yorkshire, and which became very valuable. He also wrote a treatise on the virtues of nitre, and was besides something of a poet. He died in 1615. Two of his sons, Thomas and James, were amongst the judges of Charles I.

Against the inner wall of the tower is a tablet to a gentleman named Richard Taylor, who died in 1716, and who, according to his Latin epitaph, presented a marvellous combination of Spanish firmness, Gallic promptitude, Italian sagacity, and English benevolence. Higher up on the same wall is a monument with a medallion bust, and the following inscription:—

> "If talents to make entertainment instruction, to support the credit of the stage by just and manly action, if to adorn society by virtues which would honour any rank and profession, deserved remembrance: let him, with whom these talents were long exerted, to whom these virtues were long known, and by whom the loss of them will be long lamented, bear testimony to the worth and abilities of his departed friend. Charles Holland was born March 12, 1733, dy'd Dec. 7, 1769, and was buried near this place. D. Garrick."

Holland had been trained to act by Garrick, and imitated very closely the style of his master. He is censured by Churchill, in the *Rosciad*, for his lack of originality:—

> "Next Holland came—with truly tragic stalk
> He creeps, he flies,—a hero should not walk."

ST. NICHOLAS, CHISWICK

> As if with Heaven he warred, his eager eyes
> Planted their batteries against the skies;
> Attitude, action, air, pause, start, sigh, groan
> He borrowed, and made use of as his own.
> By fortune thrown on any other stage,
> He might perhaps have pleased an easy age;
> But now appears a copy, and no more,
> Of something better we have seen before.
> The actor who would build a solid fame,
> Must imitation's servile arts disclaim;
> Act from himself, on his own bottom stand;
> I hate e'en Garrick thus at second-hand."

Holland was the son of a baker at Chiswick. In the northwest part of the churchyard is a large tomb over the family vault, bearing the names of himself, his father and mother, and many others of the family.

Thomas Bentley, who was partner with Josiah Wedgwood, and died in 1780, has a tablet in the church over the south door. Outside the church, close to the south wall, is a flat stone with the following quaint lines:—

> "Here lyes the clay
> Which the other day
> Inclosed Sam Savill's soul,
> But now is free and unconfined.
> She fled and left her clog behind
> Intomb'd within this hole."

He died on May 21, 1728, in his thirtieth year. East of the church, just outside the chancel wall, is the gravestone of Charlotte, Duchess of Somerset, who died, aged eighty, in January, 1773.

The churchyard contains a large number of tombs, several of which are of considerable interest. Pre-eminent among these is the tomb of Hogarth. The great painter, his widow, sister, and mother-in-law, Lady Thornhill, sleep beneath a large monument in that portion of the churchyard which lies immediately south of the church.

RIVERSIDE CHURCHES

On the north side are engraved a laurel-wreath and several emblems of the painter's art, beneath which are the verses written by Garrick on his deceased friend :—

> "Farewell, great painter of mankind,
> Who reached the noblest point of art ;
> Whose pictured morals charm the mind,
> And through the eye correct the heart !
> If genius fire thee, reader, stay ;
> If nature touch thee, drop a tear ;
> If neither move thee, turn away,
> For Hogarth's honoured dust lies here."

The east side is thus inscribed :—

> "Here lieth the body
> Of William Hogarth, Esq.
> Who died October 26th, 1764.
> Aged 67 years.
>
> Mrs. Jane Hogarth,
> Wife of William Hogarth, Esq.
> Obiit 13th November, 1789.
> Aetat 80 years."

The south side :—

> "Here lieth the body
> Of Mrs. Anne Hogarth, sister
> To William Hogarth Esq.
> She died August 13th 1771.
> Aged 70 years.
>
> Also, the body of
> Mary Lewis, Spinster,
> Died 25th March, 1808.
> Aged 88 years."

The west side :—

> "Here lieth the body
> Of Dame Judith Thornhill,
> Relict of Sir James Thornhill, Knight,
> Of Thornhill in the county of Dorset.
> She died Nov. 12, 1757.
> Aged 84 years."

The monument was "restored," as is recorded on a small granite slab at the base of the north side, "by William Hogarth of Aberdeen in 1856."

Hogarth's house, a red-brick mansion, is still standing. It is situated to the north of the church in a road which is called in his honour Hogarth Lane. It was inhabited for twelve years (1814-1826) by Henry Francis Cary, the translator of Dante, who was during that period curate of Chiswick.

In this part of the churchyard is an ornate altar-tomb erected by Lord Burlington to his bricklayer, Richard Wright, who died

CHISWICK FROM THE RIVER

in 1734. There have been added inscriptions to more recent members of the family—Alphonso Wright, who died in 1864, and Alphonso Matthew Wright, who died in 1888. Near to this is a large tomb bearing a poetical inscription by Arthur Murphy to the memory of Dr. William Rose. Rose, who was a native of Aberdeenshire, was an excellent classical scholar. He kept a school first at Kew, and afterwards at Chiswick, and published a translation of Sallust which his learned contemporaries highly esteemed. He was a friend of Doctor Johnson, and the father of Cowper's friend, Samuel Rose. He died, aged sixty-seven, on July 4, 1786. In the same portion of the churchyard is the tomb of Alexander Brodie, who died in 1811. He was the "first inventor of the register stoves and fire hearths for ships, and had the honour of supplying the whole British navy with the latter for upwards of thirty years." Another tombstone bears the name of Joseph Constantine Carpue, the anatomist, who died, in his eighty-second year, on January 30, 1846.

In that part of the churchyard which lies to the west of the church, and just south of the pathway, is the tomb of George, Earl of Macartney. After serving his country in several important capacities, including those of Envoy Extraordinary to Russia, Chief Secretary of Ireland, Governor of Grenada, and Ambassador Extraordinary to China, he spent his last years in tranquillity at Chiswick, and there died on March 31, 1806, in the sixty-ninth year of his age. Adjoining his monument is one of considerable size, designed by Sir John Soane, in memory of Philip James de Loutherbourgh, R.A., the landscape painter. He was born at Strasburg in 1740, but spent the best part of his life in England. He died in Hammersmith Terrace on March 11, 1812.

Chiswick Churchyard also contains the monuments of William Sharp, the historical line engraver, who died in 1824, and James Fittler, "Marine Engraver to his late Majesty George the Third," who died in 1835. Sharp's memorial is near that of Loutherbourgh; Fittler's is affixed to the south wall of the churchyard.

Towards the centre of the western part of the churchyard is the memorial of Ugo Foscolo. It is of grey granite, in shape like a coffer, and is crowned with the representation of a laurel wreath. On the east end is inscribed:—

"Ugo Foscolo
Died Sept. 10, 1827, aged 50."

On the south side:—

ST NICHOLAS, CHISWICK

> "From the sacred guardianship of Chiswick
> To the honours of Santa Croce, in Florence,
> The Government and People of Italy have transported
> The remains of the wearied Citizen Poet,
> 7th June, 1871."

On the north side :—

> "This spot where for 44 years
> The Relics of
> UGO FOSCOLO
> Reposed in honoured custody,
> Will be for ever held in grateful Remembrance
> By the Italian Nation."

Foscolo was originally buried under a flat stone. His present monument, which was designed by Marochetti, was erected in 1861, which date is inscribed on the west end.

On the south-west wall of the churchyard is a stone tablet with this inscription :—

> "This church was enlarged by an addition of twenty-five perches of ground given to the parish by His Grace William Spencer Cavendish, Duke of Devonshire, K.G., and this boundary wall built thereon by order of Vestry, A.D. 1838."

There is a similar inscription at the north-west end. Still further west, beyond this wall, is a new burying-ground, which is very tastefully laid out. Here is the grave of Admiral Sir Robert Smart, "who died September 10th, 1874, aged 78 years, after the long career of sixty years active service." His monument consists of a piece of rock, to which an anchor is fastened, surmounted by a cross. "The anchor," says the inscription, "is placed on this rock as a tribute to his memory, and a mark of respect for his high professional character, by some of those Brother Officers, who had served under him, esteemed him so much, and loved him so well."

An inscription at the entrance records that—

"This Acre of ground was presented to the Parish of Chiswick by his Grace the Duke of Devonshire, K.G., and dedicated to the service of God as a Burial Ground, Friday, March 3, A.D. 1871."

A similar gift, of a much more ancient date, is mentioned by Newcourt. "In 1349," says he, "John de Bray had the King's

A STREET IN CHISWICK, WITH EAST END OF CHURCH

license to give half an acre of ground to enlarge the churchyard."

There have been buried at Chiswick several noteworthy persons, to whom there is no memorial. Amongst them are two daughters of Oliver Cromwell, Mrs. Rich, who died in 1709, and the Countess of Fauconberg, who died in 1713. From her great-nephew, Thomas Viscount Fauconberg, the lease of the Manor of Sutton was acquired by Richard, Earl of Burlington, famous for his architectural skill, who designed Chiswick House. His daughter, Charlotte Elizabeth, who was baptized at Chiswick on

ST NICHOLAS, CHISWICK

November 24, 1731, was married in 1748 to William, Marquis of Hartington, and through her Chiswick House passed into the possession of the Dukes of Devonshire. The architect, painter, and landscape-gardener, William Kent, who was long loved and honoured by Lord Burlington, was buried at Chiswick on April 17, 1748. He died at Burlington House, Piccadilly, and was interred in his noble friend's family vault in the chancel. Barbara, Duchess of Cleveland, Charles II.'s mistress, was buried at Chiswick on October 13, 1709. Pope and his parents came from Binfield to Chiswick, and it was here, in Mawson's Buildings, a row of houses a little east of the church, on October 23, 1717, that Alexander Pope the elder met that death "instant and without a groan," which his son has lovingly recorded. Here, too, rests one of the heroes of the *Dunciad*, James Ralph:—

> "Silence, ye wolves! while Ralph to Cynthia howls,
> And makes night hideous. Answer him, ye owls!"

He was buried at Chiswick on January 31, 1762. And here also was interred, in September, 1803, Ralph Griffiths, of the *Monthly Review*, whom Goldsmith in the days of his obscurity found a not too agreeable employer.

Sir Stephen Fox resided at Chiswick, and was a benefactor to the church. In it he was married, on July 11, 1703, to Christian Hope; and in it his son Henry, afterwards Lord Holland, was baptized October 15, 1705. It was at Chiswick House that Lord Holland's illustrious son, Charles James Fox, passed away on September 13, 1806.

The vicarage of Chiswick is in the patronage of the Dean and Chapter of St. Paul's.

ST MARY
BARNES

THE church of St. Mary, Barnes, is situated to the north of the common, on the north side of Church Road. It stands in a pretty churchyard, which contains several fine trees. The tower, which perhaps dates from the end of the fifteenth century, is a very picturesque object. It is

built of red brick, and is partly covered with ivy. It is ornamented with a turret at the south east angle. On the south face beneath the clock is a sun-dial. The south and south east walls, which belong to the old church, are of flint and stone; the north side, which is of modern construction, is of red brick. The red tiles of the roof afford a very pleasing effect. The interior consists of a narrow nave and chancel, and a somewhat large north aisle, added about fifty years ago. The chancel seems to be, in part, at all events, Early English. At the east are three lancet windows, which, after having been long blocked up, were re-opened in 1852.

BARNES CHURCH, FROM THE EAST.

They are filled with stained glass, as are also the three easternmost windows of the south wall. The rest of the windows are plain, except that the topmost lights of the window at the east end of the north aisle are coloured. There are galleries on the north and west, in the latter of which the organ is placed.

On the floor of the chancel is a brass to Elizabeth and Anne, daughters of John Wylde, who both died unmarried in 1508. Above the inscription are well-executed figures of the two ladies, and beneath it is a coat of arms. There was formerly also a brass to William Millbourne, who died in 1415. He was represented in complete armour, with sword and dagger. This interesting brass has unfortunately disappeared.

In the chancel is a tablet to the memory of Sir Thomas Powell, a Cheshire Baronet, who died at Barn Elms in 1647. There is also a tablet to John Squier, Rector of Barnes. "He was invested with this care," says his epitaph, "Anno 1660, Sept. 2. He was divested of all care, Anno 1662, Jan. 9." On the south wall, near the entrance door, is an elaborate monument by Hickey in memory of Sir Richard Hoare, and his widow, Dame Frances Ann Hoare, who died in 1800. They dwelt at Barn Elms, a place celebrated as having been the residence of Sir Francis Walsing-

BARNES BRIDGE

ham, his son-in-law, the unfortunate Earl of Essex, and Abraham Cowley; and now occupied by the Ranelagh Club. There is also a monument to another occupant of Barn Elms, Vice-Chancellor Sir Lancelot Shadwell, who died in 1850.

At the north-east is a monument, on which is a figure representing a naval officer in uniform, in an attitude of sorrow. It was erected, we gather from the epitaph, by Captain William Dawson, R.N., in testimony of his grief for the loss of his wife, Letitia, who died in November, 1843. On the south wall are two brass tablets commemorating recent Rectors of Barnes. The first, which is close to the Hoare monument, is to the memory of the Rev. Lewis Taswell Lochee, who died after a rectorship of six years, on January 26, 1891. The second is farther east, by the pulpit. It is inscribed with the name of the Rev. John

ST MARY, BARNES

Ellerton, Honorary Canon of St. Alban's. He was Rector of Barnes from 1876 to 1884, and died on June 15, 1893.

On the exterior of the south wall is a tablet, protected by palings and encircled with rose bushes. It bears this inscription :—

> "Here lyeth interred Mr. Edward Rose,
> Citizen of London, who departed
> This lyfe the 3rd of July
> 1653."

Edward Rose left £20 to the parish of Barnes to purchase an acre of land for the benefit of the poor, at the same time stipulating that out of the profits of his bequest the palings before his monument should be always kept in repair and the rose bushes about it ever continued. As Lysons remarks, "this man made an innocent attempt at least to perpetuate his name."

The tombstones in the churchyard are numerous, but there are none of any special interest. One cannot but regret that the memorial of Anne Baynard has perished. She was a very learned young lady, so attached to the study of divinity that she learned Greek in order to be able to read St. Chrysostom in the original. She died in 1697 at the early age of twenty-five, and on her monument in Barnes Churchyard were engraved these lines :—

> "Here lies that happy maiden, who often said
> That no man is happy until he is dead;
> That the business of life is but playing the fool,
> Which hath no relation to saving the soul;
> For all the transaction that's under the sun,
> Is doing of nothing—if that be not done,
> All wisdom and knowledge does lie in this one."

The church of Barnes was probably originally founded about the time of Richard I. The patronage has always belonged to the Dean and Chapter of St. Paul's. Previously to 1388 the benefice had become a vicarage; since that year, in which the then vicar, John Lynne, was made rector, it has been a rectory. Hezekiah Burton was presented to the rectory in 1680, and died in the following year. He was a man much esteemed by Tillotson, who published his sermons and wrote an account of his life. Dr. Francis Hare, famous among the clergy of his time as a scholar and a controversialist, was Rector of Barnes from 1717 to 1727, resigning the living on being raised to the bishopric of St. Asaph. He was translated to Chichester in 1731, and died in 1740.

ST PAUL
HAMMERSMITH

HAMMERSMITH was originally a hamlet belonging to the parish of Fulham, but a chapel was erected here by the inhabitants, and consecrated by Laud, then Bishop of London, on June 7, 1631. In 1834, Hammersmith was created a separate parish, and the chapel of ease accordingly became the parish church. The appointment of the curate had, by the terms of the agreement made between Laud and the parishioners, been vested in the see of London, and the Bishop is now the patron of the vicarage. The old church, not being large enough for the needs of the greatly increased population of the parish, was pulled down, and a new church was commenced in 1882, and consecrated in 1886 by the present Archbishop of Canterbury, then Bishop of London. Though much altered in the course of time, the old church of Hammersmith remained to the last an interesting and picturesque building, and it is to be regretted that it could not have been left standing, and a new parish church erected elsewhere.

The two most prominent parishioners of Hammersmith at the time of the building of the chapel were the Earl of Mulgrave and Sir Nicholas Crispe. Edmund Sheffield, Earl of Mulgrave, commanded a vessel called the *Bear* in the fight against the Spanish Armada, and for his valour during that momentous conflict was made a Knight of the Garter by Queen Elizabeth. He afterwards served with distinction in Ireland, and was appointed by James I. President of the North, the duties of which office he performed for many years in a most exemplary manner. He had a house at Hammersmith, opposite the church, and promised that, as long as he should reside in the parish, he would provide the curate with lodging and diet. He died on October 6, 1646, in the eighty-third year of his age, and was buried in Hammersmith Church, where an altar-tomb of black and white

HAMMERSMITH OLD CHURCH (DEMOLISHED).

marble was erected to his memory. He was the great-grandfather of the witty and poetical Earl of Mulgrave, whom Queen Anne created Duke of Buckinghamshire, and great-great-grandfather of the second and last Duke, whose epitaph was written by Pope.

Sir Nicholas Crispe was a wealthy merchant of London, whose

devoted attachment to the cause of Charles I. won for him the admiration of Dr. Johnson. "A man of loyalty that deserves perpetual remembrance," he says in his *Life of Waller*; "when he was a merchant in the city, he gave and procured the king in his exigencies an hundred thousand pounds; and when he was driven from the exchange, raised a regiment and commanded it."

Crispe built himself a magnificent mansion at Hammersmith on the river bank in the direction of Fulham. Towards the

HAMMERSMITH CHURCH

erection of the church he was a bountiful contributor, for out of a total expense of about £2,000, he alone furnished, in money and materials, £700, and also embellished the roof with the arms of the Crown, roses, thistles, and fleur-de-lis. After having endured many perils and troubles in his sovereign's cause, he had the happiness of beholding the Restoration. He then placed in Hammersmith Church a bronze bust of Charles I. elevated on a monument of black and white marble, about eight feet high, with this inscription :—

> "This effigies was
> Erected by the special Appointment
> Of Sir Nicholas Crispe, Knight and Baronet
> As a grateful commemoration of that
> glorious Martyr King Charles
> the first of blessed
> Memory."

He died a few years afterwards, and his body was laid beside those of his parents in the family vault in St. Mildred's, Bread Street, to which church also he had been a munificent benefactor. But his heart was, in accordance with his special directions, placed in an urn beneath the bust of that royal master whom he had served so faithfully. The urn stands on a pedestal of black marble, which is thus inscribed :—

> "Within this urn is entombed the heart of
> Sir Nicholas Crispe, Knt and Baronet, a loyal
> Sharer in the sufferings of his late and present
> Majesty. He first settled the trade of gold
> from Guinea, and there built the castle of
> Cormantine. Died the 26th of February 1665.
> Aged 67 years."

Not long after the death of Sir Nicholas, his house was sold to Prince Rupert. In 1748 it was purchased by Bubb Dodington, afterwards Lord Melcombe, who called it "La Trappe." In 1792 it was bought by the Margrave of Brandenburg-Anspach, who had sold his dominions to the King of Prussia, and taken up his abode in England. From him it acquired the name of Brandenburg House, under which it was known during the last and most celebrated stage of its existence when, during the time of her trial, Queen Caroline was its occupant. She died at

Brandenburg House on August 7, 1821. The mansion was pulled down in the following year.

James Smith, a member of the Salters' Company and an Alderman of London, was buried at Hammersmith in October, 1667. His widow erected to his memory a black marble monument, surmounted by his bust, showing him in a flowing wig and the aldermanic gown, and recorded in the epitaph that he was "a good benefactor to his country, in erecting of almshouses for the relief of the poor in the parish of Bookham, near Maidenhead, where he was born. He was also very liberal to the poor children of Christ's Hospital, and to the said Company of Salters, and very free in many other charitable uses for the good of the poor. He had the blessing of many children, whereof five by Mary, his first wife, deceased; and by his second wife, Sarah, now living, fifteen."

Sarah Smith, who died in 1680, was also buried here, and is stated in her epitaph to have been "one truly joined to her husband, not only in conjugal love and virtue, but also in bountiful charity, having lately augmented the gifts of her late husband."

In 1685 Francis Lucy gave some ground to enlarge the churchyard on the west side. He was a member of the family which has been made famous by Shakespearean associations, as appears from the inscription on a brass plate found in a vault beneath the chancel in 1830, in which he is described as "Francis Lucy Esq., youngest son of Sir Thomas Lucy of Charlecote in the county of Warwick." The churchyard has been twice subsequently augmented.

Sir Edward Nevill, a Justice of the Common Pleas, who died in 1705, was interred at Hammersmith, and a monument to him was set up in the church. A tablet was likewise placed in commemoration of Thomas Worlidge, the miniature painter and engraver, who died at Hammersmith in September, 1766. Arthur Murphy, the dramatist and friend of Dr. Johnson, on whose *Life and Genius* he wrote an *Essay*, lived in Hammersmith Terrace, at the Chiswick end of the parish. He died in his seventy-eighth year, on June 18, 1805, and was buried in Hammersmith Church, "in the same vault," says the inscription, "with his mother, Mrs. Jane Murphy."

Several members of the Impey family, who resided in a house occupying part of the site of Lord Mulgrave's mansion, are buried at Hammersmith, among them Sir Elijah Impey, the Indian judge, whose history is so closely connected with that of Warren Hastings. Sir Elijah, who died on October 1, 1809, and his widow, Dame Mary, who survived him about nine years, have white marble tablets with encomiastic inscriptions.

A monument of white and veined marble, surmounted by an urn, is thus inscribed:—

> "Sacred to the memory of George Pring Esq., of Hammersmith, Surgeon, who died, November 7th 1824, aged 45. Professional skill, active benevolence, and zeal for the public welfare, were eminently united in this excellent man. The various plans for rational amusement and public benefit which originated with and were promoted by him will long endear his name to the inhabitants of this hamlet. His numerous friends, deeply lamenting his loss, have erected this tablet as a tribute of their esteem."

Mr. Pring was not buried here. He deserves to be remembered as the person who originated the scheme of a suspension bridge at Hammersmith. The work had just been commenced at the time of his death.

Sir George Shee, who filled with distinction several offices of state in England and Ireland at the end of the last and the beginning of the present century, and his widow, Elizabeth Maria, who was a descendant of Sir Nicholas Crispe, were interred in a vault beneath Hammersmith Church. They both died in their seventy-fourth year—he on February 3, 1826, and she on September 13, 1838.

In the present church, the bust of Charles I. and the urn containing the heart of Sir Nicholas Crispe are placed on the north side of the entrance to the side chapel on the south of the chancel. The monuments of Lord Mulgrave and Alderman Smith have not been as yet re-erected, owing to considerations of the expense which their re-adjustment would involve. They are, however, carefully preserved, and, when funds permit, will be brought back to the church. The inscriptions of many of the mural tablets have become almost illegible. Murphy's tablet is on the south wall; Impey's on the north wall; and Pring's at the west end of the north aisle.

The new church of Hammersmith is a large, but not particularly beautiful Gothic edifice. The tower, which contains eight bells, stands at the north-east: it is completed by a pierced parapet and four pinnacles. The central east front culminates in a gable, and at the south east rises a shaft which supports a pinnacle. At the west end is a circular projection which is used as a baptistery. There are porches in front of the main entrance doors, which are situated at the north and south, towards the west end. The aisles are separated from the nave by a series of six pointed arches on each side, supported by clustered columns of black marble. The church is lighted by lancet windows, of which there are three at the east end. Both the lower and clerestory windows are filled with tinted glass. The roof of the nave is coved and is crossed by bands. The roof of the chancel, which is coloured a bluish grey, is also crossed by bands, but of a different pattern. The organ is placed at the north of the chancel. The south of the chancel is occupied by a chapel which contains a side altar. The three windows in the south wall of this chapel and the iron screen which divides it from the nave were presented to the church in memory of Mr. William Watson, a Hammersmith solicitor, who died suddenly during the Parliamentary election of 1895, while he was zealously labouring to promote the return of General Goldsworthy, the Conservative candidate.

Hammersmith Church is situated on the west side of Queen Street, near the junction of that thoroughfare with Fulham Palace Road.

ALL SAINTS
FULHAM

FOR more than a thousand years—from the time, it is said, of the great Saxon Bishop Erkenwald—has the manor of Fulham belonged to the See of London. In its grounds on the river banks stands the Manor House, which constitutes the Bishop's Palace, and adjoining on the southeast is the parish church of All Saints. There was formerly a Rectory of Fulham, which was a sinecure in the gift of the Bishop of London, and the Rector appointed the Vicar. The Rectory has now been abolished, and the Vicarage is in the patronage of the Bishop of London.

One Rector, Richard Hill, who was presented in 1488, was consecrated Bishop of London in November of the following year. He had a long dispute with Archbishop Morton with regard to their respective authorities concerning the proving of wills, in which the Archbishop got the better of him; he died on February 20, 1496. Another Rector was a Bishop of London's son. This was Henry King, who, after holding the Rectory of Fulham about five and twenty years, resigned it in 1641, on being raised to the See of Chichester. He survived the Restoration and died Bishop of Chichester on October 1, 1669. He was buried in his cathedral. Newcourt describes him as "a most florid preacher," and says that "when he was young, he delighted much in the studies of music and poetry: when older, he applied himself to oratory and philosophy: and in his reduced age, he fixed on divinity, in which faculty he became eminent." His father was John King, Bishop of London from 1611 to 1621, whom James I., in his punning way, called "the King of Preachers." "He was a solid and profound divine," says Newcourt, "of great gravity and piety, and of a most excellent volubility of speech."

All Saints is a conspicuous object from Fulham Bridge, and the effect formed by this church on the Middlesex and the corresponding church of Putney on the Surrey side is very pleasing. The stone tower, though it has been considerably repaired in later times, may perhaps originally date from the fourteenth century. It attains a height of 95 feet, and is ornamented with battlements and with a turret at the south-west angle; upon it is placed a flagstaff. It contains ten bells. The body of the church was rebuilt in the Perpendicular style by Sir A. Blomfield in 1881, on July 9 of which year it was consecrated by Bishop Jackson. It is large and lofty, and includes two aisles separated from the nave by clustered columns and pointed arches, and two transepts. In the south transept stands the organ, which is by Jordan and dates originally from 1700. It is enclosed in a handsome oak case, and is ornamented with the Royal Arms. The font, which is placed at the west end of the north aisle, is of coloured marble, and is surmounted by a carved oak cover. It bears this inscription :—

> "This Font was erected at the charge of Thos.
> Hyll, Church-warden, 1622."

The monuments are numerous and of great interest. To the south-east wall of the nave is attached a lozenge-shaped brass plate, which displays at the top a half-length female figure, and at the bottom a coat of arms; between the figure and the arms is a Latin inscription, which states that this is the memorial of Margaret Svanders, a native of Ghent, wife of Gerard Hornebolt, also a native of Ghent, and a very distinguished painter, and mother of Susanna, wife of John Parker, the King's bowyer; and that she died on November 26, 1529. Hornebolt, who is also called Horneband, seems to have been one of those painters whom Henry VIII.'s love of art induced him to welcome to England. This brass, which is apparently of Flemish workmanship and is very finely executed, was, after having been long lost, re-discovered during some excavations in a reparation of the church in 1770.

FULHAM CHURCH AND PUTNEY BRIDGE.

Within the tower is the monument of Sir William Butts, Chief Physician to Henry VIII., who died a little more than a year before his royal master, on November 22, 1545. Sir William, who is introduced by Shakespeare in *Henry VIII.*, had an altar tomb with his figure in brass, but these have perished. A slab, however, remains, on which is engraved a Latin epitaph, which, having become decayed, was, as is stated at the conclusion, restored in 1627 by Leonard Butts, a gentleman of Norfolk. The epitaph includes the following lines :—

> "Quid medicina valet, quid herbis, quid gratia Regum,
> Quid popularis amor, mors ubi saeva venit?
> Sola valet pietas quae structa est auspice Christo,
> Sola in mort valet, caetera cuncta fluunt.
> Ergo mihi in vita fuerit quando omnia Christus,
> Mors mihi nunc lucrum, vitaque Christus erit."

Strype, in his *Life of Sir John Cheke*, conjectures that these graceful and devout lines were the work of that learned man. "And what if I should think that this was the issue of Cheke's own pious fancy, as his last respects to this man, for which he had so high and deserved a veneration?"

Butts had warmly encouraged Cheke in his studies, and had recommended him to Henry VIII., thus laying the foundation of his fortunes. The respect and gratitude with which Cheke regarded his benefactor are beautifully shown in the pious letter of consolation which he wrote to Butts—" Patrono suo singulari "—in the physician's last sickness, signing himself "Tuus animo filius."

On the wall of the north transept, near the side entrance door, is a tablet with the following quaint inscription:—

> "At Earth, in Cornwall, was my first beginninge.
> From Bondes and Carringtons, as it may apere.
> Now to Earth, in Fulham, God disposed my endinge.
> In March, the thousand and six hundred yere
> Of Christ, in whome my body here doth rest
> Tyll both in body and soule I shal be fully bleste.
>
> Thomas Bonde,
> Obiit A° Aetis suae
> 68."

Bonde left a bequest to the poor of the parish.

Near this is a monument, with kneeling figures of a man and woman, erected by William Payne "to the memory of himself and Jane his wife, who lived with him in wedlock XLIIII. yeares, and dyed the first day of Maye, in An° Dni. 1610." He describes himself as "of Pallingswick," that is, the district now known as Ravenscourt Park, where the name still survives in a corrupted form in Paddenswick Road. "The said William Payne," concludes the inscription, "has given for ever after his decease an Hande in the Ryver Thames called Mackenshaw, to the use of the Poore of this Parishe on Hammersmith side."

On the same wall is the monument of Catharine Hart, who is represented kneeling together with her four children, two sons in front of her and two daughters behind. She was the wife of John

FULHAM CHURCH AND THE BISHOPS WALK

Hart, and the eldest daughter of Edmund Powell, of Fulham, one of which family, Sir William Powell, founded in 1680 the almshouses for twelve poor widows, rebuilt in 1869, which stand to the north of the churchyard. Catharine Hart "lived vertuoslye, and dyed godlie ye 23rd daie of Octo—1605, in ye 24 yere of her age."

On the south of the chancel is a monument with a full-length life-sized figure of a lady, having in her arms an infant, while the figure of another infant is placed beside her. This is the memorial of Margaret, daughter of Sir Gilbert Gerrard, Master of the Rolls, and wife of Sir Peter Legh of Lyme, Cheshire. She died in 1603, at the age of thirty-three. Directly opposite, on the north side of the chancel, is the monument of Sir Thomas Smith, Latin Secretary, Clerk of the Council, and Master of the Requests, to James I. He died in 1609. In the tower is a large monument of alabaster and various coloured marble to William Plumbe, who died in 1593. His second wife was Elizabeth, widow of John Gresham, of Mayfield in Sussex. There is also a tablet to Edmund, youngest son of John Gresham, who died in the same year at the age of sixteen. A large black slab in the floor of the north aisle, at the west end, commemorates Humphrey Henchman, twelve years Bishop of London, who died in 1675. There is a flat stone in the chancel to Thomas Carlos, who died in 1665, son of Colonel William Careless, who concealed Charles II. in the oak at Boscobel, and was rewarded by a grant of arms on which figure an oak and three royal crowns, and by permission to change his name to Carlos.

In the tower is a life-sized statue of John, Viscount Mordaunt, a distinguished cavalier, and father of the celebrated Earl of Peterborough. He was Constable of Windsor Castle, and died, at the age of forty-eight, on June 5, 1675. The statue, which is of white marble, is elevated on a high slab of black marble; in the right hand is grasped the baton of office: two black marble pedestals in front of the statue support representations of a coronet and gauntlets: and at the sides are two oval tablets, one of which is inscribed with a long epitaph and the other with Lord Mordaunt's pedigree from the time of the Conquest. This monument was the work of Francis Bird and John Bushnell, the former of whom carved the statue, while the latter furnished the decorative part. For the statue Bird was paid £250, and the cost of the whole monument was £400.

In the corner of the tower is a tall and ornate monument of

veined marble, in memory of Thomas Winter, an East India merchant, who died in 1681. His epitaph states that he was the great-grandson of John Winter, the Elizabethan seaman. Not far off is a still larger monument of white marble, about fourteen feet in height, beautifully ornamented with festoons of flowers and figures of angels. It is by Grinling Gibbons, and cost £300. It is inscribed to the memory of Dorothy, wife, first of Sir William Clarke, Secretary at War to Charles II., and secondly of Dr. Samuel Barrow, Physician in ordinary to the same King. She died in 1695. Barrow, who was the author of the Latin verses prefixed to *Paradise Lost*, and died in 1682, is also commemorated on this monument, which was erected by George Clarke, Dame Dorothy's son by her first husband. There is, in addition, a large black stone in the floor of the south transept inscribed to his memory.

A large marble tablet, encircled by a broad frame of wood very finely carved, now placed in the porch at the north-west, is thus inscribed: "Here lyes buried Elizabeth Limpany, daughter of Robert and Isabel Limpany, who dyed October 10th 1694, and in the third year of her age." In this porch is also a tablet to Edward Limpany, who died in 1662, and Margaret Limpany, who died in 1675. Robert Limpany, who was a member of the Stationers' Company, died in April, 1735, having attained the great age of ninety four. In *The Gentleman's Magazine* for that month, it is stated of him: "He was sixty years a considerable merchant, yet never arrested any person. He owned a great part of the town of Fulham, to which he was a great benefactor; and so generous, that if any of his tenants pleaded poverty, he forgave their arrears. By his will he ordered all the parishioners to be invited to his funeral."

A tablet against the wall of the tower bears the following interesting inscription :--

"Near this place lies the body of Philip Daniel Castiglioni Maurelli, descended from an ancient family in the Kingdom of Naples. He was educated in the Church of Rome, but for the sake of the Gospel and a good conscience, having left his native country and relations, and become a sincere convert to the Protestant Faith, and a true member of the Church of England, he was entertained in the families of two successive Bishops of London, Dr. John Robinson and Dr. Edmund Gibson, in the service of whom he lived with great piety and fidelity upwards of twenty years, and died Jan. 17, 1737, aged 50 years."

Above this is a tablet to Bridget Holland, who died in 1823. She was the widow of Henry Holland, the architect of the Pavilion at Brighton and Carlton House, and daughter of Lancelot Brown, the landscape-gardener, "the omnipotent magician Brown," as Cowper calls him, whose dictatorial airs so exasperated George III.

In the tower are monuments to two Bishops of London, Edmund Gibson (1723–1748) and Beilby Porteus (1787–1809). Gibson lies in the churchyard, but Porteus was buried at Sundridge in Kent. There is also a monument to Christopher Wilson, Bishop of Bristol, who died in 1792, and his wife and family. He married Anne, daughter of Bishop Gibson, and was buried in his father-in-law's tomb. In the floor of the middle aisle is a stone bearing the name of Jeffrey Ekins, Dean of Carlisle, who died in 1791. In the vestry is a monument to a daughter of his. On the south wall is a handsome tablet to Catherine Elizabeth, Viscountess Ranelagh, who died in 1805. In the south transept is a brass tablet to Francis Blomfield, son of Bishop Blomfield, lost in the wreck of the *Northerner* off Cape Mendocino, North America, January 5, 1860, in his thirty-third year. To the wall of the north transept a brass plate has been affixed in memory of William Sharp of Fulham House, surgeon to George III., his brother Granville Sharp, the philanthropist, and his sister, Mrs. Elizabeth Prowse, children of Dr. Thomas Sharp, Archdeacon of Northumberland, and grandchildren of John Sharp, Archbishop of York, who are all three buried in a vault on the western side of the churchyard.

The east window is in memory of Bishop Blomfield, Bishop of London 1828–1856. One of the windows in the south wall is in memory of Bishop Jackson, Bishop of London 1869–1885. That at the west end of the south aisle is in memory of Arch-

FULHAM AND PUTNEY CHURCHES FROM THE RIVER

bishop Tait, Bishop of London 1856–1868, Archbishop of Canterbury 1868–1882, and Catherine, his wife. The westernmost window in the north wall was contributed by the children of the parish in commemoration of the rebuilding of the church in 1881.

The churchyard is even more interesting than the church. Here, to the east of the church, is a notable array of dignified Episcopal tombs. Here sleep Henry Compton, Bishop of London 1675–1713, the stout prelate who signed the invitation to the Prince of Orange, and rode with drawn sword in front of the Princess Anne; John Robinson, 1713-1723, the skilful diplomatist, who was Plenipotentiary at Utrecht; the learned Edmund Gibson, 1723-1748; Thomas Sherlock, the famous preacher, 1748-1761; Thomas Hayter, whose brief episcopate of three months terminated on January 9, 1762, and in whom, says Churchill, "mankind lost a friend"; Richard Terrick, 1764-1777; the elegant scholar, Robert Lowth, 1777-1787; and John Randolph, 1809-1813. The two most imposing of these tombs are those of Bishop Lowth and Bishop Sherlock. The practice of interment outside the church which thus prevailed among the bishops was originated by Compton, who, with a wisdom beyond that of most of his contemporaries, declared that the church was for the living, the churchyard for the dead, and therefore directed that his remains should be buried in the churchyard.

Against the east wall of the church is a tablet, the inscription on which is now much defaced, to one Thomas Cornwallis, who, if we may believe his epitaph, was a perfect paragon of virtue and amiability. "His person," we are told, "was graceful, his soul sublime; honor, virtue and complacency guided all his actions. A lover of his country, most tender and indulgent to his wife and children, obliging and serviceable to his friends, hospitable and generous to his neighbours, just, charitable and courteous to all he conversed with. He lived beloved and died lamented by them all ye 16 of July, 1703. His noon was night, being made perfect in 33 years." His daughter Laetitia seems to have taken after her father, for of her we read that "she dyed as she had lyved, a bright example of every virtue and accomplishment that make life happiness and death a blessing."

To the south of the tombs of the bishops are those of two distinguished citizens of London—Sir Francis Child, the first banker of that family, Lord Mayor 1698, and one of the representatives of the city in the first Parliament of Queen Anne, and Sir William Withers, Lord Mayor 1707, and a representative of the city in five Parliaments. The tomb of Child, who died in 1713, is ornamented with the insignia of the mayoralty. That of Withers, who departed this life in 1720, is surmounted by sword-rests. On the sides are inscriptions to some of his descendants, the Ravenshaws.

In the very midst of the bishops lies Theodore Hook. His grave is marked by a plain headstone merely inscribed—

> "Theodore Edward Hook
> Died 25th August 1841
> In the 53rd year of his Age."—

and by a small stone at the foot bearing his initials and the year of his death. He died at that residence in Fulham which the genial Ingoldsby spied from the river:—

> "As Dick and I
> Were a-sailing by,
> At Fulham Bridge, I cocked my eye,
> And says I, 'Add-Zooks !
> There's Theodore Hook's
> Whose Sayings and Doings make such pretty Looks."

Hook's house was pulled down fourteen years after his death.

In Fulham Churchyard are also buried two persons closely connected, one with the boyhood, the other with the middle age of Cowper. These are Vincent Bourne, who was one of the Westminster masters when the poet was at school there, and whose elegant Latin poems were subsequently turned into equally graceful English verse by his old pupil; and Joseph Johnson, Cowper's publisher. Bourne died in 1747, Johnson in 1809.

At the extremity of the additional burying-ground on the

north-west, rest side by side Bishop Blomfield (died 1857), by whom this new cemetery was consecrated; Bishop Jackson; and Colonel Thomas Forsyth Tait, a distinguished Indian soldier, who breathed his last on March 16, 1859, in the house of his youngest brother, then Bishop of London.

ST MARY
PUTNEY

PUTNEY CHURCH (THE SUNDIAL)

THE church of St. Mary, Putney, is situated at the bottom of High Street, on the east side, and is close to the bridge, the north side of the churchyard extending to the edge of the river. Like that of Mortlake, it was originally built as a chapel of ease to Wimbledon: but its foundation was earlier, as it is mentioned in 1302, almost half a century before Mortlake Church was commenced. Of the present church the most ancient portion is the tower, which was probably erected in the fifteenth century. It is of stone, and has a handsome appearance. It is finished with battlements, and has a turret at the north-east angle; and on the south face, under the clock, is a sundial. There are eight bells.

RIVERSIDE CHURCHES

The body of the church, which mostly dated from the early part of the sixteenth century, and was famous as having been used, while the Parliamentary army was encamped at Putney (from August 27 to November 13, 1647), as a council chamber by Cromwell, Fairfax, and the other leading officers, was pulled down in 1836, and the present edifice erected from the designs of Edward Lapidge, the architect of Kingston Bridge, St. Peter's Hammersmith, and St. Andrew's Ham. It is a commonplace building in the Perpendicular style, principally constructed of pale-coloured brick. It includes two aisles, and has galleries on the north, west, and south. The walls are painted a lightish blue, the roof of the chancel, which is ornamented, a somewhat richer blue; the roof of the nave is coved, and is crossed by beams. The organ is placed at the south of the chancel. The east window is filled with painted glass, inserted in memory of his mother by Archbishop Longley, then Bishop of Ripon.

The church is redeemed from absolute dreariness by Bishop West's chapel. Nicholas West was born at Putney, where his father pursued the trade of a baker. He was educated at King's College, Cambridge, where he first distinguished himself by the liveliness of his frolics, but subsequently to a much greater degree by his uncommon learning and abilities. Having taken orders, he became in 1502 vicar of Kingston on-Thames. Henry VII. made him one of his chaplains, and both that sovereign and his son and successor despatched him to the Continent on missions of importance, in the conduct of which he showed himself a skilful diplomatist. In 1515 his services were rewarded with the bishopric of Ely. In his later years he zealously espoused the cause of Catherine of Aragon: he was one of that Queen's advocates, and wrote a book in opposition to the divorce. He died in April, 1533, and was buried in Ely Cathedral.

Bishop West embellished the church of his birthplace by the

addition of a side chapel, which he built at the south of the chancel. When the church was rebuilt, this chapel, for some reason not easy to discover, was re-erected on the north side of the chancel. It is about fifteen feet long by ten feet wide, and about fifteen feet high. The roof is ornamented with extremely beautiful fan-groining, and upon it are displayed in two circles the

PUTNEY CHURCH

arms of West quartered with those of the See of Ely. On the east wall is an inscription which states that—

"This chapel was restored A.D. 1878, in loving memory of Sarah and Ann Lewis of Putney."

These two ladies caused the windows in the north wall of the chapel to be filled with stained glass, as we learn from another inscription :—

"These windows were set up by two sisters, Sarah and Ann Lewis, many years resident in Putney, as a thank-offering to God at the close of a long and honoured life spent in the work of education."

Under one of these windows has been affixed to the wall a brass representation of a man in armour. The figure is perfect, and the inscription has also been preserved and placed above it. This gives the name of John Welbeck, who died in 1477, and Agnes, his wife, who died in 1478. When Lysons wrote his account of Putney, in 1792, the figure of Agnes Welbeck, "habited," he says, "in a long robe," was still in existence, but it has now disappeared. Aubrey, in his *Natural History and Antiquities of the County of Surrey*, mentions, on the authority of Vincent's MS. *Visitation of Surrey*, written towards the end of James I.'s reign, four other brasses to members of this family: Jane, wife of William Welbeck, haberdasher of the city of London, who died in 1485; Richard Welbeck of the Middle Temple, who died in 1488; Johanna, wife of Richard Welbeck, who died in 1489; and John, son of Richard Welbeck, a member of the Inner Temple, and servant to Archbishop Morton, who died in 1494.

Within the tower, on the south wall, is a large monument to Richard Lussher, who died in 1615. On the opposite side is a very ornate monument with black marble columns, in memory of Catherine, wife of Sir Anthony Palmer, who died in 1613. On the walls of the tower are also tables of benefactors. On the west wall, north of the tower, behind the font, is the monument of Sir Anthony Palmer's second wife, Margaret, who died in 1619, and of Philadelphia, his daughter by his first wife, who died in 1621. On the north wall is a monument, prominently displaying a skull, to Sir Thomas Dawes, who died in 1655. On the wall at the east end of the south aisle is a large tablet to James Martyn, who died in 1651; and close to it is a brass plate of a much more recent period, for it commemorates Emily Louisa Henley, wife of Robert Henley, Vicar of Putney, who died on August 20, 1893.

ST MARY, PUTNEY

In the west gallery is a monument to Robert Gale, Chaplain to Christian, Countess of Devonshire, who died in 1659, and also one to Edward Martyn, who died in 1655. In the north gallery are tablets to Leicester Burdet, a merchant, who died in 1691; Daniel, son of Sir Robert Belt, of Bossall, Yorkshire, who died in 1697; Thomas Payne, "Serjeant at Arms for thirty-six years to the Crown," who died on Christmas Day, 1698; and Sir John Dick, Bart., who was for twenty-two years British Consul at Leghorn, and afterwards Comptroller of Army Accounts and

PUTNEY CHURCH AND BRIDGE

Auditor of Public Accounts, and who died at his seat at Roehampton, aged eighty-five, on December 2, 1804. In the south gallery is a monument, with half-length medallion portrait, inscribed to Maria Cary, but bearing no date.

John Toland, the deistical writer, spent the last four years of his life at Putney, and there wrote *Pantheisticon*. He died at Putney on March 11, 1722, and was buried in the churchyard two days later. He has no memorial. Shortly before he died he composed a Latin epitaph for himself, in which he praised his own virtues very highly and set forth his views about a future state; it was not, however, inscribed over his grave.

On the south wall of the churchyard is the following inscription:—

> "The Ancient Riverside Boundary
> Of this Churchyard was restored, and the
> Western Boundary Wall was straightened
> At the Building of Putney New Bridge
> By the Metropolitan Board of Works,
> 1886
> W. J. Lancaster) Churchwardens
> W. H. Cutler)
> Robert Henley,
> Vicar."

In 1763 Dr. Roger Pettiwand bestowed upon the parish a piece of land for an additional burying ground. It is situated in the Upper Richmond Road, to the west of Putney High Street, and on the south side of the way. The most conspicuous monument in it is a huge marble sarcophagus, which bears the following inscription, from the pen of Horace Walpole:—

> "To the beloved memory of Robert Wood, a man of supreme benevolence, who was born at the Castle of Riverstown near Trim, in the County of Meath, and died Sept. 9th 1771, in the fifty-fifth year of his age: and of Thomas Wood, his son, who died Aug 25th, 1772, in his ninth year; Ann, their once happy wife and mother, now dedicates this melancholy and inadequate memorial of her affection and grief. The beautiful editions of Balbec and Palmyra, illustrated by the classic pen of Robert Wood, supply a nobler and more lasting monument, and will survive those august remains."

Wood travelled in the East in 1751, and gave to the world the results of his travels in two very elaborate folios, *The Ruins of*

ST MARY, PUTNEY

Palmyra otherwise Tadmor in the Desert, published in 1753, and *The Ruins of Balbec otherwise Heliopolis in Coelosyria*, published in 1757. In 1759 he was made Under Secretary of State, and in this capacity he was concerned in the issue of the celebrated general warrant against Wilkes, who in consequence brought an action against him and gained a verdict with £1,000 damages. Wood owned a large house with extensive grounds, situated between the roads to Wimbledon and Wandsworth. He bought it from the executors of Edward Gibbon, whose son, the historian, was born in it on April 27, 1737, and baptized at Putney Church on May 13 following.

The Vicarage of Putney, like that of Mortlake, is in the patronage of the Dean and Chapter of Worcester.

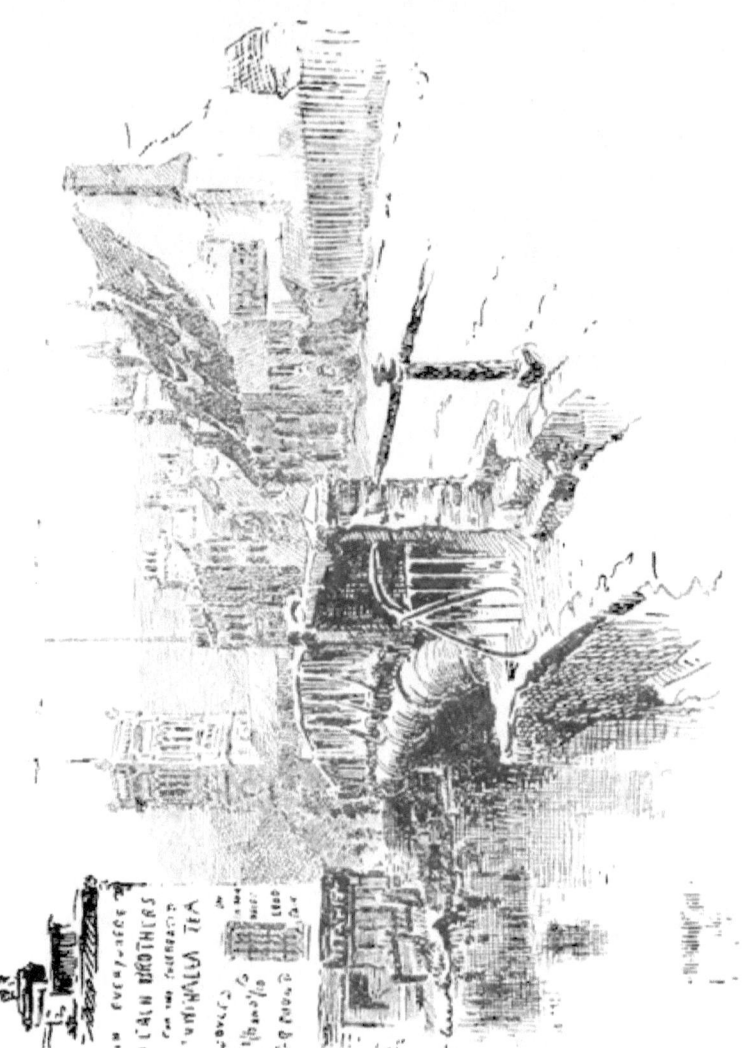

WANDSWORTH AND THE WANDLE

ALL SAINTS
WANDSWORTH

THE church of All Saints, Wandsworth, stands on the north side of High Street. At the west end is a brick tower, which was built in 1630, and was, as we are informed by an inscription on the south face, "repaired and heightened" in 1841, when the Rev. D. C. Delafosse was vicar. He was the son of the Rev. R. M. Delafosse, whose monument, by Flaxman, is in Richmond Church. The additional storey, then imposed, is poorly executed, and by no means improves the tower's appearance. There are eight bells, cast by Thomas Mears at the Whitechapel Bell Foundry in 1842. In the basement storey remnants of an older stone and flint tower have been discovered beneath the coating of brick, by the present vicar, when letting a safe into the vestry wall. The body of the church was rebuilt in 1780. It is of brick, and is very ugly. In front of the south entrance is a mean portico. The interior contains two aisles, which extend the whole length of the church, and a nave and chancel, between which there is no perceptible division. The ceiling of the nave is coved, those of the aisles are flat. There is a large round-headed central east window, which is filled with stained glass, as is also a small circular window above it. The large windows at the east end of the north and south aisles are plain. There are galleries on the north, west, and south. On the front of the west gallery are fixed the Royal Arms. The organ is placed at the north of the chancel.

Though in itself it possesses very little that is pleasing, Wandsworth Church is well worth a visit for the sake of its monuments. The most interesting of these is a brass on the floor of the chancel with the figure of a man in armour, the head unfortunately being missing. It disappeared long ago, for Strype, in noticing this brass, remarks that the head had been "torn off." The inscription also is imperfect, the surname of the warrior being lost, and all we are able to ascertain is that his Christian name was Richard, and that he was an officer in the army of Henry V., and died in 1420. Also on the chancel floor, a little to the north of this ancient memorial, are two brass plates commemorating respectively John Powell and Robert Knaresbrough, who both died in 1611. On Powell's plate are inscribed the following quaint lines:—

> "Under a stone, within this place,
> Doth lie John Powel, who, for the space
> Of Thirty years before her death,
> Did serve the Queen Elizabeth;
> And to King James, of worthy fame,
> For nine years more he did the same;
> And when the years of seventy-four
>   Were now come to an end,
> Into the hands of God above
>   His soul he did commend.
>   Obiit 25 die Junii
>   Anno Dom. 1611."

Knaresbrough's epitaph, which is in Latin, merely states that he had been a servant of Queen Elizabeth, and was patron of the church, and that he died on January 11, 1611.

These brasses are preserved with laudable care, being covered with thick floor cloth, so as to protect them from being injured by persons walking over them.

At the north of the chancel is a monument, with kneeling effigy, to Susanna Powell, John Powell's widow, who died in 1630. She " was a gracious benefactor unto this town of Wandsworth,"

WANDSWORTH CHURCH

and the particulars of her benefactions are recorded on her monument, "that God might be glorified, the memorial of the Just might be blessed, and the living stirred up to such like good works of piety and compassion." She owned the rectory of Wandsworth, and charged it with the payment of her charitable bequests, as appears by her epitaph: "These foresaid donations are to issue out of the benefits and profits of the rectory of Wandsworth." She was the "daughter of Thomas Hayward of Wandsworth, Yeoman of the Guard unto King Henry the Eighth, King Edward the Sixth, to Queen Mary, and to Queen Elizabeth, of ever precious memory."

Next to this monument, on the north side, is the memorial of Sir Thomas Brodrick, who died in 1641, and Katherine, his wife, who died in 1678. On it are displayed their busts in white marble, and very finely sculptured. Several of this family have been buried at Wandsworth, among them Allan Brodrick, who was raised to the peerage as Viscount Middleton, and died in 1747, and George, the second Viscount, who died in 1765. Sir Allan Brodrick, Surveyor-General of Ireland, who died in 1680, left a charitable bequest to the parish.

On the south of the chancel is the monument of Alderman Henry Smith, with a figure of him, clad in a gown and ruff, and kneeling at a desk. Smith, who was born at Wandsworth, began life in poverty, but gradually amassed great wealth. In 1620, being then a widower, and having no children, he assigned his estate to trustees for charitable uses, only reserving £500 per annum for his own use. He died, in his seventy-ninth year, on January 30, 1628, at his house in Silver Street, in the city of London, and on February 14 following he was interred, as he had desired, in the church of his native place. Nearly every parish in Surrey received benefit from his charity, and he also bequeathed £10,000 "to buy impropriations for Godly preachers"; £1,000 "to buy lands for perpetuity to redeem poor captives and prisoners from the Turkish tyranny"; and £150 to found a fellowship at Cambridge for his own kindred. His epitaph contains particulars of his benefactions, and designates his conduct as "a pattern worthy the imitation of those whom God has blessed with the abundance of the goods of this life to follow him therein."

On the same wall, a little farther south, is a tablet to a centenarian, William Plank, of whom the inscription says that he was "Father and for 52 years a member of the Court of Assistants of the Worshipful Company of Salters, and for 78 years a Liveryman of the same Company and a Freeman of the city of London;" that he was "born at Wandsworth 7th November A.D. 1767 at 3 p.m.," and "died at Harrow on the Hill, where he had resided 56 years, 20th November A.D. 1867 at 5.10 a.m. aged 100 years and 12 days"; and that he was "interred at Harrow in the old churchyard."

At the west end of the north aisle is a monument to Samuel Palmer, F.R.S., surgeon of St. Bartholomew's Hospital, who died in 1738. At the north-west of the nave, above the vicar's pew, and near the entrance to the vestry-room, is a tablet, the inscription on which is worth quoting:—

> "Near this place are deposited the remains of Mr. Somerset Draper, who departed this life greatly lamented Jan. 31st 1756, aged 49 years. In the year 1742 he married Elizabeth, youngest sister to the Friend of his heart, James Clutterbuck Esq. who in grateful remembrance of his affection to her and of his other truly amiable qualities hath caused this monument to be erected to his memory."

The church of Wandsworth was anciently appropriated to the Abbey of Westminster. The advowson of the vicarage belonged, at the commencement of the seventeenth century, to Robert Knaresbrough, as his epitaph records. About 1630 it was in the possession of the Crown, but before many years had passed it again became private property, and such it has ever since remained.

RIVERSIDE CHURCHES

One vicar of Wandsworth, Griffith Clerke, came to a tragic end. He was hanged and quartered on July 8, 1539, apparently for denying the King's supremacy. With him suffered his chaplain, his servant, and a friar named Ware.

ST MARY BATTERSEA

BATTERSEA CHURCH, WEST FRONT

THE church of St. Mary, Battersea, stands by the waterside, a little to the west of Battersea Bridge. The old church was taken down about 1775, and the present edifice was erected in its stead, and first used for Divine worship in November, 1777. It is built of brick, with stone quoins and cornices. At the east is a circular projection, which forms the chancel. At the west is a portico, behind which rises a brick tower, pierced by windows with louvres; the tower is concluded by a cornice with pineapples at the angles; above this is a pedestal in which are the clock-faces, and next comes an octagon which supports a lead-covered obelisk, terminating in a ball and vane. This steeple is a very conspicuous object from the Chelsea side of the river. There are eight bells. The churchyard, which is well furnished with trees, has a very pretty appearance in summer.

The interior of the church is plain, with a flat roof and no aisles. There are galleries on the north, south, and west. The north and south walls each have two rows of windows. The large east window is filled with painted glass preserved from the old church. In the lower portion are portraits of Henry VII., his grandmother, Margaret Beauchamp, and Queen Elizabeth; over these are the Royal Arms in the centre, and at the sides the arms and quarterings of the St. John family. Below the portraits are inscriptions setting forth the relationship of the St. Johns to

LITTLE EA CHURCH

Margaret Beauchamp and the Bullens. At the north-east and south-east are small circular windows. The lower parts of the walls are panelled, and above they are coloured a light green; the roof is coloured blue, and has a large ornament in the centre. In front of the chancel arch are affixed the Royal Arms. The font stands in the north-east of the nave, and the pulpit is on the opposite side. The organ occupies the east end of the south gallery.

ST. MARY, BATTERSEA

Some interesting monuments, which belonged to the old church, still remain. The earliest of these is that of Oliver St. John, who was General of the Forces, Lord High Treasurer and Lord Deputy of Ireland; and was created Viscount Grandison in the peerage of Ireland by James I., and by Charles I. Baron St. John in the peerage of England. He married Joan, widow of Sir William Holcroft, and daughter and heiress of Henry Roydon, to whom the manor of Battersea had been granted by Queen Elizabeth; thus it was that the manor came into the hands of the St. Johns. Lord Grandison's monument is over the north gallery. It displays white marble busts of himself and his lady in a recess under a canopy supported by black marble columns. His arms are shown at the top of the monument in front of the pediment. Behind the bust is a Latin inscription. He died, aged seventy, on December 29, 1630, and Lady Grandison only survived him about two months.

BATTERSEA CHURCH, WINDOW IN WEST FRONT

Lord Grandison left no children. His nephew, Sir John St. John, was buried in Battersea in 1648. So magnificent was his funeral that the heralds instituted a prosecution against his executor for causing him to be buried in a manner above the degree of a baronet. Sir Walter St. John, nephew of Sir John, inherited the Battersea Estate. He married a daughter of Lord Chief Justice St. John, and died at the age of eighty-seven, in 1708. He was a man, says Lysons, "eminent for piety and moral virtues," and founded a free school at Battersea. His son, Henry St. John, was created Viscount St. John in 1716, and attained an even greater age than his father, being almost ninety when he died in April, 1742. He was succeeded by the most celebrated man of the whole family, his son, Henry, Viscount Bolingbroke, Queen Anne's minister, and Pope's "guide, philosopher and friend." Bolingbroke, who was nearly sixty-four when his father died, spent his remaining years at Battersea, and, dying here on December 12, 1751, was buried in the family vault six days later. Sir John St. John, Sir Walter St. John, and Lord Bolingbroke's father have no monuments, but there is one to Bolingbroke and his second wife next to Lord Grandison's. It is the work of Roubiliac, and is of grey and black marble. At the sides of the inscription are medallion profiles of Bolingbroke and his Viscountess, above is an urn, and at the summit are displayed his arms. Bolingbroke's epitaph, which probably was his own composition, has often been quoted. It runs as follows:—

"Here lies Henry St. John, in the reign of Queen Anne, Secretary of War, Secretary of State, and Viscount Bolingbroke: in the days of King George the First and King George the Second, something more and better. His attachment to Queen Anne exposed him to a long and severe persecution; he bore it with firmness of mind, the enemy of no national party, the friend of no faction; distinguished (under the cloud of a proscription, which had not been entirely taken off) by zeal to maintain the liberty and to restore the ancient prosperity of Great Britain. He died the 12th of December, 1751, aged 73."

Lady Bolingbroke was a French lady, a niece of Madame de Maintenon. Her epitaph is as follows:—

> "In the same vault are interred the remains of Mary Clara des Champs de Marcelly, Marchioness of Villette, and Viscountess Bolingbroke, of a noble family, bred in the court of Lewis 14th. She reflected a lustre on the former by the superior accomplishments of her mind; she was an ornament to the latter by the amiable dignity and grace of her behaviour. She lived, the honour of her own sex, the delight and admiration of ours: she dyed, an object of imitation to both: with all the firmness that reason, with all the resignation that religion can inspire; aged 74, the 18th of March, 1750."

Over the south gallery is a monument to Bolingbroke's half-brother, the Hon. Holles St. John, equerry to Queen Caroline, who died in 1738, aged twenty-seven.

In 1763 the manor of Battersea was sold by Bolingbroke's nephew, the second Viscount, to the trustees of Lord Spencer, and it has ever since remained the property of that noble family.

Bolingbroke House, the mansion of the St. Johns, in the yard of which its owner burned Pope's clandestine edition of the *Patriot King*, was situated to the east of the church. It was mostly pulled down in 1778, and now nothing remains of it except the name, which survives in Bolingbroke Road and Bolingbroke Terrace.

Over the south gallery, near Holles St. John's monument, is that of Sir Edward Wynter, a man of marvellous prowess, as his epitaph records:—

> "Born to be great in fortune as in mind,
> Too great to be within one isle confined;

Young, helpless, friendless, seas unknown he tried;
But English courage all those wants supplied;
A pregnant wit, a painful diligence,
Care to provide, and bounty to dispense:
Join'd to a soul sincere, plain, open, just,
Procur'd him friends, and friends procur'd him trust:
These were his fortune's rise, and thus began
This hardy youth, rais'd to that happy man.
A rare example, and unknown to the most,
Where wealth is gain'd and conscience is not lost.
Nor less in martial honor was his name
Witness his actions of immortal fame:
Alone, unarm'd, a tyger he oppress'd,
And crush'd to death the monster of a beast.
Twice twenty mounted Moors he overthrew
Singly on foot, some wounded, some he slew.
Dispers'd the rest. What more could Sampson do?
True to his friends, a terror to his foes,
Here, now in peace his honor'd bones repose!"

The prose part of his epitaph informs us that he was a merchant in the East Indies, and after an absence of forty-two years returned to England and married Emma, daughter of Richard Howe, a gentleman of Norfolk; and that he died, at the age of sixty-four, on March 2, 1686. The monument is surmounted by a large bust of Sir Edward. Beneath the inscription is a bas-relief in which he is represented in the performance of his two mighty exploits—crushing to death the tiger, and overthrowing the mounted Moors. At the bottom is an inscription stating that Catherine, relict of William Wynter, Sir Edward's grandson, who died in 1771, and her son, William Woodstock Wynter, who died in 1747, were also buried here, and that the monument was re-erected and repaired by Edward Hampson Wynter, a great-grandson of Sir Edward.

Sir Edward Wynter lived at York House, Battersea, which had

ST MARY, BATTERSEA

formerly been a residence of the Archbishop of York, and which has given its name to York Road.

On the east wall above the north gallery is a large monument to Sir John Fleet, who was Lord Mayor of London in 1692. He died, at the age of sixty-five, on July 6, 1712. Over the staircase leading to the south gallery, is another large monument to James Bull, a London merchant, who died in 1713. His widow, Frances, who died in 1738, has a smaller monument on the north wall below the gallery.

A considerable number of memorials have been added since the building of the present church. The most striking of these is one over the south gallery, marked "Coade, Lambeth, 1792," and displaying an urn and a beautifully executed female figure. It bears an epitaph in prose and verse to Elizabeth, wife of James Neild, of St. James's Street, who died June 30, 1791, in her thirty-sixth year. On the south wall, beneath the gallery, is a slab, bearing an urn, inscribed tablet, and arms, to the memory of Thomas Astle, F.R.S., F.S.A., Keeper of the Records of the Tower of London, and one of the trustees of the British Museum. He died, in his sixty-eighth year, on December 1, 1803. In the west gallery is a monument, with kneeling angels, to Richard Rothwell, Alderman of London, and Sheriff in 1819, who died in 1821, and Eleanor, his widow, who died in 1834; and also one to his eldest daughter, Margaret Susanna, wife of Henry Pounsett of Stockwell, who died in 1820, and her second daughter, Ellen Anne Pounsett, who died in 1834. Over the staircase leading to the north gallery is a lozenge-shaped tablet in memory of John Ambrose, for fifty-seven years sexton and steeple-keeper, who died in 1875. A representation of a bell is very appropriately introduced beneath the inscription.

The manor of Battersea was given to Westminster Abbey by William the Conqueror. Both the manor and the church remained in the possession of the abbot and convent till the Dissolution of Monasteries. The advowson of the vicarage was granted, together with the manor, to the St. Johns, and from them it has come to the present patron, Earl Spencer.

In the south vestibule beneath the tower are two tables giving a list of the vicars from Thomas de Sunbury, 1301, to the present time. Among them are some distinguished names. Thomas Temple, instituted in 1634, was a brother of Sir John Temple, Master of the Rolls in Ireland, and uncle to Sir William Temple. He was one of the Assembly of Divines, and frequently preached before the Long Parliament. He was succeeded, in 1658, by Simon Patrick, domestic chaplain to Sir Walter St. John. Patrick remained in Battersea till 1676, and three years later he was made Dean of Peterborough. In the reign of James II. he, in conjunction with Dr. Jane, argued, in the King's presence, in favour of the reformed doctrines against two Roman Catholic priests, in which discussion the Protestant divines had so palpably the superiority that the King could not help observing that he "never heard a good cause so ill defended, or a bad one so well." His zeal and ability were not forgotten at the Revolution: in 1689 he was raised to the See of Chichester, and in 1691 translated to Ely. He died in 1707. Of Dr. Thomas Church, the following account is given by Lysons:—

"Dr. Thomas Church, of Brasenose College, Oxford, who was instituted to the vicarage of Battersea in the year 1740, distinguished himself much in the field of controversy, in which he engaged against Wesley, Whitfield, and Middleton: for his successful attack upon the latter, and his defence of the miraculous powers during the early ages of Christianity, the University of Oxford conferred on him the degree of D.D. by diploma. He was too zealously attached to his religion to let the opinions of Lord Bolingbroke pass unnoticed, notwithstanding he had been his patron. His publication upon this subject, however, was anonymous; it was called 'An Analysis of the Philosophical Works of the late Lord Bolingbroke,' and came out in 1755. Dr. Church published likewise several single sermons. He died in 1756, aged forty-nine, having never obtained any further preferment than the vicarage of Battersea and a prebendal stall in St. Paul's Cathedral. . . . Dr. Church, soon after he was instituted to the vicarage, began to transcribe a considerable part of the registers, which for many years preceding had been kept by a very ignorant parish clerk. He proceeded so far as to copy the whole of the baptisms, and, with great industry, rectified a vast number of mistakes, and supplied many deficiencies. The difficulty of transcribing the burials, of which indeed for some years there were no entries, discouraged him from proceeding any further in this laudable undertaking."

In the present century two vicars have quitted Battersea for the episcopal bench. Joseph Allen was, in 1835, promoted to the bishopric of Ely; and his successor, Robert John Eden, became Bishop of Sodor and Man in 1847. Bishop Eden succeeded to the Barony of Auckland in 1849: in 1854 he was translated to Bath and Wells: he resigned his see in 1869, and died in the following year.

William Blake, the poet and painter, was married in Battersea Church, on August 18, 1782, to Catherine Sophia Boucher.

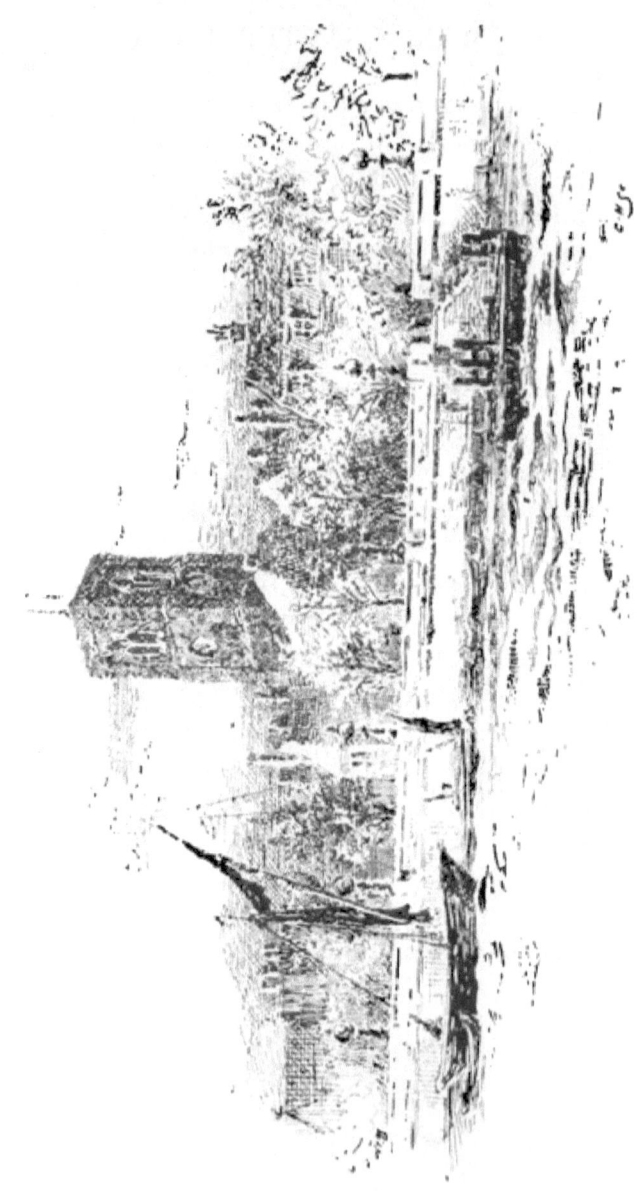

CHELSEA FROM THE RIVER

ST LUKE
CHELSEA

THE BRAY TOMB

CHELSEA Old Church stands at the south-east end of Church Street at its junction with Cheyne Walk. It is now a chapel of ease, having ceased to be parochial in 1824, when a new church of St. Luke was consecrated. It consists of a nave, chancel, and side-chapels at the north-east and south-east, and has a red-brick tower at the west end. The walls of the nave are of red brick, but those of the eastern portions are of stone. The architecture of various periods is here represented. The north-east chapel may very probably have been built in the fourteenth century; the chancel appears to date from the early years of the sixteenth century, and the south-east chapel is but little later, having been added by Sir Thomas More. Between the years 1667 and 1674 the church was considerably enlarged, and it was then that the present tower was erected.

Chelsea Church has fortunately escaped the modern restoration craze which has destroyed the interest of so many historical edifices; and, with its old-fashioned altar-piece and wooden altar-rails, its fine oak pulpit, its organ in the west gallery, its pews, the hatchments on the walls, and the banners of the Chelsea Volunteers of the period of the great French War, it presents an old-world appearance which is extremely refreshing. The special attraction of St. Luke's, however, is not the building itself, but the grand collection of monuments which are contained within its walls, and which render it second in interest to no church in the metropolis.

On the north side of the chancel is an altar-tomb, of which the inscription has long perished. It is probably that of Edmund, Lord Bray of Eaton, son of John, the brother of Sir Reginald Bray, Henry VII.'s minister, who was Lord of the Manor of Chelsea. Weever, who wrote early in Charles I.'s reign, copied from his tomb this brief inscription: "Of your charitie pray for the soul of Edmund Bray, Knight, cosin and heire to Sir Reignold Bray, Knight of the Garter." "His brother Reignold Bray, Esquire," he adds, "lieth buried by him, but their monuments are so defaced, that I can finde no farther remembrance, neither of their lives, nor of the time of their death."

Affixed to the same wall, a little farther east, is a monument with small kneeling figures to Thomas Hungerford of Chelsea, who died, at the age of seventy, in 1581. His epitaph states that he "served King Henry the 8. in the rometh of a gentilman pencioner, and was with his Matie at the wining of Bologne, and King Edward the 6. at Musslbroughe feild, besides Quene Mary and Quene Elizabeth in their affaires."

On this wall is the monument of Dr. Adam Littleton, Rector of Chelsea from 1669 to 1694, a very learned divine who published a *Latin, Greek, Hebrew, English Dictionary*, which enjoyed great celebrity; and there is also a tablet with medallion bust to a much more recent D.D.—Dr. Richard Wilson, Fellow of St. John's College, Cambridge, and many years Sunday evening Lecturer here, who died in 1879, aged eighty-one. On the east wall, to the north of the altar, is a small and elegant white marble monument "in memory of two affectionate sisters," Lucy Smith and Anne Wilton, who both died in 1781 and were buried in a vault beneath the chancel.

On the south side of the chancel is the monument which has made Chelsea Church, as Newcourt remarks, "most famous"— that of Sir Thomas More. Sir Thomas, when Chancellor, used to sing here in the choir in a surplice, for which the Duke of Norfolk called him a parish clerk, and told him that he dishonoured the King and his office. "Nay," rejoined Sir Thomas, "you may not think your master and mine will be offended with me for serving God, his master, or thereby count his office dishonoured." He erected this monument for himself in 1532 after his resignation of the Chancellorship. Under a flat Gothic arch, surmounted by his crest, a Moor's head, and his arms and those of his two wives, is a slab of black marble whereon is engraved the Latin inscription which he himself composed.

"It used to strike me, however," says Henry Kingsley, in his description of Chelsea Church in *The Hillyars and the Burtons*, "that, among the known or the unknown, Sir Thomas More was the most obstinately determined that posterity should hear his own account of himself." And certainly he has here placed on record a very full history, not only of his doings, but also of his thoughts and sentiments. He tells us of his birth and family, and recounts every step of his public career: states that he so behaved himself that his sovereign approved his labours, and neither the nobility nor the people disliked him, but that he was severe towards thieves, homicides and heretics; that after his father's death he began to feel older in mind, and weaker in body, and therefore obtained the King's permission to resign his offices, so that, being satiated with earthly things, he might spend his declining years in undisturbed contemplation of the world to come: that he caused this tomb to be erected that it might daily keep him in mind of the ever nearer approach of death, and that he had transferred hither the remains of his first wife. He concludes by entreating that, both alive and dead, he might receive the benefit of the reader's pious prayers.

Weever, writing in 1631, describes this inscription as "now hardly to be read," but a few years afterwards it was restored by one of the Lawrence family, and it was again renewed in 1833 by public subscription. On both occasions the words "hereticisque," in which he alluded to his persecution of heretics, were omitted, a blank space being left where they had been originally engraved. It is uncertain whether More's body was interred here or in the chapel of the Tower, but the latter was most probably his place of burial. His head was deposited in St. Dunstan's Church, Canterbury. His widow was buried at Northall in Hertfordshire. A portrait of Sir Thomas More, copied from the painting by Holbein, hangs in the vestry of Chelsea Church.

In consequence of More's attainder, his house at Chelsea, together with his other property, was forfeited to the Crown. It was granted to the Marquis of Winchester, the Lord High Treasurer, and after the death of his widow in 1586 it came into the possession of Lord Dacre, who had married the Marchioness's daughter by her first husband, Sir Richard Sackville. Lord Dacre died in 1594, and Lady Dacre in the following year. She bequeathed the house to Lord Burleigh, and from him it descended to his son, Robert Cecil, Earl of Salisbury, by whom it was rebuilt. Cecil sold it to the Earl of Lincoln, from whose hands it passed into those of his son-in-law Sir Arthur Gorges. Sir Arthur disposed of it to Lord Cranfield, subsequently Earl of Middlesex and Lord Treasurer. He sold it in 1625 to Charles I., who gave it to the Duke of Buckingham. During the Commonwealth it was held by Sir Bulstrode Whitelocke, but the second Duke of Buckingham, Dryden's Zimri, recovered it at the Restoration. In 1674 it was transferred to the Earl of Bristol, whose widow sold it in 1682 to Henry, Marquis of Worcester, afterwards Duke of Beaufort. From him it was called Beaufort House. In 1738 it was purchased by Sir Hans Sloane, and in 1740 it was demolished. The site is still marked by Beaufort Street, the second street to the west of the church. The gate, which Inigo Jones had built for Lord Middlesex, was presented by Sir Hans Sloane to Lord Burlington, who set it up at Chiswick—an occurrence commemorated by Pope in some sportive lines:—

> "O gate, how cam'st thou here?
> I was brought from Chelsea last year,
> Battered with wind and weather.
> Inigo Jones put me together.
> Sir Hans Sloane
> Let me alone;
> Burlington brought me hither."

On the south wall of the chancel, above Sir Thomas More's tomb, is a monument to Elizabeth, daughter of Sir Theodore Mayerne, physician to James I. and Charles I., and wife of Peter de Caumont, Marquis de Cugnac, a Huguenot, who had taken refuge in England. She died in 1653. Affixed to a pillar at the north-west of the chancel is the monument of Dr. Baldwin Hamey, an eminent physician who died in 1676. It was erected by Ralph Palmer of the Middle Temple, his great-grandson, who died in 1715, and to whom there is an inscription on the same pillar. Dr. Hamey was a bountiful contributor to the reparation of the church, and acted with great liberality towards the College of Physicians. Beneath his monument is a tablet stating that it was restored in 1880 by the Royal College of Physicians of

RIVERSIDE CHURCHES

London, "in grateful remembrance of their munificent benefactor."

In More's chapel against the south wall is the monument of Jane, Duchess of Northumberland, widow of John Dudley, Duke

THE MORE CHAPEL.

of Northumberland—who was executed for his attempt to place Lady Jane Grey on the throne—mother of Lord Guildford Dudley, Lady Jane's husband, and Robert, Earl of Leicester, Queen Elizabeth's favourite, and grandmother of Sir Philip Sidney. The manor of Chelsea was granted by Edward VI. to

ST LUKE, CHELSEA

the Duke of Northumberland, and his widow appears to have been allowed to retain it. Her epitaph says that "she departed this transitory world at her Maner of Chelse ye 22 daye of January, in ye second yere of ye reigne of our Sovereyne Lady Quene Mary the first, and in Ano. 1555." Her monument is covered with a Gothic canopy, which must have been very handsome, but is now in a dilapidated state. Above the epitaph are brass plates with kneeling figures of the Duchess and her children, the workmanship of which is not the best. Adjoining on the east is the altar-tomb of the Duchess's daughter, Catherine, Countess of Huntingdon, who died in 1620. Upon it is a slab of white marble inscribed with her epitaph.

CHAINED BOOKS

At the east end of the chapel is a magnificent monument to Sir Robert Stanley, who died in 1632. He was the second son of William, Earl of Derby, and brother to Earl James, the gallant Cavalier, who was beheaded after the battle of Worcester. He resided at Chelsea in a house which he obtained through his marriage with a daughter of Sir Arthur Gorges, and this branch of the Stanleys remained here till almost the close of the century. Sir Robert's bust in veined marble appears on his monument, which is also ornamented with busts of two of his children.

At the junction of More's chapel with the south aisle is a brass plate with kneeling figures of Sir Arthur Gorges, his second wife Elizabeth, daughter of the Earl of Lincoln, six sons and five daughters. Sir Arthur, who died in 1625, was a cousin of Sir Walter Raleigh, a friend of Spenser, a sailor, a scholar, a poet, and a member of several Parliaments. Among his works are a narrative of one of his voyages, which appears in Purchase's *Pilgrimes*, and a translation of Lucan's *Pharsalia*. Below are two stone slabs with English inscriptions—one in prose, the other in verse—to the memory of his grandson, Arthur Gorges, who died in 1668. Sir Arthur Gorges, who became possessed of the More chapel, together with the house which had been the Chancellor's, retained it when he sold the mansion to Lord Middlesex; but in 1664 it was sold by his grandson, subject to a right of burial for his family. Later owners were the Milmans, of whose connection with Chelsea we are still reminded in Milman's Street, the next street on the west beyond Beaufort Street. There are tablets on the south wall of the chapel to Sir William Milman, who died in 1713, and others of the family.

Against the wall of the south aisle is a large and elaborately executed monument in memory of Gregory, Lord Dacre, and Anne, his wife. Beneath an arch, upheld by pillars of veined marble, are placed their recumbent life sized effigies. Lord Dacre is represented in armour, while his lady is wrapped in a long cloak and has a ruff round her neck. The feet of each rest on a dog. Lord Dacre died September 25, 1594, and Lady Dacre followed him on May 14, 1595. She was sister to Thomas Sackville, created successively Baron Buckhurst and Earl of Dorset, and distinguished both as a statesman and as a poet. Emanuel Hospital at Westminster was founded in accordance with instructions in her will. This good work had been projected by her and her husband, but they did not live to execute it themselves.

At the side of one of the windows of this aisle is one of the smallest monuments ever seen. It consists of a minute brass tablet surrounded by a marble frame, and bears an inscription to the memory of Humphrey Peshull, a gentleman of Staffordshire, who died of a fever in London in 1650, at the age of fifty-one.

On the south wall is a tablet commemorating John Woolley, aged thirty-five, John Wells Lambe, aged twenty-nine, and William Bruce, aged twenty-nine, "who were drowned opposite this church through the swamping of their boat in a squall of wind," on June 20, 1839. The original tablet which recorded this sad accident is still, the inscription states, on the exterior wall. But the three hapless oarsmen have been honoured with this additional and more prominent memorial. Next to this is a tablet to Rear-Admiral Mathew Squire, who died in 1800. On the floor is the gravestone of Francis Thomas. The inscription is now illegible, but a copy of it is printed on a card which is attached to the wall over his tomb. He was "Director of the China Porcelain Manufactory, Lawrence Street, Chelsea," and "surely the tenderest husband, the best of fathers and the sincerest friend." He died on January 6, 1770, in his forty-fifth year. His epitaph is concluded by these four lines :—

> "Oh, but when the great God does call,
> And summons us both great and small,
> Therefore let us, my friends, prepare
> Like this the best of fathers here."

The Manor of Chelsea was granted by Queen Elizabeth to the Duchess of Somerset, widow of the Protector. After her death, in 1588, it was bestowed on one of her relations who was made Lord Stanhope of Harrington, and then on Katherine, Lady Howard, wife of the Lord Admiral. In Charles I.'s time it came into the possession of the Duke of Hamilton, whose loyalty brought him to the block in 1649. In 1660 it was sold by the then Duke to Charles Cheyne, afterwards created Viscount Newhaven of the Kingdom of Scotland, from whom Cheyne Walk has obtained its name. Cheyne's wife was Jane, daughter of William Cavendish, Duke of Newcastle, the Royalist commander, and it was through her large dowry that he was enabled to purchase the manor. Lady Jane Cheyne was a liberal benefactress to her parish church. She died in 1669, and has a beautiful monument in the north aisle, executed by Bernini at a cost, it is said, of £500. Under an arch sustained by columns of veined marble is a black sarcophagus, and upon this is placed a life-sized figure in white marble of Lady Jane, reclining upon her elbow, with her hand on a Bible. There is a long Latin epitaph, and also an inscription to her husband, who died in 1698.

On the wall of this aisle is a tablet to Richard Guildford, who died in 1680. He bequeathed £8 per annum to be distributed amongst sixteen poor people of the parish on December 5, that being the anniversary of his marriage with his last wife.

Between the north aisle and the chancel is a large monument overshadowed by an arch decorated with handsome carving and about ten feet high. It bears an inscription to the memory of Richard Gervoise, who died, at the age of twenty-seven, in 1563. It may very probably have been first erected to his father, Richard Gervoise, who was Sheriff of London in 1546, and was buried at Chelsea in 1557.

In the chapel at the north of the chancel is a monument on the north wall, with kneeling figures, to Thomas Lawrence, who died in 1593. Beside it is that of his daughter, Sarah, wife of Richard Colvill of Newton, in the Isle of Ely, who died in 1631. She has a monument of white marble, on which she is represented rising from her tomb, habited in a winding sheet, with hands upraised and eyes gazing fervently towards heaven. On the east wall is the monument of her brother, Sir John Lawrence, who died in 1638. The Lawrences were long the owners of this chapel. They resided at Chelsea for many generations in a

house which had been the manor house, before Henry VIII.
built a new mansion farther eastward, near where the Pier Hotel
now stands. The site of their house is shown by Lawrence
Street, the next street to the church on the east. The More

LAWRENCE CHAPEL.

chapel and the Lawrence chapel are now integral parts of the
church, having been purchased from their private possessors—the
former about twenty years ago, the latter more recently.

On the outside of the church, affixed to the south wall, are monuments to Dr. Edward Chamberlayne, Susannah, his widow, his sons, Peregrine Clifford, Edward and John, and his daughter Anne, wife of John Spragge. Dr. Chamberlayne has a long Latin epitaph written by his friend Walter Harris, M.D. In this we are informed that he wished to be buried, after the fashion of the ancients, without the city boundaries, near the high road, in an elevated tomb: that he was an Englishman, a Christian, and a Doctor of Laws; that he sprang from a Norman family, was born at Oddington in Gloucestershire in 1616, and became versed in grammar at Gloucester, in jurisprudence at Oxford, and in polite learning in London; that he travelled through France, Spain, Italy, Hungary, Bohemia, Germany, Denmark, and Sweden; that he married Susannah Clifford, a lady belonging to a knightly family, in 1658; that he begot nine children, and composed six books; that he at length departed this life in 1703; and that he was so anxious to benefit all men, even those who should come after him, that he ordered some of his books to be enveloped in wax and buried with him, in the hope that they might at some time be of service to remote posterity. His most celebrated work was *The Present State of Great Britain*, thirty-eight editions of which were published. His sons Peregrine Clifford and Edward were in the Navy, and both died young—the former in 1691, and the latter in 1698. John survived his father, and died, at the age of fifty-seven, in 1723. He was a Fellow of the Royal Society, and is described in his epitaph as "some time Gent. Waiter to Prince George of Denmark, Gent. of the Privy Chamber to Queen Anne and to King George." "He was," it is added, "given to hospitality and doing good offices, especially to foreigners." He revised and enlarged his father's book on *The Present State of Great Britain*, and published at Amsterdam a collection of versions of the Lord's Prayer in a great number of languages, together with Dissertations upon the Origin of Languages; he also translated from the Dutch Brandt's *History of the Reformation in the Low Countries*. Anne was a very warlike young lady. On June 30, 1690, on board a fire ship commanded by one of her brothers, she fought in man's clothes against the French for six hours. She married shortly afterwards, and died a few days after the birth of her first child, on October 30, 1692.

At the eastern extremity of the south wall a stone at the base is inscribed to the memory of Henry Sampson Woodfall, the publisher of the *Letters of Junius*, who died on December 12, 1805. He was buried in the churchyard without a monument, and this memorial was placed here in 1884 by his grandson, Henry Woodfall. At the east end of the churchyard is a tall obelisk, set up in 1815 by the Fellows of the Linnæan and Horticultural Societies of London, in memory of Philip Miller, author of *The Gardener's Dictionary*, who, after having been for almost half a century gardener of the Apothecaries' Company's gardens at Chelsea, died, in his eightieth year, on December 18, 1771, and was interred in the churchyard four days later.

At the south-east corner of the churchyard, close to the railings, stands a very conspicuous monument, which no one who passes along Cheyne Walk can fail to observe. It has very much the appearance of a fountain. From the four corners of a pedestal rise pillars supporting a canopy, and under the canopy, in the recess thus formed, is placed an urn wreathed with serpents. On the south side of the pedestal, facing the road, is the following inscription :—

"In memory of Sir Hans Sloane, Bart., President of the Royal Society and of the College of Physicians, who in the year of our Lord 1753, the 92nd of his age, without the least pain of body, and with a conscious serenity of mind, ended a virtuous and beneficent life, this monument was erected by his two daughters, Eliza Cadogan, and Sarah Stanley."

On the north side is an inscription to Elizabeth, Lady Sloane, who died in 1724, almost thirty years before her illustrious husband.

Sir Hans Sloane, whose connection with Chelsea is commemorated in the names of Hans Place, Sloane Square and Sloane Street, purchased the manor from the second Lord Newhaven in 1712. He spent his last years at Chelsea, and there, in the Manor House, he kept that magnificent collection, the purchase of which after his death, by Parliament, brought about the establishment of the British Museum. The manor was divided between his two daughters, Lady Cadogan and Mrs. Stanley, the latter of whom was the mother of Elizabeth Stanley, whose epitaph was written by Thomson, and whose early death gave occasion to one of the most beautiful passages in *Summer*. By the extinction of the Stanleys, the whole property came into the possession of the Cadogan family.

In 1733, Sir Hans Sloane gave the parish a cemetery, which is situated on the north side of King's Road, at the east corner of Arthur Street. The most prominent monument therein is an obelisk in the centre, which marks the resting-place of the famous bookseller, Andrew Millar, Thomson's fellow-countryman, friend and publisher, who died in 1768. It also contains a memorial to Dr. John Martyn, Professor of Botany in the University of Cambridge, who died in the same year as Millar, and one erected by Francis Bartolozzi, the engraver, to his friend and fellow-worker, John Baptist Cipriani, a Florentine artist, who died in 1785.

Elizabeth, wife of Richard Fletcher, Bishop of London, and mother of John Fletcher, the dramatist, was buried at Chelsea in 1595, but without a monument. Neither is there any memorial to a far more celebrated lady, Dame Magdalen Danvers, whose virtues have been immortalised by Izaak Walton in his life of her son, George Herbert, and of whom, in her middle age, Donne wrote :—

> "No spring nor summer beauty has such grace,
> As I have seen in an autumnal face."

After the death of her first husband, Richard Herbert, "she continued," says Walton, "twelve years a widow," and "she then married happily a noble gentleman, the brother and heir of the Lord Danvers, Earl of Danby, who did highly value both her person and the most excellent endowments of her mind."

Sir John Danvers, her second husband, resided at Chelsea in a large mansion called Danvers House. It was pulled down in 1696, and on its site was built Danvers Street, the street between Church Street and Beaufort Street. She was buried on June 8, 1627, and her funeral sermon was preached by Donne and attended, as he tells us, by Walton :—"I saw and heard this Mr. John Donne (who was then Dean of St. Paul's) weep, and preach her funeral sermon, in the parish church of Chelsea, near London, where she now rests in her quiet grave."

The burials are also noted in the register of Thomas Shadwell (died 1692), the poet laureate, and hero of Dryden's *Mac Flecknoe*; Henry Mossop (died 1774), whose acting Churchill ridiculed in the "*Rosciad*,"—"with more severity than justice," Lysons thought: William Kenrick (died 1779), the miscellaneous writer; and Sir John Fielding (died 1780), the famous blind magistrate of Bow Street, Henry Fielding's half-brother.

The register likewise records the baptism, on February 13, 1598, of "Charles, a boy, by estimacon, 10 or 12 yers olde, brought by Sir Walter Rawlie from Guiana"; and the marriage, on August 21, 1633, of Charles, Viscount Wilmot of Athlone, and Frances Merton, the parents of the celebrated Earl of Rochester. There are several entries relating to the family of

Lord Robartes of Truro, who distinguished himself on the Parliamentary side during the Civil Wars, and having been a favourer of the Restoration, was made Lord Privy Seal in 1661, subsequently held the offices of Lord Lieutenant of Ireland and Lord President of the Privy Council, and was created Earl of Radnor in 1679. Pepys went on business to Lord Robartes's house at Chelsea on September 30, 1661, "and found it to be the prettiest contrived house that I ever saw in my life."

Francis Atterbury, the Jacobite Bishop of Rochester, of whom Pope was so fond, resided at Chelsea, as Thackeray has not forgotten to notice in *Esmond*. He lived in Church Lane, now called Church Street, and here he became acquainted with Swift, who in 1711 took lodgings opposite his house. The entries in the register which relate to him are some years earlier. They comprise the records of two baptisms and two burials of children of his between the years 1701 and 1705. Charlotte, widow of Judge Jeffreys, was married at Chelsea, on August 28, 1703, to Lord Windsor of Blankcastle, and their children were baptised here. In this church also, the younger George Colman was married on November 10, 1788, to Miss Clara Morris, more than four years after their private wedding at Gretna Green.

The Rectory of Chelsea was anciently in the patronage of the Abbot and Convent of Westminster. On its becoming vacant in 1530, they allowed Sir Thomas More to nominate the next rector. He appointed John Larke, Rector of St. Ethelburga, Bishopsgate, whom he had a few years before presented to the rectory of Woodford in Essex, which Larke, however, soon resigned. Larke died for the same cause as his friend and patron, being executed at Tyburn for refusing to acknowledge the King's supremacy, on March 7, 1544. He had resigned his rectory of St. Ethelburga about two years previously, but that of Chelsea he retained till his death. In 1538 the advowson came

ST LUKE, CHELSEA

into the hands of King Henry VIII. by means of an exchange, and since then it has always gone with the manor. Consequently, the present patron is Lord Cadogan.

The new parish church of St. Luke, in Sydney Street, consisting of nave and aisles with tower at the west end, was designed by James Savage in the Perpendicular style. Although not exempt from errors of detail—which, nevertheless, are fewer than might have been expected from the period of its erection—the loftiness of the building, with the stone groined roof of its nave internally and the external flying buttresses, give it a far greater dignity than most modern churches, however correct in detail they may be, can boast.

The tower contains ten bells. There were originally eight at the old church, but six went to the bell founder in part of the cost of the bells for the new church, and of the remaining two only one is now used. The other, to which a rather curious history belongs, stands on a bracket in the porch. It bears the following inscription:—

"The Guift of the Honorable William Ashburnham Esquire Cofferer of His Maiesties Houshold, 1679."

Ashburnham, passing through Chelsea one evening in winter, missed the road, and got into the river. Not knowing in the darkness which way to turn to regain solid land, he was in a situation of considerable peril, when, providentially, he heard the church clock as it struck nine. Guided by the friendly sound, he soon extricated himself from danger, and in gratitude for his escape, he presented this bell, and bequeathed a sum of money to the parish to have it rung nightly at nine o'clock from Michaelmas to Lady Day. It was so rung up to 1825. It was placed in its present position in 1862, and its story is told on a tablet attached to the bracket.

LAMBETH PALACE GATEWAY AND LAMBETH CHURCH.

ST MARY LAMBETH

THE Manor of Lambeth is said to have been given by the Countess Goda, sister of Edward the Confessor, and her husband, Eustace of Boulogne, to the Bishop and Convent of Rochester. But they do not appear to have had settled possession of it, till it was confirmed to them by William Rufus, as a compensation for the damage he had done to the cathedral when he besieged Rochester. In 1197 Hubert Walter, Archbishop of Canterbury, obtained the manor and the advowson of the church from the Bishop and Convent in exchange for those of Darenth in Kent; and from that time they have appertained to the Archiepiscopal See.

The church of St. Mary, Lambeth, stands on the river bank immediately south of the Palace; and the effect presented from Lambeth Bridge by the stone tower of the church and the red-brick gateway of the Palace, built by Archbishop Morton, is remarkably picturesque. The body of the old church, which dated from the fifteenth century, but had been many times altered and repaired, was pulled down, and the present edifice erected between the years 1850-1852 from the designs of Mr. Philip Charles Hardwick. The tower is now the only remnant of the ancient edifice, beneath the walls of which Mary of Modena, James II.'s Queen, sought shelter from the storm on the night of her flight from England, December 6, 1688. The total height of the tower is 87 feet: it contains eight bells.

The present church is a large and lofty Gothic building, consisting of a nave, chancel, and two aisles. The aisles are divided from the nave by four arches on each side, extending as far as the chancel arch. Beyond the chancel arch is a similar arch on each side, reaching to the easternmost recess, in which the altar is placed. The organ, a handsome instrument, is located in a gallery at the west. The font stands at the south-west, beneath the tower. Its sides are elaborately carved with representations of Scriptural subjects, and its cover is very gracefully executed. It was presented when the church was rebuilt.

In the south wall, just within the chancel, is a pane of glass, measuring about 24 inches by 16, on which is painted the portrait of a pedlar with his staff and pack, and his dog at his heels. There is a tradition that a pedlar gave an acre of ground to the parish on condition that his portrait and that of his dog should be always preserved in one of the windows of the church; and it is also said that he stipulated that his canine companion should be buried in the churchyard. But for these stories there seems to be no foundation. The date of the first erection of the pedlar's likeness is unknown, but it must at least have been as early as 1607, for in the parish accounts for that year it is noted that two shillings was "paid to the glazier for a pannell of glasse for the window where the picture of the pedlar stands." It is also recorded that on March 6, 1703, £2 was "paid Mr. Price for a new glass pedlar."

On each side of the communion table there stands against the wall a stately altar-tomb. These are the oldest monuments in the church, and commemorate Hugh Peyntwin, Doctor of Laws, an officer of the Archbishop's Court, under Morton, Dene, and Wareham, who died in 1504; and John Mompesson, a member of the household of Archbishop Wareham, who died in 1524. At the north of the chancel, against the east wall, is the figure in

ST MARY, LAMBETH

brass of a lady. This represents Katherine (died 1535), wife of Lord William Howard, a son of Thomas, Duke of Norfolk. The inscription and the remainder of her monument have perished. This Duke of Norfolk, the second of the Howard family, who had, as Earl of Surrey, commanded the English army at Flodden, added a chapel to Lambeth Church in 1522, and many of the

LAMBETH CHURCH

family were buried there. In the same part of the church, against the north wall, is a brass effigy of a man in armour. It is that of Thomas Clere, who died in 1545. He was a friend of the poetical Earl of Surrey, who wrote his epitaph in English verse; but the tablet on which it was engraved disappeared long ago. On the same wall is a brass plate with the following quaint inscription:—

"Here lyeth the body of Margret Chute, daughter of S⟨t⟩ George Chute of Stockwell in the Coun— of Surrey K⟨t⟩ and Dame Anna his wife, who departed this life the second of March 1638 being aged 6 yeares and one moneth.

" If Virtue, Beauty, Heavenly Grace and Witt
Could have procurd long life, this Child had yet
Liv'd heere the wonder of her time and age,
But God did thinke it fit to disingage
Soe pure a Soule from humane frailities bands
And place her w⟨th⟩ his Saints, where now she stands
Praysing his Glorious Name, and sings those hymnes
Which blessed Angels use and Cherubims."

Six Archbishops of Canterbury—Richard Bancroft (died 1610), Thomas Tenison (died 1715), Matthew Hutton (died 1758), Thomas Secker (died 1768), Frederick Cornwallis (died 1783), and John Moore (died 1805)—were buried in Lambeth Church; so likewise was Margaret, wife of Archbishop Parker (died 1570), but Parker himself was interred in the chapel of the Palace. Bancroft's gravestone is within the communion rails, those of Tenison, Hutton, and Cornwallis just outside; Secker's is in the passage which leads from the church to the Palace. In the chancel of Lambeth Church were also laid the remains of Bishops Cuthbert Tunstall and Thomas Thirlebye, who were deprived of their sees by Queen Elizabeth for their opposition to the Reformation, and committed to the custody of Archbishop Parker. Tunstall, who was appointed Master of the Rolls in 1516, and was several times employed as a diplomatist, was made Bishop of London in 1522, and translated to Durham in 1530; he was ejected by Edward VI., restored by Mary, and ejected again by Elizabeth. He died a few months afterwards, in November, 1559, being more than eighty years old. He was loved and revered by Sir Thomas More, who accompanied him on an embassy to Flanders, as he mentions in his *Utopia* and in his

epitaph in Chelsea Church, in both which places he speaks of
Tunstall in terms of the warmest affection and the most profound
veneration. Thirlebye is noteworthy as having been the only
Bishop of Westminster; when that short-lived bishopric was
created by Henry VIII. in 1543, Thirlebye was appointed to it;
he was translated to Norwich in 1550, and thence to Ely in
1554. He survived Tunstall several years, and died in August,
1570. His body, which, having been embalmed, was in perfect
preservation, and was attired in ecclesiastical garments, was

LAMBETH AND WESTMINSTER FROM THE RIVER

accidentally discovered in 1783, when the grave of Archbishop
Cornwallis was being dug.

A large slab of blue marble at the east end of the south aisle,
close to the vestry door, is the gravestone of Elias Ashmole, the
founder of the Ashmolean Museum at Oxford. His epitaph
states that he was Comptroller of the Excise and for many years
Windsor Herald, and that his third wife was the daughter of Sir
William Dugdale, Garter King at Arms. It concludes thus:
"Mortem obiit 18 Maii 1692 anno aetatis 76: sed durante
Musaeo Ashmoliano Oxon, nunquam moriturus."

Just within the chancel, on the north side, is a large monument, surmounted by a bust, to Thomas Lett, who was High
Sheriff of Surrey in 1817 and died in 1830. On the wall of the

south aisle is a very pretty little monument, a small bas-relief showing little children being brought to our Lord—"erected by parishioners and former pupils, in memory of Mercy Weller, Infants' School Mistress," who died on December 16, 1887, aged thirty-nine.

There are several monuments in the south porch. The most conspicuous is that of Robert Scott, whose history is thus narrated in his epitaph :—

> "Nere to this place lyeth interred the body of Robert Scott Esq'., descended of the ancient Barrons of Bawerie in Scotland. He bent himselfe to travell and studie much, and amongst many other thinges, he invented the Leather Ordnance and carried to the Kinge of Sweden 200 men, who after two yeares service for his worth and valour was p'ferred to the office of Quarter Mr Generall of His Matie Army wch he possessed 3 yeares : from thence wth his favour he went into Denmarke (where he was advanced to the Gen'all of that King's Artilerie): theire beinge advised to tender his service to his owne Prince, wch he doinge His Matie willinglie accepted and p'ferred him to be one of ye Gent. of his most honorable Privie Chamber & rewarded him with a pension of 600^l l^i. An'um : this deserving Spirit adorned with all endowments befitting a gentleman in the prime of his flourishinge age surrendred his soule to his Redeemer 1631 :

> > "Of his great worth to knowe who seeketh more
> > Must mount to Heaven where he is gone before.

> "In France he tooke to wife Anne Scott, for whose Remembrance shee lovinglie erected this Memoriall."

The monument displays his bust. The face is an unmistakably Scottish one.

ST MARY, LAMBETH

Here also is a tablet to Sir Peter Rich, Alderman of London, who died in 1692. He was one of the Tory Sheriffs whom Charles II., with the assistance of the Lord Mayor, Sir John Moore, succeeded in forcing on the citizens in 1682, with the object of getting the London juries packed in the interests of the Court—a proceeding fraught with momentous results.

On the outside of the tower, on the south face, is a tablet with this inscription:—

"Bryan Turbervile late of St. James's Westminster, Gent. deceased, did by his last will and testament bearing date the 20th of October 1711, give and bequeath to this Parish of Lambeth One Hundred Pounds for ever to be laid out in a purchase and the interest thereof for the putting out yearly two poor boys apprentices.

"His children also have given One Hundred Pounds more for the better putting out the said boys as aforesaid—provided the Rector and Churchwardens shall maintain this or a like stone on this place, fairly carved in a legible hand, setting forth this bequest, in default of which the said legacy is to become the right of St. Margaret's Westminster.

"N.B. None to be put to Chimney-Sweepers, Watermen or Fishermen, and no Roman Catholic to enjoy any benefit thereof.

"And in default of issue to his children and grandchildren hath also left certain freeholds and other incomes, for the augmentation of the said charity &c, Anno Domini 1719."

The wishes of this charitable gentleman have been punctually complied with. The "stone" is certainly "fairly carved" in a most "legible hand."

Beneath it is a smaller tablet thus inscribed:—

"Ann Richards, upwards of sixty years Midwife in this Parish, died 28th December 1794 aged 88 years. In the exercise of her professional skill she was deservedly esteemed for humanity and disinterested benevolence, especially towards the poor. This stone was placed at the expense of some of the inhabitants as a mark of respect to the memory of so valuable a character."

In the eastern portion of the churchyard is a table monument of stone, the sides of which are adorned with bas-reliefs representing Egyptian and Grecian ruins, animals, trees, and shells. On the top is a slab of black marble bearing the names of John Tradescant (died 1638), Jane Tradescant (died 1634), John Tradescant (died 1662), John Tradescant (died 1652), and Hester Tradescant (died 1678). Below these names are engraved the following lines :—

> " Know stranger, ere thou pass, beneath this stone
> Lye John Tradescant, grandsire, father, son :
> The last dy'd in his spring : the other two
> Lived till they had travell'd Art and Nature through,
> As by their choice collections may appear :
> Of what is rare, in land, in sea, in air :
> Whilst they (as Homer's Iliad in a nut)
> A world of wonders in one closet shut :
> These famous Antiquarians that had been
> Both Gardiners to the Rose and Lily Queen,
> Transplanted now themselves, sleep here : and when
> Angels shall with their trumpets waken men,
> And fire shall purge the world, these hence shall rise,
> And change this Garden for a Paradise."

Beneath the verses is an inscription stating that the monument was restored by subscription in 1773, and again in 1853. It was originally erected by Hester, the widow of the second John Tradescant, who is herself here commemorated.

Tradescant is said to have been a Dutchman. He was a great

traveller and a great botanist and collector of curiosities of all kinds. He settled in England, and became gardener to Charles I. His son inherited the tastes of his father, and sailed to Virginia in search of new plants. Their collection, which was very celebrated, was bequeathed by the younger Tradescant to Elias Ashmole, by whom it was, together with some curiosities of his own, presented to the University of Oxford, whither it was transferred in 1682.

Near the Tradescant monument is a large tomb surmounted with an urn, and bearing on the south side a coat of arms. On the west side is this inscription : —

"Sacred to the memory of William Bligh, Esquire, F.R.S., Vice Admiral of the Blue : the celebrated Navigator who first transplanted the Bread Fruit Tree from Otaheite to the West Indies, bravely fought the battles of his country, and died beloved, respected and lamented, on the 7th day of December 1817, aged 64."

On the south side is an inscription as follows :—

"Sacred to the memory of Mrs. Elizabeth Bligh, the wife of Rear-Admiral Bligh, who died April 15th 1812, in the 60th year of her age.

"Her spirit soared to Heaven, the blest domain,
Where virtue only can its meed obtain,
All the great duties she performed thro' life,
Those of a child, a parent, and a wife."

Beneath is an inscription to Anne Campbell Bligh, their youngest daughter, who died, aged fifty-nine, in 1844. On the east side appear the names of two sons and one grandson, who died in infancy.

This was the celebrated commander of the *Bounty*, who, with a few faithful officers and seamen, was turned adrift in an open boat by his mutinous crew, but contrived by his courage and seamanship to bring the greater part of those who had adhered to him back to England. Subsequently, as Governor of New, South Wales, he was again troubled by mutineers, who forcibly deposed him, but on his return home he obtained full redress.

In Lambeth Churchyard is also the tomb of Patrick Nasmyth, the landscape painter, termed the "British Hobbema," who died in 1831. Here, too, were buried Simon Forman, the notorious astrologer and quack-doctor, who died in 1611; Thomas Cooke, the translator of Hesiod, satirized by Pope—

> "From these the world will judge of men and books,
> Not from the Burnets, Oldmixons and Cookes"—

who died in 1756; and Edward Moore, the dramatist and fabulist, who died in the following year.

The rectors of Lambeth include two divines who came in time to occupy the See of London—Edmund Gibson, presented in 1703, who resigned the living in 1717, a year after he became Bishop of Lincoln; and Beilby Porteus, who was rector from 1767 to 1777—and also Dr. Christopher Wordsworth, who was instituted in 1816, and resigned in 1820, on being chosen Master of Trinity College, Cambridge; he was the poet's youngest brother—father of Charles Wordsworth, Bishop of St. Andrew's, and Christopher Wordsworth, Bishop of Lincoln, and grandfather of the present Bishop of Salisbury.

ST JOHN THE EVANGELIST WESTMINSTER

ST. JOHN'S, WESTMINSTER. M. E. FROST

THE church of St. John the Evangelist occupies the centre of Smith Square, Westminster. It was one of the churches built under Queen Anne's Act, its parish being taken out of St. Margaret's; it was commenced in 1721, and consecrated in June, 1728. The architect was Thomas Archer, a pupil of Vanbrugh. It is a large, heavy looking edifice without a steeple, but with four towers, one at each angle, which give it a most singular aspect. This peculiarity has elicited some very unfavourable criticisms. "The *chef d'œuvre* of his (Archer's) absurdity," says Horace Walpole, "was the church of St. John's, with four belfreys, in

RIVERSIDE CHURCHES

Westminster." "A church with four belfreys," says Peter Cunningham, "resembling a parlour table upset, with its legs in the air." "A very hideous church," says Charles Dickens, "with four towers at the four corners, generally resembling some petrified monster, frightful and gigantic, on its back with its legs in the air."

It has secured, however, the approbation of Benjamin Disraeli, who describes it as a "church of vast proportions, and built of

ST. JOHN'S, WESTMINSTER, VIEW FROM RIVER

hewn stone in that stately, not to say ponderous style, which Vanbrugh introduced."

The towers do not deserve the contempt which they have excited. They did not form part of the original design, and they were erected, not for ornament, but from necessity. When the building was first set up, the foundations not being strong enough, it sank unevenly in the marshy ground, and therefore these weighty towers were constructed to equalize the pressure. It cannot, however, be denied that they are more useful than beautiful. They look better when seen from a distance than when one is close under them. St. John's viewed from Lambeth Bridge is much more pleasing than St. John's viewed from Smith Square. The north and south fronts, which contain the entrance doors, possess Doric porticos with broken pediments. They are approached by steps, and give a dignified effect to the sides of the building. There is not much room to see the south portico, but the north presents a picturesque aspect as seen from North Street. The church has no aisles. The ceiling of the nave is flat, and is divided into compartments: in the middle is a large circular panel, with a great ornament at its centre. There are galleries on the north, south, and west, in the last of which the organ is located. The pulpit, which stands on the north side, is of carved wood, and has an imposing appearance. The interior was severely damaged by a fire on September 26, 1742, and is much plainer now than it was in its original condition. The reparation of the chancel was not completed till 1825, when the long-unfinished work was accomplished under the care of William Inwood, the architect of St. Pancras New Church.

In the east window are figures in stained glass of St. John the Evangelist and St. Paul, which came, we are informed by a notice in the table of benefactors at the south west, "from the old church at Rouen," and were presented in 1818 by Mr. Thomas Green. The font, which stands at the south-west, was given by Mr. Henry Arthur Hunt in 1847. Against the west wall is a tablet, with a medallion portrait, "in memory of the Ven. John Jennings, M.A., Archdeacon of Westminster—For fifty-one years Rector of this Parish. Died March 26th 1883 in the 85th year of his age." In the vestry are a picture of the ruins of the church after the fire of 1742, and a copy of the picture by Murillo in the chapel of Magdalen College, Oxford, representing Christ bearing the cross. The latter was given to the church as an altar-piece by Mr. Simon Stephenson in 1827.

The rectory house – No. 32, Smith Square – the southernmost on the west side, is the one which Disraeli introduces in *Sybil*, as the London lodging of his heroine and her father.

"In the extreme corner of this area, which was dignified by the name of Smith's Square, instead of taking a more appropriate title from the church of St. John, which it encircled, was a large old house, that had been masked at the beginning of the century with a modern front of pale-coloured bricks, but which still stood in its courtyard, surrounded by its iron railings, withdrawn as it were from the vulgar gaze, like an individual who had known higher fortunes, and blending with his humility something of the reserve which is prompted by the memory of vanished greatness.

"'This is my home,' said Sybil. 'We lodge here with some kind people that we were recommended to by the good priest at Mowbray. It is a still place, and suits us well.'"

The burial ground of St. John's lies between Horseferry Road and Page Street; it now serves as a recreation ground. In it is the tomb of Alderman John Johnson and his parents. Alderman Johnson was chosen Sheriff of London in 1836, and Lord Mayor in 1845. He died, in his fifty-seventh year, on December 30, 1848.

The rectory of St. John the Evangelist, to which a canonry of Westminster is attached, is in the patronage of the Crown. An early rector was Dr. Edward Willes, who was presented in 1736, and resigned the living in 1742 on being elevated to the See of St. David's; two years later he was translated to Bath and Wells. He died in 1773. His brother John was Chief Justice of the Common Pleas.

Churchill is said to have alluded to the Bishop's skill as a decipherer, when, commenting on the ignorance of many of the nobility, he remarks : —

ST JOHN THE EVANGELIST, WESTMINSTER

> "Others can write, but such a Pagan hand,
> A Willes should always at our elbow stand."

But the most memorable person connected with St. John's is Churchill himself. Charles Churchill was a Westminster man born and bred. His father was curate and lecturer of St. John's, and he himself was born in February, 1731, hard by the church in Vine Street.

> "More famed Vine Street,
> Where Heaven the utmost wish of man to grant
> Gave me an old house and an older aunt,"

he says. Vine Street, the title of which commemorated the vineyard of the Royal Palace of Westminster, was stupidly re-named Romney Street some five-and-twenty years ago. He was educated at Westminster School, where Cowper was one of his schoolfellows. He was ordained by Bishop Willes. In 1758 the elder Churchill died, and his son succeeded him as curate and lecturer of St. John's. He had been, he tells us,

> "Bred to the church, and for the gown decreed,
> Ere it was known that I should learn to read."

But nature had never intended him for the clerical profession, into which his father seems very injudiciously to have forced him. His distaste for his duties he has very plainly expressed:—

> "E'en whilst I kept those sheep
> Which, or my curse, I was ordained to keep,
> Ordained, alas, to keep through need, not choice,
> Those sheep which never heard their shepherd's voice;
> Which did not know, yet would not learn their way;
> Which strayed themselves, yet grieved that I should stray;
> Those sheep which my good father (on his bier
> Let filial duty drop the pious tear),
> Kept well, yet starved himself; e'en at that time
> Whilst I was pure and innocent of rhyme,
> Whilst, sacred dulness ever in my view,
> Sheep at my bidding crept from pew to pew."

And his natural disinclination for his profession was aggravated by the scantiness of the remuneration which it afforded him:

> "Condemned (like many more and worthier men,
> To whom I pledge the service of my pen)
> Condemned (whilst proud and pampered sons of lawn,
> Crammed to the throat, in lazy plenty yawn)
> In pomp of reverend beggary to appear,
> To pray and starve, on forty pounds a year."

For three years, overwhelmed with debt and wretchedness, he remained the obscure curate of St. John's. As Cowper afterwards wrote,—

> "Churchill, himself unconsciouss of his powers,
> In penury consumed his idle hours."

But at length, with the publication of the *Rosciad* in March, 1761, he entered on that brilliant though brief career in which he "blazed the comet of a season." At the beginning of 1763 he resigned the curacy and lectureship of St. John's, and devoting himself entirely to political satire, laboured with marvellous force and energy, till, on November 4, 1764, his mortal course was abruptly terminated by a violent fever.

Churchill had his faults, as he himself frankly confessed, but he was honest, courageous, and a true patriot. He said truly:—

> "Let private sorrows rest.
> As to the public, I dare stand the test,
> Dare proudly boast, I feel no wish above
> The good of England and my country's love."

And because he loved his country well, and wielded in her cause his powerful pen, we pause, ere we quit St. John's Church, to do honour to the memory of that right English poet, "the great Churchill."

ST. MARGARET
WESTMINSTER

"THE parish church of St. Margaret," says Stow, "sometime within the Abbey, was by Edward the Confessor removed, and built without, for ease of the monks. This church continued till the days of Edward I., at which time the merchants of the staple and Parishioners of Westminster built it all of new, the great chancel excepted, which was built by the Abbots of Westminster; and this remaineth now a fair parish church, though sometime in danger of downpulling."

The church was, as Weever tells us, "re-edified for the most in the reign of King Edward the Fourth, especially the south aisle, from the piety of the Lady Mary Billing and her second husband, Sir Thomas Billing, Chief Justice of England in that King's time." Lady Billing died in 1499, and a monument was set up in St. Margaret's, bearing figures of her and her three husbands, William Cotton, Sir Thomas Billing, and Thomas Lacy. "Her last husband," the inscription stated, "erected this monument to the memory of her and her two former." It was beautifully executed, and there is an excellent illustration of it in Weever. Hatton, in his *New View of London*, published in 1708, mentioned it as then still existing, but unhappily it has long since altogether perished.

Another tomb that has disappeared is that of John Skelton,

the famous satiric poet of Henry VIII.'s time, "orator regius, poeta laureatus," as he called himself. He died in 1529, and Weever has preserved his epitaph, in which he is styled "vates Pierius." Another poet, of whom now no memorial remains, the unfortunate Thomas Churchyard, was buried at St. Margaret's in 1604. He was interred beside Skelton "in the quire," says Weever, "and not in the church porch, as the rimes following would approve:

> "'Come, Alecto, and lend me thy torch,
> To fynde a Church yard in a Church porch.
> Povertie and Poetrie this tombe doth enclose,
> Therefore, gentlemen, be merry in Prose.'"

A north gallery was built in 1641, in which the members of the House of Commons sat when they came to the church. During the troubled years which followed, they were in the habit of resorting to St. Margaret's frequently, and in 1647 they voted £200 for repairing it. There were further repairs in 1651. In 1682 Sir John Cutler built a south gallery at his sole expense for the poor of the parish—one of those charitable acts which show he was far from being the miser that Pope maliciously represents him. In the eighteenth century Parliamentary grants for repairs were numerous. In 1735 the tower was cased and mostly rebuilt, and other repairs were executed, at a cost of £3,500, voted "in consideration of its being, as it were, a national church for the use of the House of Commons." In 1737 the House granted a further sum of £1,500 18s. 5d., and in 1739 they supplied £2,000 more. In 1758 they bestowed £4,000, with which the church was newly pewed and decorated, and fresh galleries were erected. In 1799 the Commons displayed even greater liberality, granting no less than £6,721 for repairs. But the church seems to have perpetually required repairs, for in 1813 funds were again needed, and the House

ENTRANCE GATEWAY TO THE MOAT OF WARWICK CASTLE

came to the rescue with £3,059. During the next thirty years the parishioners managed to consume £15,000 in renovating the sacred edifice; and in 1845 they obtained another £1,200 from the House of Commons. In 1878, as a brass plate on the south wall records, the church was restored and the galleries were removed. Such multitudinous reparations few churches have experienced; but it may well be questioned whether St. Margaret's has been improved by this everlasting tinkering.

The church of St. Margaret, Westminster, is, as almost every Londoner knows, a stone edifice, standing close to the Abbey, on the north side of it. At the north-west is a square tower, consisting of four stories, and completed by a pinnacle at each angle; in the centre, between the pinnacles, is placed a small cupola, from which rises a flagstaff. The altitude to the summit of the pinnacle is 85 feet. There are ten bells. In the bottom story of the tower, in the north face, is the main entrance: above it is a tablet with a high flown Latin inscription, now obscured by smoke and dirt, setting forth that the tower was repaired in 1736, at the public expense, under the patronage of the most gracious King George II., by the authority of the British Parliament.

Internally the church measures in length 130 feet, in breadth 65 feet, and in height 45 feet. The aisles are separated from the nave by pointed arches resting on clustered columns of Perpendicular character, with a clerestory above. Indeed, in spite of all the alterations which it has endured, the whole church still retains the Perpendicular character which it acquired by being "re-edified in the reign of King Edward the Fourth." A window over the vestry door, at the south-east of the building, retains old Perpendicular mullions and tracery, but the windows of the aisles had otherwise lost their tracery long before the restoration of 1878, when new mullions and tracery, not altogether happy in design, were inserted. The chancel was originally separated from the

ST MARGARET, WESTMINSTER

nave by a rood screen entirely crossing the church, and the position of the staircase to the rood-loft is marked by the recesses in the

ST MARGARET'S, WESTMINSTER, WEST END

south aisle wall, behind and above Lady Dudley's monument. Nearly opposite to this, under a window in the north aisle, is a square recess in the wall with an iron grille in front of it, and on the remains of the sill of the tomb is the matrix of a small brass, which has disappeared. The decorative stone carving and canopy, which once adorned and surmounted the tomb, have been hacked away flush with the wall. The most remarkable object in the church is the magnificent east window, which demands attention, not only because it is one of the most splendid examples of glass painting in the world, but also on account of its very curious history.

The subject of the window is the Crucifixion. In the centre is the figure of our Lord on the cross; the blood from His wounds is being received in chalices by three angels. At the sides are the crucified thieves; an angel above is taking charge of the soul of the Penitent Thief, while that of the other is being carried off by the devil. On the right of the cross—that is to say, on the left hand as one faces the window—is the Roman centurion mounted on a horse, and piercing with a spear our Lord's side. Beneath the cross are Roman soldiers and Jewish rulers, and also our Lord's mother, her sister Mary, the wife of Cleophas, and Mary Magdalene. Behind the cross, on the other side, is a distant view of Jerusalem. On the left of the Crucifixion scene as one faces the window, is a figure of St. George in armour, holding a white banner with a red cross, and trampling on a red dragon. Corresponding to this, on the opposite side of the window, is a figure of St. Catherine. Below these saints are two royal figures kneeling in prayer. The lady beneath St. Catherine is unquestionably meant for Catherine of Arragon, but whether the male figure represents Henry VIII. or his elder brother, Prince Arthur, does not certainly appear. At the top of the window are introduced the red and white rose united, and the pomegranate, the badge of Catherine of Arragon.

The history of this noble window is as surprising as its workmanship is superb. It is said to have been made at Dort in

ST. MARGARET'S, WESTMINSTER (INTERIOR)

Holland, with a view to its erection in Henry VII.'s Chapel in Westminster Abbey. But, when it arrived in England, it was placed, not in the Abbey of Westminster, but in that of Waltham. This circumstance would lead one to suppose that the window was not made for Henry VII. but for Henry VIII., and that it was not completed until the King had become anxious for the dissolution of his marriage with Catherine, whose portrait he would not then have been desirous of publicly setting up in conjunction with his own. At Waltham Abbey it remained until the suppression of that house, and was then conveyed to the chapel of New Hall, in Essex. New Hall, which had been the property of the Butlers, Earls of Ormond, passed into the possession of Thomas Bullen, Earl of Wiltshire, Anne Bullen's father, and afterwards into that of the Ratcliffs, Earls of Sussex. George Villiers, Duke of Buckingham, bought it from the Ratcliffs, and his son, the second Duke, sold it to General Monk. Monk, who appreciated the window, is said to have had it buried, for fear the exuberant zeal of the Puritan soldiers should move them to destroy it. After the Restoration he re-erected it. After the death of Monk's son, Christopher, the last Duke of Albemarle, the estate was sold to one John Olmius, who pulled down the chapel, but preserved the window, and subsequently sold it to a gentleman named Conyers, who had it repaired by one of the Prices, at that time the best glass-painters in England, and placed it in his private chapel at Copthall, near Epping. By his son, it was, in 1758, sold for 400 guineas to the parishioners of St. Margaret, Westminster, and thus, after travelling to and fro upwards of two centuries, it at last found a permanent habitation hard by the spot for which it was originally designed.

It was not, however, erected without powerful opposition. Zachary Pearce was then Dean of Westminster, a man of considerable learning as a classical scholar, but utterly devoid of taste, as he proved not long afterwards, when he contemplated the removal of the tomb of Aylmer de Valence, Earl of Pembroke, from the Abbey, in order to make room for General Wolfe's monument, "being told," as Walpole puts it, "that hight Aylmer was a Knight Templar, a very wicked set of people, as his Lordship had heard—though he know nothing of them, as they are not mentioned by Longinus." He got it into his head that the window was something Popish, and instigated a prosecution against the churchwardens under the Act of Edward VI. "for abolishing and putting away divers books and images." Hence Churchill, in *The Ghost*, speaks of him as one—

"Who his Redeemer would pull down."

Happily, the Churchwardens, after a lengthy lawsuit, at last worsted the iconoclastic Dean.

Above the altar, underneath the window, is a copy in plaster, by Alkin, of Titian's picture of the "Supper at Emmaus."

St. Margaret's, Westminster, is one of the most interesting parish churches in the Metropolis, for it is full of memorials of the mighty dead, both those of times long past and those who have but recently entered into their rest. The examination of these may well be commenced by entering the church by way of the porch at the south-east.

This porch is itself a memorial. It was erected, as we learn from a Latin inscription on its south wall, by Caroline, Viscountess Sherbrooke, in memory of her distinguished husband, better known as Robert Lowe. The inscription claims for him that he "faithfully discharged the highest offices of state, and always put country before party." Against the north wall of the porch is Lord Sherbrooke's bust. When we have passed through into the south aisle, the first object which presents itself is a brass tablet on the right, here placed to remind all who enter that St.

Margaret's was the burial place of Sir Walter Raleigh. The inscription is as follows:—

> "Within ye chancel of this church was interred the body of the great Sr Walter Raleigh, K^t, on the day he was beheaded in Old Palace Yard, Westminster, Octr 29th, An Dom. 1618.
>
> "Reader: Should you reflect on his errors,
> Remember his many virtues,
> And that he was a mortal."

This was formerly inscribed on a painted board; the brass tablet was substituted in 1845.

On the east wall of the south aisle is a marble tablet to another never-to-be-forgotten Englishman. It is thus inscribed:—

> "To the memory of William Caxton, who first introduced into Great Britain the art of Printing: and who, A.D. 1477 or earlier exercised that art in the Abbey of Westminster. This tablet in remembrance of one to whom the literature of his country is so largely indebted was raised Anno Domini MDCCCXX. by the Roxburghe Club—Earl Spencer K.G. President."

It is stated by the Rev. M. E. C. Walcott, in his *History of the Parish Church of St. Margaret in Westminster*, that "this tablet was originally intended to have been placed in Westminster Abbey; but the fees attending its erection there were so great that application was made to the Churchwardens of St. Margaret's, who, as a mark of their respect to his memory, allowed it to be erected without any of the customary fees."

Caxton died in 1491, and was buried in St. Margaret's; the parish accounts note the expenditure at his funeral of 7s. 2d. — 6s. 8d. for torches, and 6d. for ringing the bell. The window at the east end of the south aisle is a memorial to Caxton; it was erected in 1882 by public subscription, most of the contributors being members of the printing and publishing trades. It contains a figure of Caxton in the centre, and at the sides those of the Venerable Bede, a typical scholar of the old days of manuscripts, and Erasmus, a leader of the great revival of learning, to which the invention of printing afforded so powerful an impetus; and it bears the arms of Kent, Caxton's native county; of the City of London, of which he was a freeman; of Bruges, where he studied the art of printing; and of Westminster, where he pursued it after his return to England.

On the south wall, near the east end, is a monument with kneeling figures to Thomas Seymour, second son of Edward, Earl of Hertford, who died in 1600, and his wife, Isabel, who died in 1619. The easternmost window of the south wall is in memory of William the next Earl's unhappy wife, Arabella Stuart. Beneath this window is a large brass tablet with figures of a husband and wife, one son, and two daughters, and a long rhyming epitaph, from which it appears that this tablet was set up by Margaret Cole to the memory of her husband, a Member of Parliament, who died in 1597. A little farther west is a tablet ornamented with arms, an urn, a skull and cherubs' heads, and bearing an inscription to Nicholas Dering of Dorset, who died in 1588. At the sides of Dering's monument are placed, against the wall, two old painted figures in frames, representing our Saviour and Moses. Under the former are the words, "Grace and Truth came by Jesus Christ," and under the latter, "The Law was given by Moses." The next window is in memory of the eminent American bishop, Phillips Brooks: under it are these four lines composed by the lamented Archbishop Benson:—

> "Fervidus eloquiis, sacra fortissimus arte
> Suadendi gravibus vera Deumque viris,
> Quaereris ad sedem populari voce regendam,
> Quaereris ad sedem raptæ domumque Dei."

Below is a tablet commemorating one of the heroes of the Indian Mutiny—"Louis Henry Bedford, Captain in Her Majesty's 37th Regiment. Born 7th June, 1819; killed on the 27th March, 1858, in a sortie from the intrenchments at Azimghur in the East Indies." A little beyond is a handsome altar-tomb, on which is the recumbent figure, beautifully executed, of a beautiful woman. The inscription is as follows:—

> "Here lieth entombed Marie La: Dudley, Daughter of Willĩ. Lo: Howarde of Effinghã, in his tyme Lo: High Admyrail of Englande, Le Châberlayne, & Lo: Privy Seale. She was grandchilde to Thomas D. of Norff—the 2— of that surnae: & sister to Charles Howarde, Erle of Notĩ: Lo: High Admyrail of Englãd: by whose prosperous direcciõ, through the goodn of God in defendinge his handãyde Q. Elizab—, the whole fleete of Spayne was defeated & discomfited.
>
> "She was firste maried to Edw. Sutton- Lo: Dudley, & after to Rich: Mompesson Esq. who in the memorie of her virtues, & testimony of his love, erected this monument. She slept in Christ Jesus in the yere of our Lord 1600 & the 21 of Aug. attending the joyfull day of her Resurrection."

The next window is to the memory of William Page, Baron Hatherley, the Lord Chancellor. "He was a good Man," says the inscription simply. The succeeding window is to his wife, Charlotte, Lady Hatherley. There is a big tablet, with arms, to Richard Willis, who died at the Star Chamber, in Westminster, in 1640. Then comes a window to "Anne Wainwright, of Dean's Yard, who died in 1875." Beyond is a monument, with kneeling figures of a man and wife, and two daughters, the male figure much injured: it commemorates Hugh Haughton, who died in 1616. The next window is to the memory of Sir Thomas Erskine May, who was in 1886 raised to the peerage as Baron Farnborough, and died in the same year. He was for more than a half-century in the service of the House of Commons, and filled for fifteen years the important position of Clerk of the House. As a historian he performed much valuable work, particularly by his *Treatise on the Law and Usage of Parliament*. We next come to the monument, with bust, of Mary Brocas, daughter of William Brocas of Feddingworth, Leicestershire, who died in 1654.

The succeeding window was erected in commemoration of Her Majesty's Jubilee. Beneath is a brass tablet in memory of the Right Honourable Charles Shaw Lefevre, who was for nearly eighteen years Speaker of the House of Commons, and, on his retirement in 1857, was created Viscount Eversley: he was in his ninety-fifth year when he died, December 28, 1888. Beyond is a tablet to Edward Reynolds, who died in 1623: then comes a window to Sir Henry Arthur Hunt, C.B., who died in 1889, and members of his family: and at the west end of the south wall we may perceive a tablet to a Welsh gentleman, Owen Jones by name, who died in 1633.

Beneath the window at the west end of the south aisle is the following inscription:—

> "Dedicated by his Fellow Members of the House of Commons to the beloved memory of Frederick Charles Cavendish, son of William seventh Duke of Devonshire, Member for the Northern Division of the West Riding of Yorkshire for 17 years: and Chief Secretary for Ireland. Born on the Feast of St. Andrew 1836, and like him permitted in singleness and humility of heart to follow his Lord and with his blood to seal a life devoted to duty. On the day of his arrival in Dublin, in company with and

in attempted defence of his Colleague, Mr. T. N. Burke, he was murdered in the Phœnix Park, May 6th 1882."

Below are tablets to Lieutenant-Colonel John Probyn, who shared " in the glorious defence of Gibraltar against the united efforts of France and Spain," and after serving his country for thirty-six years, "fell a victim to a malignant fever contracted on an expedition to the Coast of France," January 23, 1796; James Nares, " Doctor of Music, many years Organist and Composer to their Majesties King George II. and III. and twenty-three years Master of the Children of the Royal Chapels," who died, aged sixty-seven, in 1783; and Captain Francis Hamilton Elliot, of the 94th Regiment, who died at Jullunder, in the East Indies, March 29, 1863, aged twenty-five. This memorial was erected by his brother officers.

The great west window of the nave forms another and more worthy memorial to Sir Walter Raleigh. It was subscribed for by Americans, and erected a little earlier than the window to Caxton. Beneath this window, on the south side of the west door, is a kneeling figure of a lady, with an inscription to Blanche Parrye, "Chiefe Gentlewomā of Queene Elizabethe's moste honorable Privie Chamber & Keper of her Ma^{tes} Juells." " She died a maide " in 1589, in her eighty-second year. North of the west door is a monument, with figure of a lady kneeling at a desk, and beneath it a bas-relief showing three sons and three daughters. The epitaph is to a lady of very noble birth, and of a character worthy of her birth, " Dorothee Stafford, wife & widdowe to Sr William Stafford, Knight, daughter to Henry Lord Stafforde, ye only sonne of Edward ye last Duke of Buckingham. Her mother was Ursula, daughter to ye Countesse of Salsburie, ye only daughter to George Duke of Clarence, brother to King Edward ye 4th. She continued a true widdowe from ye age of 27 till her death. She served Q. Elizabeth 40 yeares lying in her Bed-chamber, esteemed of her, loved of al, doing good al she coulde to everybody, never hurted any, a continual remembricer of ye sutes of ye poore : as she lived a religious life in great reputation of honor & vertue in ye world, so she ended in continual fervent meditation & hearty prayer to God, at wch instant (as all her life) so after her death she gave liberally to ye poore, & died aged of 78 years ye 22 of September 1604 ; in whose remembrance Sr Edwarde Stafforde her sonne hath caused ye memoriall of her to be set up in ye same forme & place as she her self long since required him."

The window at the west end of the north aisle was erected, in memory of John Milton, by George W. Childs of Philadelphia, in 1888. Beneath this window is the monument of Sir Peter Parker, Captain of H.M.S. *Menelaus*, who fell at the early age of twenty-eight, on August 30, 1814, while landing British troops on the American coast. On the monument appears his bust, and his death-scene is shown in bas-relief. It was erected by his officers and sailors, and bears a long inscription, but his noblest memorial is contained in Byron's beautiful lines :—

> "There is a tear for all that die,
> A mourner o'er the humblest grave :
> But nations swell the funeral cry,
> And triumph weeps above the brave.
>
> For them is sorrow's purest sigh
> O'er Ocean's heaving bosom sent :
> In vain their bones unbaried lie,
> All earth becomes their monument.
>
> A tomb is theirs on every page,
> An epitaph on every tongue :
> The present hours, the future age,
> For them bewail, to them belong.

RIVERSIDE CHURCHES

> For them the voice of festal mirth
> Grows hushed, their name the only sound
> While deep remembrance pours to worth
> The goblet's tributary round.
>
> A theme to crowds that knew them not,
> Lamented by admiring foes,
> Who would not share their glorious lot?
> Who would not die the death they chose?
>
> And, gallant Parker, thus enshrined
> Thy life, thy fall, thy fame shall be,
> And early valour, glowing, find
> A model in thy memory.
>
> But there are breasts that bleed with thee
> In woe, that glory cannot quell,
> And shuddering hear of victory
> Where one so dear, so dauntless, fell.
>
> Where shall they turn to mourn thee less?
> When cease to hear thy cherished name?
> Time cannot teach forgetfulness,
> While grief's full heart is fed by fame.
>
> Alas, for them, though not for thee:
> They cannot choose but weep the more;
> Deep for the dead the grief must be,
> Who ne'er gave cause to mourn before."

Next is a brass plate recording the charitable deed of Mrs. Joice Goddard, who in 1621 bequeathed "to the Churchwardens and Sidesmen of St Margaret's certain funds, out of which she directed them to pay to sixteen poor women every Sunday in the year after morning prayer sixpence a piece to every one of them." Adjoining is a tablet to another benefactress to the parish, "Joane Barnet, Widdow," who died in 1674. Close to this is a brass plate commemorating Susanna Gray, daughter of Henry Gray of Enfield in the county of Stafford, who died in

1654, aged ten years. The reasons why this little girl was honoured with a monument are thus set forth:—

"First, that such virtues as she practised may encourage others to imitate her. 2 That they may not fall into oblivion. 3 That others may see 'tis not in vaine to be such: ye most imp'tiall of them y' knew her thought it justice to her memory to leave this testimony that she was ye most modest, pious & learned that hath beene knowne of her yeares."

In the north-west corner is the monument of Dr. Patrick Colquhoun, who died in 1820, at the age of seventy-six. He had been Provost of Glasgow, a Deputy-Lieutenant of Middlesex, and a Westminster magistrate: and was the author of some works on the Police and the Condition of the Poor. Above his epitaph is inscribed the famous line of Horace—

"Integer vitæ, sceleris que Purus,"

and at the top is a bas-relief displaying a bee-hive and emblems of Justice and Commerce.

On the north wall, a little to the east of the doorway beneath the tower, is a handsome monument, with bust, thus inscribed:—

"Dedicated to the memory of the Rev^d. William Conway M.A., Canon of Westminster—for twelve years Rector of this Parish, by his Parishioners and friends, in affectionate remembrance of the blessed influence which by his meekness of wisdom, gentleness of spirit, and sincerity of purpose, he exercised over all classes. 'Thanks be to God which giveth us the victory through our Lord Jesus Christ.' 'He was a good man, and full of the Holy Ghost and of faith.' Born 16th April 1815. Canon of Westminster and Rector of this Parish 31st August 1864. Died 22nd March 1876."

Above Canon Conway's monument are tablets to Sir Richard

Corbett, of Longnor, in the county of Salop, who died in 1683, and his grand-daughter Elizabeth, daughter of Sir Uvedale Corbett of Longnor, and Lady Mildred, daughter of James Cecil, Earl of Salisbury, who died in 1724. The epitaph of Elizabeth Corbett was written by Pope:—

> "Here rests a woman, good without pretence,
> Blest with plain reason and with sober sense:
> No conquest she, but o'er herself, desired;
> No arts essayed, but not to be admired.
> Passion and pride were to her soul unknown,
> Convinced that virtue only is our own.
> So unaffected, so composed a mind,
> So firm, yet soft, so strong, yet so refined,
> Heaven, as its purest gold, by tortures tried:
> The saint sustained it, but the woman died."

Dr. Johnson's remarks on this epitaph contain so much solid wisdom that they cannot be too often quoted:—

"I have always considered this as the most valuable of all Pope's epitaphs: the subject of it is a character not discriminated by any shining or eminent peculiarities: yet that which really makes, though not the splendor, the felicity of life, and that which every wise man will choose for his final and lasting companion in the languor of age, in the quiet of privacy, when he departs weary and disgusted from the ostentatious, the volatile and the vain. Of such a character, which the dull overlook, and the gay despise, it was fit that the value should be made known, and the dignity established. Domestic virtue, as it is exerted without great occasions, or conspicuous consequences, in an even unnoted tenor, required the genius of Pope to display it in such a manner as might attract regard and enforce reverence. Who can forbear to lament that this amiable woman has no name in the verses?

"If the particular lines of this inscription be examined, it will appear less faulty than the rest. There is scarcely one line taken from commonplaces, unless it be that in which 'only virtue' is said to be 'our own.' I once heard a lady of great beauty and elegance object to the fourth line, that it contained an unnatural and incredible panegyric. Of this let the ladies judge."

On the same wall, a little farther east, are the figures of a man and his wife kneeling at a desk under a canopy. This is the monument of Thomas Arnwaye, who died in 1603: his epitaph is in rhyme :—

"Interred here in grave doth Thomas Arnwaye lye,
Who in his life tyme loved the poore, and in that love
(did dye,
For what he left, to helpe the poore, he did devise
(the same,
Not idell folke, but such as woulde them selfs to
(goodness frame :
The thriftie peopell by his will, that in this Parishe
(dwell
Fyve Poundes for ther comforte may have, if yt they
(use it well,
From yeare to yeare if carefullie they looke unto their
(charge.
Of suche men as this Arnwaye was God make the number
(large."

Beyond is a window in memory of Sir Goldsworthy Gurney, who died in 1875, aged eighty-two. "He originated," says the inscription, "the electric telegraph, high speed locomotion, and flashing light signalling. He invented the steam jet and oxy-hydrogen blowpipe." A fine manly countenance next greets us in the image of James Palmer, who has a handsome monument and this epitaph :—

"Here under is interred the Body of James Palmer, Bachelor in Divinity, born in this Parish of St. Margaret's in July 1581. A most pious and charitable Man, expressed in several places by many remarkable Actions, and particularly to this Parish, in building fair Almshouses for 12 poor old People, with a Free School, and a commodious Habitation for the Schoolmaster, and a convenient chapel for Prayers and Preaching, where he constantly, for divers years before his Death, once a week gave a comfortable sermon. He endowed the same with a competent yearly Revenue of Free-hold estate committed to the Trust and Care of 20 considerable Persons, to be renewed as any die.

"He cheerfully ended this life, the 5th of January 1659.

"Erected at the charge of Sir William Playter, Knight and Baronet."

Palmer, says Hatton, on the authority of a person who knew him, "was a very frugal person, and being Vicar of St. Bride's used to lye in the steeple."

But what he saved by his frugality he devoted to the assistance of the needy; nor did he stay his bountiful hand when, on the outbreak of the Civil War, he was ejected by the Parliament from his vicarage, which he had held for upwards of a quarter of a century. He was a member of Magdalene College, Cambridge, and Fuller, in his History of that University, pays the following tribute to his benevolence :—

"Amongst the worthies of this House Mr. Palmer B.D. late Minister of St. Brigit's (commonly Bride's) must not be forgotten, a pious man and painfull preacher, who (besides many and great benefactions to Ministers' Widdowes) hath built and well endowed a neat Almes-house at Westminster. Verily I have found more charity in this one sequestered Minister than in many who enjoy other men's sequestrations."

The next window commemorates Edward Lloyd, for many years one of the chiefs of journalism, who died on April 8, 1890.

aged seventy-five. On a tablet below are these four lines by Sir Edwin Arnold :—

> "A Master Printer of the Press, he spake
> By mouth of many thousand tongues; he swayed
> The pens which break the sceptres. Good Lord, make
> Thy strong ones faithful and Thy bold afraid."

Then comes the finely executed, but somewhat time worn bust of Cornelius Vandun, who is represented with a kindly, thoughtful face, and a long beard. He died in 1577, at the advanced age of ninety-four, and is thus described by his epitaph :—

> "Cornelius Vandun lieth here, borne at Breda in Brabant, Souldiour with K— Henry at Turney, yeoman of the gard and usher to K. Henry, K. Edward, Q. Mary, and Q. Elizabeth : of honest and vertuous lyfe, a carful man for pore folke, who in the ende of this towne dyd buyld for pore widows 20 howses of his owne coste."

The succeeding window is to the memory of one of the greatest among England's naval heroes, Admiral Robert Blake. After the victory of Santa Cruz, his last and most glorious achievement, he died on his homeward voyage, just as his fleet entered Plymouth Sound. He was buried in Henry VII.'s chapel with the honours due to his mighty deeds in his country's cause; but after the Restoration, the impotent and ungrateful rulers, who enjoyed the fruits of his labours, in a childish ebullition of factious malice, cast out from the Abbey the remains of the illustrious seaman, and thrust them into an undistinguished grave in St. Margaret's Churchyard. Thus a second time did tyranny and injustice serve to enrich St. Margaret's : it had been graced with the body of Raleigh, and now it was still further honoured with the dust of Blake. The inscription beneath the window is as follows :—

RIVERSIDE CHURCHES

"To the glory of God, and to the Memory of Colonel Robert Blake, Admiral at Sea, Chief Founder of England's Naval Supremacy. Died August 7th 1657. Ejected from his grave in the Abbey and buried in St Margaret's Churchyard Sepr 1661.

> "Kingdom or Common-wealth were less to thee,
> Than to crown England Queen o'er every sea.
> Strong sailor, sleeping sound as sleep the just,
> Rest here. Our Abbey keeps no worthier dust.
> *Lewis Morris.*"

Next we are confronted by the figure of a bulky knight, on his knees in prayer, with his right hand on his heart. This is the effigy of Sir Francis Egioke of Egioke, in the county of Worcester, who died in 1622. The window beyond is in memory of Edward Ashurst Morris, who died in 1890. The last monument on this wall displays the kneeling effigies of two men in gowns and ruffs, and one lady. The following epitaph records their history :—

> "To the memory of Robert Peter Esq, Auditor of the Receipt, her first husband, who gave to th' use of ye poore of this Parishe One Hundred Pound, & of Edmund English her secōd husband a gentleman kinde courtious & of great hospitallitie who gave 12 poundes in annuitie for ever to ye same use, Margaret their loving wife, daughter of S— John Tirell of Gipping Knight, who likewise hath bequeathed One Hundred Pound for the purchasinge of one yearlie anuitie of 20 Nobles for ever to the aforesaid poore, lametinge their death and for testification of her dutifull love hath erected ye monumēt."

The westernmost window of the north aisle at present remains unoccupied. In the chancel hang the ancient colours of the Queen's Westminster Volunteers, which were presented to the corps by George III. in 1798, when a French invasion was anticipated. As a memorial of the patriotism manifested by the corps in that season of national peril, they were here erected in 1887, the year of Queen Victoria's Jubilee.

Catherine Milton, the poet's second wife, "my late espoused saint," as he calls her in the sonnet which he wrote after her decease, was buried at St. Margaret's on February 10, 1657. Milton, while Latin Secretary to the Protector, lived in Westminster, in Petty France, afterwards called York Street. His house was purchased by Jeremy Bentham. From 1812 to 1819, during Bentham's ownership, it was occupied by William Hazlitt. It was pulled down in 1877, and the site is now covered by Queen Anne's Mansions.

James Harrington, the author of *Oceana*, who died September 7, 1677, was buried in the chancel of St. Margaret's. The parish register records the burial, on August 27, 1680, of the audacious Colonel Thomas Blood, famous for his daring attempts to hang the Duke of Ormond and carry off the crown.

The burials are also noted, of Sir John Cutler, in 1693, and Dr. George Hickes, the Jacobite divine and Anglo-Saxon scholar, in 1715. Among the baptisms are those of Thomas Betterton, the famous actor (1635), and Henry Aldrich, the celebrated Dean of Christ Church (1647). Lady Elizabeth Lee, daughter of the Earl of Lichfield, whose baptism here is recorded on June 26, 1693, was married, in 1731, to Young, the poet. He seems to have been very fond of her.

"The longer known, the closer still she grew,"

he says himself, and his son told Boswell that after her death he was never cheerful. She died in 1741, and it was under the influence of this crushing sorrow that he commenced the *Night Thoughts*.

Edward Hyde, afterwards Earl of Clarendon, was married at St. Margaret's, July 10, 1634, to his second wife, Frances Aylesbury, the mother of Anne Hyde, and grandmother of Queen Mary and Queen Anne. Here were also married Edmund Waller, the poet, July 5, 1631, to his first wife, Anne Bankes: Samuel Pepys, December 1, 1655; and Thomas Campbell, "the Bard of Hope," September 10, 1802.

Another interesting association connected with St. Margaret's is that the churchyard was the scene of a memorable event in Cowper's boyhood. "As I was crossing St. Margaret's Churchyard," he says in his *Memoir* of his early life, "late one evening, I saw a glimmering light in the midst of it, which excited my curiosity. Just as I arrived at the spot, a gravedigger, who was at work by the light of his lanthorn, threw up a skull which struck me upon the leg. This little accident was an alarm to my conscience; for that event may be numbered among the best religious documents which I received at Westminster."

It is not easy now to picture to oneself the appearance which St. Margaret's churchyard must have presented when Cowper was at Westminster School. Walcott, writing in 1847, gives the number of gravestones then remaining as 1,167: now, with one solitary exception, they have all been swept away.

The Rectory of St. Margaret, which is united with a Canonry of Westminster, is in the patronage of the Crown.

ST MARTIN-IN-THE-FIELDS

THE church of St. Martin-in-the-Fields must have been originally in the vast parish of St. Margaret, Westminster; but it early obtained an independent position, for in 1222, when Stephen Langton, Archbishop of Canterbury, settled the respective boundaries of the Bishop of London and the Abbot of Westminster, he specially excepted from St. Margaret's "the church and cemetery of St. Martin." The vicarage, however, continued in the patronage of the Abbot and Convent, till Queen Mary completed the separation by bestowing the advowson on the See of London, to which it has ever since appertained. Henry VIII. greatly enlarged St. Martin's parish at the expense of that of St. Margaret, for having appropriated land belonging to St. Martin's for his park of St. James, in consequence of which the tithes were diminished, he, in 1542, transferred to St. Martin's, as a compensation for this loss, all that portion of the parish of St. Margaret which was situated between his palace of Whitehall and the church of St. Clement Danes. He had also another and less disinterested reason: he was vexed because dead bodies from the farther part of the parish were borne in front of his palace to their burial in St. Margaret's Churchyard, and by making this district a part of St. Martin's he freed himself from the annoyance which the funerals of its inhabitants had caused him.

As London increased, this large parish became densely populated, and its disintegration was rendered necessary. First, in

1660, St. Paul's, Covent Garden, was taken out of it; but, notwithstanding this diminution, it was said by Burnet, about 1680, to be "the greatest cure in England," while Baxter lamented that "it had a population of 40,000 persons more than could find room in the church, and that neighbours lived here like Americans, without hearing a sermon for many years." Shortly afterwards, it was further subdivided by the formation of the parishes of St. James, Westminster, in 1684, and St. Anne, Soho, in 1686; and it was yet again lessened when the parish of St. George, Hanover Square, was created in 1725.

The continuation of Stow's *Survey*, published in 1633, records an "enlargement" of St. Martin's Church in the years 1607-8, "to the which enlargement our said Sovereign Lord King James and our most noble Prince Henry were most gracious benefactors." The "enlargement," it is added, consisted in taking some ground from the churchyard, and making upon it "a beautiful chancel." Newcourt, a century later, describes the church as "now very old, and fitter to be taken down and new built than repaired." This seems to have been the view of the parishioners, who obtained an Act of Parliament for rebuilding it at the expense of the parish, four-fifths of the cost to be contributed by the landlords and one-fifth by the tenants.

James Gibbs was selected as architect, and laid before the Commissioners several plans, one of which they agreed on. The work was commenced under royal patronage, for on March 19, 1721, King George I. deputed his Lord Almoner, the Bishop of Salisbury, and his Surveyor General, Sir Thomas Hewyt, to lay the first stone on his behalf, and ordered one hundred guineas to be distributed among the workmen. His Majesty also gave the parishioners £1,500 to buy an organ with, but the instrument purchased with the royal donation did not wear well, and had already been replaced by a fresh one at the beginning of the

ST MARTIN-IN-THE-FIELDS

183

present century. The church was completed in 1726, and "notwithstanding the great economy of the Commissioners," who had, as Gibbs tells us, rejected two designs which he had made " for a Round Church," "upon account of the expensiveness of executing them, though they were more capacious and convenient than what they pitched upon," the total expense amounted to £36,891 10s. 4d.—close upon £2,000 more than the sum which they had been empowered to raise by the Act of Parliament, and the additional £1,500 which had been presented by the King. The extra amount was, however, obtained by subscriptions and the sale of seats in the church.

St. Martin's is a very large edifice, measuring in length from the base of the steps at the west 168 feet 4 inches, and in breadth 79 feet 4 inches, while the height of the steeple is 185 feet. It is advantageously placed, for its open, prominent position at the east of Trafalgar Square is excellently adapted to reveal its great proportions in the most impressive manner. Its most striking ornament is its magnificent western portico, formed by eight Corinthian columns, six in front, and one on each flank. The breadth of this portico is 64 feet 10 inches, and the columns are 33 feet 4 inches in height. On the frieze above the columns is this inscription:—

"D. Sacram Aedem S. Martini Parochiani extrui Fec. A.D. MDCCXXVI. Jacobo Gibbs, Architecto."

Within the spacious pediment which completes the portico are displayed the Royal Arms. The ceiling of the portico is divided into panels, and very richly ornamented. The steps which lead to the portico from the street have been objected to of late years as unduly narrowing the thoroughfare ; but as there is in reality abundant room for the necessities of the traffic, and as any curtailment of this approach would materially damage the effect of the portico, any attempt to tamper with it must deserve the most emphatic reprobation.

The steeple consists of a tower in two stories, the second of which is decorated with Ionic pilasters; a stylobate; an octagonal story with Corinthian columns, at the angles; another stylobate; and a tall obelisk crowned with a ball and vane. It is certainly imposing, but as it rises from the roof just behind the portico it undoubtedly tends by its overpowering size to dwarf and weaken the latter, which is an unfortunate circumstance, since the portico is a far more beautiful object than the steeple. There are twelve bells.

The east front is crowned with a pediment, within which is a circular window. Beneath, in the centre, is a Venetian window; on each side of it are two windows, one above the other. The north and south walls each contain two rows of windows, and, at the western extremity, a side door, approached by a flight of steps.

The interior consists of a nave, chancel, and two aisles, which are divided from the central portion by Corinthian columns on high bases. There are galleries on the north, west, and south. The organ is in the west gallery. "The ceiling," remarks Gibbs, in his *Book of Architecture*, "is elliptical, which I find by experience to be much better for the voice than the semi-circular, though not so beautiful. It is divided into panels, enriched with fretwork by Signori Artari and Bagutti, the best fretworkers that ever came into England." The fretwork of the "Signori" is indeed extremely ornate. The font, which stands at the northwest, is a relic of the old church. Its cover, which is of oak, decorated with gilding, is inscribed: "This Font was the gift of William Bridgeman, 1689." At the north-east is a fine oak pulpit, but it has lost its sounding-board. The lower parts of the walls are panelled. The east window is filled with stained glass.

The north and south walls have each two rows of windows, five in each row. Those on the north are plain. The easternmost window on the south side in the upper row was presented by public subscription in honour of Her Majesty's Jubilee. The window immediately beneath it was given by Mr. George James, a former churchwarden. The succeeding pair of windows are a memorial to the late eminent statesman, Mr. W. H. Smith. Beneath the lower one is the following inscription :—

> "To the Glory of God, and in Memory of William Henry Smith; Born June 24th 1825; Died October 6th 1891; For many years the Representative of this Borough in Parliament; this window is erected in grateful recognition of distinguished services rendered to his Constituents and his Country."

The middle couple of windows are in memory of the late Vicar, the Rev. William Gibson Humphry, B.D., who died on January 10, 1886. The next window to the west in the lower row was given by another churchwarden, Major Probyn; the corresponding upper window is in course of construction.[1]

There are no monuments in the church, but against the west wall on the south side is a bust of Gibbs by Rysbraeck, with this inscription on the pedestal :—

> "This Bust (by Rysbraeck) of James Gibbs (1674–1754), the Architect of this Church of St. Martin-in-the-Fields, was presented to the Church by William Boore, A.D. 1885."

Francis Bacon, who was born on January 22, 1561, at York House, in the Strand, was baptized at St. Martin's; so also was Thomas Stothard, the painter, September 7, 1775. Here, on November 11, 1657, Oliver Cromwell's youngest daughter,

---

[1] Colonel Probyn has given another stained glass window to the Church, in commemoration of Her Majesty's Diamond Jubilee.

Frances, was married to the Honourable Robert Rich; and here, on March 25, 1811, Tom Moore married Bessie Dyke. Among the burials recorded are those of George Heriot, James I.'s Goldsmith (died 1624); Sir John Davies, poet and statesman (died 1626); William Dobson, who succeeded Vandyck as serjeant-painter to Charles I. (died 1646); Nicholas Stone, that Sovereign's master-mason (died 1647); Sir Theodore Mayerne, physician to James I. and Charles I. (died 1655); John Lacy, the actor (died 1681); before the Civil War he belonged to the King's servants, and when hostilities broke out was one of those who, as Wright puts it, "like good men and true, served their old master, tho' in a different yet more honourable capacity," being a lieutenant and quartermaster in the King's army; Henry Coventry, third son of Lord Keeper Coventry, who was Secretary of State to Charles II., and whose name is commemorated in Coventry Street, where his mansion stood (died 1686); Nell Gwynne (died 1687); Robert Boyle, the philosopher (died 1691); George Farquhar, the dramatist (died 1707); Charles, Lord Mohun, who fought the fatal duel with the Duke of Hamilton, in which both fell (died 1712); Louis Laguerre, the painter (died 1721), who figures in Pope's description of *Timon's Villa*:—

> "On painted ceilings you devoutly stare,
> Where sprawl the saints of Verrio or Laguerre";

Louis François Roubiliac, the famous sculptor (died 1762); James Stuart, the architect, joint author with Nicholas Revett of the *Antiquities of Athens* (died 1788); John Hunter, the great surgeon (died 1793);[1] Charles Bannister, the actor (died 1804); and James Smith, of the *Rejected Addresses* (died 1839).

Among the Vicars of St. Martin-in-the-Fields have been some distinguished divines. Thomas Lamplugh, who was presented in 1670, was advanced to the See of Exeter in 1676; on the landing

---

[1] Hunter's remains were removed to Westminster Abbey in 1859.

of the Prince of Orange, he hastened to London to join James II., who thereupon gave him the vacant Archbishopric of York; he died in 1691. William Lloyd, who succeeded Lamplugh at St. Martin's, was promoted to the See of St. Asaph in 1680, and was one of the "Seven Bishops"; he was translated to Lichfield and Coventry in 1692, and again, in 1700, to Worcester; he died in 1717, being upwards of ninety years old. Thomas Tenison, the next Vicar, became Bishop of Lincoln in 1691, and in 1694, on the death of Tillotson, was raised to the Archbishopric of Canterbury. While Vicar of St. Martin's he founded a grammar school and library in Castle Street, Leicester Square. In 1861 the library was sold for the benefit of the school, and in the same year the old buildings were pulled down for the extension of the National Gallery. The present premises of the school are on the east side of Leicester Square, and occupy the site of Hogarth's house. As a secondary school it is now proving itself a most excellent and valuable institution. Zachary Pearce was appointed to the vicarage in 1724; he was made Bishop of Bangor in 1748, but continued to hold the living till 1756, in which year he was created Dean of Westminster, and translated to Rochester. The deanery he resigned in 1768, and six years later he died, having almost completed his eighty fourth year.

In the council chamber of St. Martin's Town Hall are portraits of the vicars of St. Martin-in-the-Fields from Lamplugh to Humphry, and likewise portraits of George I., the royal patron, and James Gibbs, the able architect of the rebuilding of the church.

ST MARY-LE-STRAND

THE parish of St. Mary-le-Strand has had a singular history. A "Church of the Innocents" existed in the Strand at least as early as the year 1222. Subsequently it obtained a further dedication to St. Mary.

"Next beyond the which" (Arundel House), says Stow, "on the street side, was sometime a fair cemetery or churchyard, and in the same a parish church called of the Nativity of Our Lady, and the Innocents of the Strand, and of some, by means of a brotherhood kept there, called St. Ursula at the Strand."

This church and all the adjacent buildings, he goes on to tell us, "were by commandment of Edward, Duke of Somerset, uncle to Edward VI., and Lord Protector, pulled down and made level ground in the year 1549: in place whereof he built that large and goodly house, now called Somerset House."

The Protector is said to have promised the parishioners to build a new church for them, but he did not do so. The speediness of his downfall and death left him but little time. They were thus without a church of their own, and many of them resorted to the Chapel of the Savoy. In 1564 Bishop Grindall arranged for their being regularly joined to the Savoy, and in consequence the chapel, although dedicated to St. John the Baptist, received the name, which is even now sometimes applied to it, of St. Mary-le-Savoy. At the Savoy the parishioners remained, until the present church of St. Mary-le-Strand was erected for them under the provisions of Queen Anne's Act, and then they departed, taking with them their bell, which they had brought from their old church and hung in the tower of the chapel.

The building of the new church occasioned the removal of the Strand maypole—a circumstance to which Pope alludes in the *Dunciad*:—

> "Amid that area wide they took their stand,
> Where the tall maypole once o'erlooked the Strand.
> But now (so Anne and piety ordain)
> A Church collects the saints of Drury Lane."

"The which Church being now built," says Strype, "the aforesaid memorable Maypole, reckoned somewhat incommodious standing near on the west thereof, was bought by Sir Isaac Newton Knt, the great mathematician; and April 1718 carried away upon a carriage through London unto Wanstead, to the Rector, Mr. Pound, who obtained leave of Sir Richard Child, Bart., (now Lord Castlemain) to set it up in his park at Wanstead House, in a place of advantage, for the better use of a fine telescope to be raised on it: which is 125 foot long: and was given to the Royal Society by Monsieur Hugon, a member thereof."

The church of St. Mary-le-Strand, which is built of Portland stone, was designed by James Gibbs. The first stone was laid on February 25, 1714, and the steeple was completed on September 7, 1717. The edifice was not, however, consecrated till January 1, 1723-4. The graceful steeple, so familiar an object to every Londoner, was not a part of the original design; we are indebted for it to a change of plan—and a very fortunate change it turned out—on the part of the Commissioners, as Gibbs himself has recorded in his *Book of Architecture*.

"The new Church in the Strand," he says, "called St. Mary-le-Strand, was the first public building I was employed in after my arrival from Italy; which being situated in a very public place, the Commissioners for building the Fifty Churches (of which this

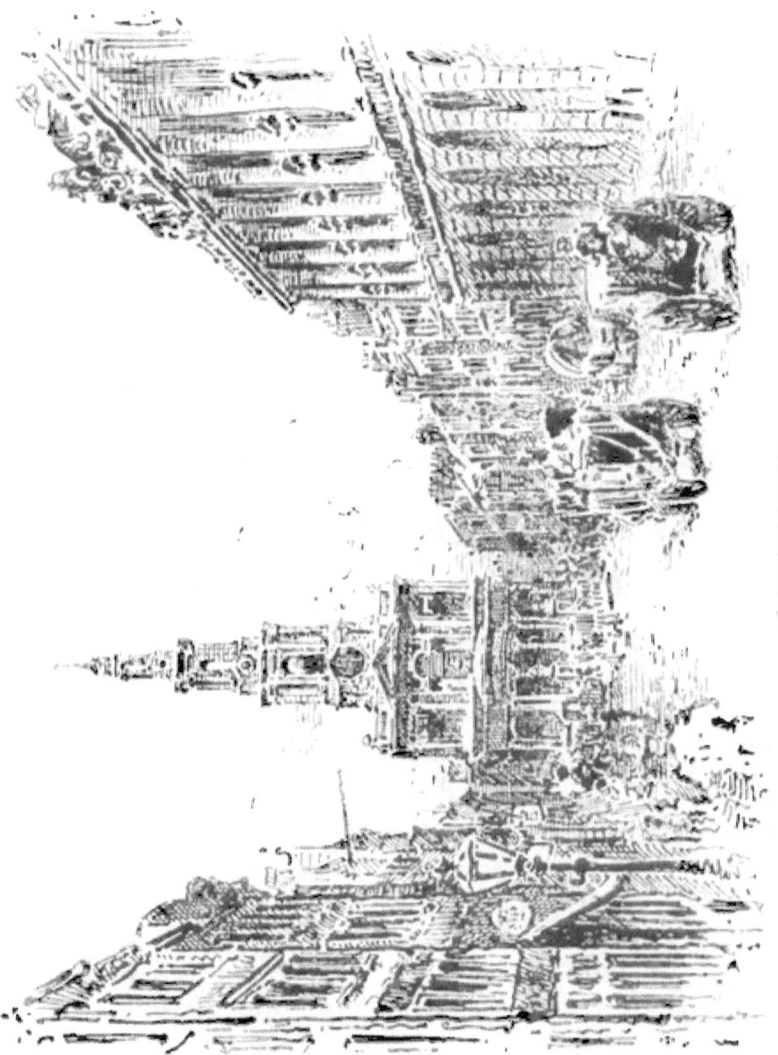

ST. MARY-LE-STRAND.

is one) spared no cost to beautify it. . . . There was at first no steeple designed for that Church, only a small campanile, or turret for a bell, was to have been over the west end of it—but at the distance of eighty feet from the west front there was a column, 250 feet high, intended to be erected in honour of Queen Anne, on the top of which her statue was to be placed. My design for the column was approved by the Commissioners, and a great quantity of stone was brought to the place for laying the foundation of it; but the thoughts of erecting that monument being laid aside upon the Queen's death, I was ordered to erect a steeple instead of the campanile first proposed. The building being then advanced 20 feet above ground, and therefore admitting of no alteration from east to west, which was only 14 feet, I was obliged to spread it from south to north, which makes the plan oblong, which otherwise should have been square."

Gibbs, who seems to have been a man not easily satisfied with his own designs, has included in his book "five draughts of steeples made for St. Mary-le-Strand, with their plans." His final selection in this case was judicious, and every one who views this elegant steeple, as he walks towards it along the Strand, must be heartily thankful that the Commissioners abandoned their monstrous column, which would have been nearly fifty feet higher than the Monument, and their statue of Queen Anne.

The west front of St. Mary-le-Strand is approached by a flight of steps, at the top of which is a circular portico formed by four Ionic columns, and surmounted by a shallow dome on which is placed an urn. An arched doorway within the portico gives access to the interior. Above the portico is the west window, which has on each side of it a pair of attached Corinthian columns, and above it a pediment. From behind the balustrade, which is broken by the pediment, rises the steeple; it includes three diminishing stories, and is completed by a small cupola and vane.

There are in this front four windows, two on each side of the portico, arranged in two tiers. The centre of the east front is occupied with the circular projection of the chancel; in the lower story are three windows, in the upper three niches. To the north and south of this projection are a doorway in the lower and a window in the upper story. This front is richly decorated. The church stands on a plinth, and is lighted from the north and south by windows inserted in the upper story. "It consists," says the architect himself, "of two orders, in the upper of which the lights are placed; the wall of the lower, being solid to keep out noises from the street, is adorned with niches." There are seven windows in each of these two walls, those at the extremities being smaller than the other five. The north and south fronts are each ornamented with three pediments, the central elliptical, the others pointed.

Entering the church at the west, one passes beneath a small gallery which is sustained by four Corinthian columns on high wainscotted bases. This gallery formerly contained the organ, which has now been removed to the north-east, close to the arch which forms the entrance to the eastern recess. On either side of this arch are two orders, one consisting of coupled Corinthian pilasters similar to those of the lower order throughout the church, and above this coupled composite attached columns supporting, above the arch, an entablature and pediment, in the tympanum of which are the Royal Arms. The three windows at the east are filled with stained glass; the west window, which appears above the gallery, and the five windows in the north and the five in the south wall are also tinted. The lower parts of the walls are panelled. The upper parts are much decorated; the pilasters, of which there are two rows on the north and south walls, one below and one between the windows, are gilded. The arched ceiling is divided into compartments and lavishly decorated. The pulpit, which is of oak and handsome, is placed in the south-east corner, opposite the organ. Beside it is the lectern, which displays an eagle of carved wood. The font stands at the south-west. On the north wall is a brass plate thus inscribed :—

"In grateful Memory of Julia Sherley, who lovingly and untiringly worked in this Parish, among the sick, needy and afflicted, for over 50 years. She fell asleep October 14th, 1894. Aged 75 years.

'I was sick and ye visited me.'"

St. Mary-le-Strand is not majestic, but it is a building of singular refinement and excellent proportions. Here Gibbs' talents appear to greater advantage than in his larger and more pretentious St. Martin's, the noble portico of the latter church of course excepted.

The benefice is a Rectory, in the patronage of the Lord Chancellor.

ST CLEMENT DANES

THE church of St. Clement Danes, standing at the east end of the Strand, in the middle of the roadway, immediately opposite the Courts of Justice, and only just outside the City boundary, is one of the best known and most conspicuous of the ecclesiastical edifices of London. It must have anciently formed a part of the wide-stretching domains of the Abbey of Westminster, but it early became an independent parish. As to the origin of the name, we know nothing certain, except that it is derived from the Danish invaders of England. Stow explains the title from its having been the burial-place of Harold Harefoot and other Danes, and also quotes a story from William of Malmesbury, that a band of Danes, who had burnt the Abbey of Chertsey and killed the monks, were themselves intercepted and slain at this spot. Strype mentions another tradition to the effect that " when the Danes were utterly driven out of this kingdom "—alluding apparently to the slaughter of them by the order of King Ethelred —the few who were left " were constrained to inhabit between the Isle of Thorne (that which is now called Westminster) and Caer Lud, now called Ludgate. And there they builded a synagogue, the which, being afterwards consecrated, was called ' Ecclesia Clementis Danorum.' " " This account of the name," he adds, " did the learned antiquarian Fleetwood, some time Recorder of London, give to the Lord Treasurer Burleigh who lived in this parish."

Descending to better authenticated history, we read that the church of St. Clement Danes was given by Henry II. to the

RIVERSIDE CHURCHES

ST. CLEMENT DANES, HOLYWELL STREET

Knights Templars, and that after their dissolution the church, together with the Outer Temple, became the property of the Prior and Canons of the Church of the Holy Sepulchre at Warwick. Not many years later the Prior and Canons exchanged this distant possession for some lands in their own county with Walter Stapleton, Bishop of Exeter, whom the citizens of London, in their ardour for the cause of Queen Isabella, beheaded "at the Standard in Cheape" as an adherent of Edward II.'s favourites, the De Spencers, in 1326. The Bishops of Exeter continued patrons of St. Clement's till the first year of Edward VI., when the advowson was procured by the Protector Somerset. After Somerset's attainder it was granted to Sir Thomas Palmer, who

ST CLEMENT DANES

was in his turn attainted when Queen Mary came to the throne. Queen Elizabeth gave it to Lord Burleigh, and the advowson has ever since remained in the Cecil family, being now the property of the Marquis of Exeter, the descendant of Burleigh's eldest son, Thomas, Earl of Exeter. The site of Burleigh's house in the Strand, which was after his time called from his son Exeter House, is marked by Burleigh Street and Exeter Street.

Henry Smith, whose life was written by Fuller, was lecturer at St. Clement Danes. He inclined somewhat in opinion to the Puritan party, which was the cause of his embracing this situation, as his biographer informs us :—

"But a greater scruple troubled him, as unsatisfied in the point of subscription, and the lawfulness of some ceremonies. He was loath to make a rent either in his own conscience or in the Church, wherefore he resolved on this expedient, not to undertake a pastoral charge, but contented himself with a lecturer's place at St. Clement Danes without Temple Bar."

Holding views of this kind, he was naturally not very acceptable to the rulers of the Church, but he found in Lord Burleigh a constant protector :—

"William Cecil, Lord Burleigh, and Treasurer of England (to whom he dedicated his sermons) very favourably reflected upon him, and he was often the screen who saved Mr. Smith from the scorching; interposing his greatness betwixt him and the anger of some episcopal officers; and it is argument enough to prove the eminency of Mr. Smith, that so great a statesman as this Lord Treasurer set a character of his peculiar respect upon him."

Smith's powers as a preacher are described by Fuller with characteristic quaintness :—

"He was commonly called the silver tongued preacher, and that was but one metal below St. Chrysostom himself. His Church was so crowded with auditors, that persons of good quality brought their own pews with them, I mean their legs to stand there upon in the alleys. Their ears did so attend to his lips, their hearts to their ears, that he held the rudder of their affections in his hand, so that he could steer them whither he was pleased, and he was pleased to steer them only to God's glory and their own good."

Suffering from consumption, he left St. Clement's a little before his death, and went into the country. The date of his decease Fuller was unable to ascertain, but conjectured that it was "about the year 1600."

"The care of those," says Stow's *Continuator*, "that by an annual succession have the charge and oversight of this church, hath continually been such, as upon the least defect or failing, either in strength or beauty, it hath instantly been employed both in repairs and adornment."

And he proceeds to give the details of "repairs and adornments," executed in 1608, 1616, 1631, and 1632-33—"the sum of all these repairs, all being the sole cost of the parishioners, £1.586." But the fabric was too far decayed to derive much benefit from being patched up. The steeple had to be recased, and, in 1680, it became necessary to completely take down the body of the church. It was rebuilt of stone from the designs of Sir Christopher Wren, who gratuitously placed his valuable services at the disposal of the parishioners, and was completed in 1682 at a cost of £8,786 17s. 0½d. The upper part of the steeple is due to James Gibbs, by whom it was built in 1719. The church is stated to measure in length 64 feet, in breadth 40 feet, in height to the ceiling 34 feet; the altitude of the steeple is 116 feet.

The steeple stands at the west of the church. The tower contains five stories, the first four of which belong to the earlier steeple, but the fifth forms the commencement of the additions of Gibbs. Above the tower are three diminishing stages, octangular in shape, of which the lowest is of the Ionic order, the second Corinthian, and the third Composite. The transition from the square tower to the octagon is softened by vases at the angles, and there are also vases on the first and second stories of the octagon. Above the third story is a low cupola, from which rises a lantern culminating in a ball and vane. The tower contains ten bells. At the base of the tower is a porch with an arched doorway, which forms the main entrance to the sacred building. At the sides of the porch are vestibules, each consisting of two stories, and each crowned with a lead-covered dome. The north and south walls have each a doorway and four smallish windows in the lower, and five large round-headed windows in the upper story. They are finished by a cornice and pierced parapet. In the east front is a large round-headed window, formed into three divisions by stone-work; over the pediment is elevated a shield, which bears an anchor, the emblem of St. Clement, and the letters S.C.D. Altogether, the exterior of St. Clement Danes is very handsome, and the effect is enhanced by its situation, which is a grand one, admirably calculated to display all its merits to the best possible advantage.

The interior is pervaded by that peculiar air of dignity which distinguishes all the works of Wren. It includes a nave and chancel, and two aisles, each of which is separated from the main body by five Corinthian columns, rising from piers at the height of the gallery. The roof is arched, and highly decorated, especially over the chancel, where it is embellished with the Royal Arms and roses and thistles. The altar-piece is of oak, and finely carved; beneath the pediment is the representation of a pelican. The three windows above it are filled with poor stained glass by Collins, inserted in 1844. The font, which is placed at the north-west, has a well-carved cover. The dark oak pulpit—"an extraordinary fine pulpit," as Strype calls it—is elaborately carved; and the woodwork of the pews and galleries is solid and handsome. The eagle of the lectern is also a good specimen of wood-carving. In the west gallery is a fine organ, the work of Father Smith, which has been recently renovated.

The most interesting association attached to St. Clement Danes is that it was the church attended by Dr. Johnson. Here it was that he conducted Boswell, on Good Friday, 1773, as the latter has recorded :—

"He carried me with him to the Church of St. Clement Danes, where he had his seat; and his behaviour was, as I had imaged to myself, solemnly devout. I never shall forget the tremulous earnestness with which he pronounced the awful petition in the Litany—'In the hour of death, and in the day of judgment, Good Lord deliver us.'"

Johnson's seat was in a front pew of the north gallery at the east end, immediately above the pulpit, which was considerably higher in his time than it is now. The pew is marked by a brass plate, with the following inscription by Dr. George Croly, the late poetical rector of St. Stephen's, Walbrook :

"In this pew
and beside this pillar, for many years,
attended Divine Service,
The celebrated Doctor Samuel Johnson,
The Philosopher, the Poet,
The great Lexicographer,
The profound Moralist, and Chief Writer
of his time,
Born 1709 — Died 1784.

In remembrance and honour
of noble faculties, nobly employed;
Some inhabitants of the Parish
of St. Clement Danes
have placed this slight Memorial
A.D. 1851."

On the north side of the altar is a tablet in commemoration of the rebuilding of the church, and on the south side one in memory of Dr. Richard Dukeson, rector from 1634 to 1678. These memorials are, as Strype very reasonably complained, "placed so high as not to be read." The inscriptions are thus given by the late Mr. Diprose, in his *Account of the Parish of St. Clement Danes* :—

"To the Glory of God and for the ye solemn worship of his Holy Name, this old Church, being greatly decayed, was taken down in ye yeare 1680, and rebuilt and finished in ye yeare 1682 by the pious assistance of ye Reverend Dr. Gregory Haskard, Rector, and ye Bountifull Contributions of ye Inhabitants of this Parish and some other Noble Benefactors—Sir Christopher Wren, his Majesty's Surveyor freely and generously bestowing his great care and skill towards ye contriving and building of it ; Which good Work was all along greatly promoted and incouraged by ye zeal and diligence of ye Vestry. Hugh Owen, Hall Jarman, Thomas Cox, William Thomson, John Padford, being churchwardens,

II. Chronicles XXIV XIII.

'So ye workmen wrought and ye work was perfected by them and they set the house of God in his state, and strengthened it.

Soli Deo Gloria.

This was erected in ye yeare 1684. Roger Franklin, James Parman, Churchwardens."

"To the Memory of Richard Dukeson, D.D. Late Rector of this Parish fortie and four yeares, a Reverend and Learned Divine, eminent for his great devotion towards God, his firm zeal to the Church, his unshaken loyalty to the King, his unwearing endeavour for the good of his flock, from which he was separated by the iniquity of ye times during the late unnatural rebellion by near seventeen yeares sequestration. But being restored he continued to the end of great age a contrite preacher both by his doctrine and life. He died September 17th Anno Domini 1678. Ætat suae 86.

"And of his only Wife, Anne, the Daughter of Anthony Hickman Esq., Dr of Lawes. She was a virtuous and goodly Matron, with whom he lived in holy matrimony 46 yeares, and had three sons and 12 daughters. She died September 22nd Anno Domini 1670. Ætat suae 66.

Their bodies lye interred on the right side of the Communion table:

<blockquote>In verbo tuo spes mea."</blockquote>

In the chancel is also a tablet to Sir Edward Leche, a Master of Chancery and Member of the House of Commons, who died, in his eightieth year, in 1652.

At the west, above the entrance into the church, is a representation of St. Clement's anchor. The anchor also appears over the door of the vestibule. Over the poor-box is an ancient tablet of carved wood, probably a relic of the old church, which is thus inscribed:—

<blockquote>
"As you have opportunity,
Do good unto All, But especially
To them of the houshold of ffaith.
For to do good and to distribute,
With such sacrifices, God
Is well pleased."
</blockquote>

On the north side of the chancel is a tablet, on which is the following inscription:—

"In Memory of Mr. Thomas Prout, who departed this life July 25th 1859, aged 74 years. Such was the high estimation in which he was held, that for 30 years he was the most influential elector of the great and patriotic City of Westminster. This tablet is erected by General Sir De Lacy Evans G.C.B. in grateful recollection of his deceased friend."

Mr. Prout, who resided for forty years in the parish of St. Clement Danes, was a prominent member of the Anti-Corn Law League and the Ballot Society, and worked zealously for the Liberal cause at eleven Westminster elections. Sir De Lacy Evans was for about thirty years a Parliamentary representative of Westminster.

On one of the pillars of the south aisle is a tablet to Mr. John Diprose, "late of this Parish—Compiler of *Some Account of the Parish of St. Clement Danes.*" He died, aged sixty-four, June 20, 1879.

The parish register contains many interesting entries. Here were baptized two sons of Lord Burleigh, William Cecil (April 23, 1661), who died young, and (June 6, 1563) Robert Cecil, who lived to occupy his father's office of Lord Treasurer, and was created Earl of Salisbury; Sir Charles Sedley, the wit of Charles II.'s Court (March, 1639); and the third Earl of Shaftesbury, the author of the *Characteristics* (March, 1671). At St. Clement Danes, October 10, 1676, Sir Thomas Grosvenor was married to Mary Davies of Ebury, the heiress of the Pimlico property, which thus came to the Grosvenor family.

Dr. Donne's wife was buried at St. Clement Danes in August, 1617:—

"His first motion from his house," says Walton, "was to preach where his beloved wife lay buried (in St. Clement's Church, near Temple Bar, London) and his text was a part of the prophet Jeremy's Lamentations: 'Lo I am the man that have seen affliction.' And indeed his very words and looks testified him to be truly such a man: and they, with the addition of his sighs and tears, expressed in his sermon, did so work upon the affections of his hearers, as melted and moulded them into a companionable sadness."

A monument, by Nicholas Stone, was erected to her memory in the chancel, but it perished when the old church was demolished.

At St. Clement's were also interred Sir John Roe, who died in 1606 in Ben Jonson's arms, and whom the poet lamented in some very noble lines; Marchamont Needham, who during the Civil Wars wrote *Mercuries*, sometimes for the King and sometimes for the Parliament, and always heartily abused the party to which he happened, for the time being, to be opposed; he died in 1678; Nicholas Byer, the painter, who died in 1681, and was the first person buried in the newly built church; Thomas Otway (died 1685) and Nathaniel Lee (died 1692), the dramatic poets; William Mountfort, the actor, who was stabbed by Lord Mohun's friend, Captain Hill, in 1692; Thomas Rymer, author of the *Foedera*, who died in Arundel Street in 1713; Henry Cromwell, Pope's early friend and correspondent, " honest, hatless Cromwell with red breeches," as Gay calls him; he died in 1728; and another encourager of Pope's budding genius, George Granville, Lord Lansdowne, to whom he dedicated " Windsor Forest," and whom he afterwards styled " Granville the polite": Granville, who was himself a maker of verses, and whose life was written by Johnson among those of the poets, died in January, 1735.

In the parish burying-ground in Portugal Street, the site of which is now occupied by King's College Hospital, were laid the remains of Joe Miller, the comedian, on whom have been fathered innumerable jests, scarcely one of which he made himself. He died, aged fifty-four, in 1738, and Stephen Duck, Queen Caroline's poet, wrote his epitaph.

ST SAVIOUR'S, SOUTHWARK (SOUTH ASPECT)

ST SAVIOUR'S SOUTHWARK

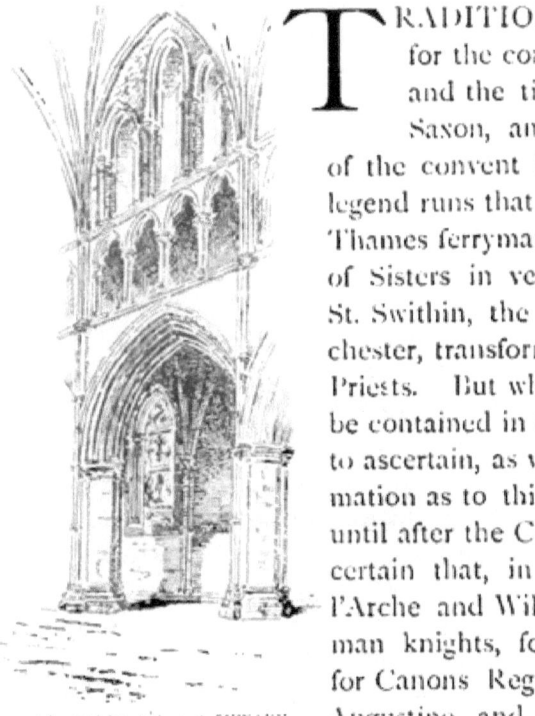

ST. SAVIOUR'S, SOUTHWARK
(ONE BAY OF NAVE)

TRADITION claims a Saxon origin for the convent of St. Mary Overy, and the title "Overy" is certainly Saxon, and denoted the situation of the convent by the waterside. The legend runs that Mary, the daughter of a Thames ferryman, founded here a House of Sisters in very early times, and that St. Swithin, the famous Bishop of Winchester, transformed it into a College of Priests. But what amount of truth may be contained in the story it is impossible to ascertain, as we have no reliable information as to this religious establishment until after the Conquest. It is, however, certain that, in 1106, William Pont de l'Arche and William Dauncey, two Norman knights, formed here a monastery for Canons Regular of the Order of St. Augustine, and William Giffard, Bishop of Winchester, co-operated with them, and built a portion of the church. The name of the first Prior was Aldgod: he held the office for four-and-twenty years. The neighbouring church of St. Margaret, in Southwark, was given to the Canons by a charter of Henry I. At the beginning of the following century the Priory suffered severely from fire, but the brethren had a zealous friend in Peter de Rupibus, Bishop of Winchester from 1205 to 1243. Bishop Peter built the choir and the Lady Chapel, and reconstructed the nave, and he also founded the chapel of St. Mary Magdalene, which stood on the south side of the choir, and was afterwards used as a parish church. In 1260 the consecration of Henry de Wengham, as Bishop of London, took place in the priory church. In the fourteenth century the transepts were built, but towards the close of it, in Richard II.'s reign, there was another fire, which did not, however, extend much beyond the nave. John Gower, the poet, who spent his later years within the precincts of the Priory, was a bountiful contributor towards the cost of the repairs which were thus necessitated; and he likewise founded a chantry in the chapel of St. John the Baptist, which was on the north side of the nave. Another liberal benefactor was Henry de Beaufort, Bishop of Winchester, the Cardinal, who is now best known to us from that terrible death-scene in *Henry VI.*, but who seems, in reality, to have been a statesman of a far better type than Shakespeare has represented him. He restored the south transept.

In 1407 the Priory Church was the scene of a magnificent wedding, that of Edmund Holland, Earl of Kent, and Lucia Visconti, daughter of a Duke of Milan. King Henry IV. gave away the bride, and after the ceremony there was a sumptuous feast in the adjacent mansion of the Bishop of Winchester. This Edmund, a son of Richard II.'s half-brother, was the last Earl of Kent of the Holland family; little more than a year after his marriage he died from a wound received in Brittany. Some years later a still more illustrious pair were united at St. Mary Overy; for it was here, on February 12, 1424, that James I. of Scotland married Joan Beaufort, daughter of John, Earl of Somerset, the Cardinal's brother.

ST SAVIOUR'S SOUTHWARK

In 1469 the roof of the nave, which was of stone, collapsed, and a roof of oak was soon afterwards constructed in its place.

ST SAVIOUR'S, SOUTHWARK (NAVE AND TRANSEPT)

Richard Fox, Bishop of Winchester from 1502 to 1528, the founder of Corpus Christi College, Oxford, gave the reredos, and in his time, very probably through his munificence, the tower was completed.

In 1539 the Priory was surrendered to Henry VIII. In the following year the parishes of St. Margaret and St. Mary Magdalene, Southwark, were united into one parish with the name of St. Saviour's; and the King granted the Priory Church and the Rectory to the parishioners on a twenty-one years' lease at an annual rent of £47 5s. 4d. Thus St. Mary Overy's became St. Saviour's. The lease was several times renewed, until finally, in 1614, the parishioners purchased the church and rectory for £800 from James I.

The Lady Chapel was devoted by the parochial authorities to "such use," as Stow's *Continuator* puts it, "as in respect of that it was built to, divine and religious duties, may very well be branded with the style of wretched, base, and unworthy." In fact, "this house of God" was "made a bakehouse," for it was let to four bakers in succession, all of whom employed it "in the way of their trade." But after it had been thus shamefully treated for "three-score and some odd years," the parishioners, in 1624, "repaired, renewed, well and very worthily beautified" it, and restored it to its proper use. Hence, in spite of its antiquity, it acquired the title of "the New Chapel." The chapel of St. Mary Magdalene, which, after the Priory Church had become parochial, had been utilized as a vestibule, was pulled down in 1822. There was another chapel, at the extreme east, which was known as the "Bishop's Chapel," because it was the burial place of Bishop Andrewes. This appeared to date from the fourteenth century, and it has been surmised that it was the original Lady Chapel. It was demolished in 1830 when the approaches to the New London Bridge were being made. The destruction of the Lady Chapel also was proposed, but happily this barbarous suggestion was not acceded to; and in 1832 the restoration of

ST SAVIOUR'S SOUTHWARK

the chapel, which stood in great need of repair, was commenced under the direction of George Gwilt. In 1831 the groined oak roof of the nave, the erection of which has been already noticed, was pronounced no longer safe, and accordingly removed. The nave was left roofless for seven years, and then taken down altogether, and a new nave, only remarkable for its excessive ugliness, was built in 1839.

In 1877 St. Saviour's, Southwark, was, with the rest of the South London parishes, transferred from the diocese of Winchester to that of Rochester. In the same year Dr. Thorold was

LONDON BRIDGE, WITH ST SAVIOUR'S AND ST OLAVE'S CHURCH, SOUTHWARK

appointed to the latter See. The new Bishop ardently desired an adequate restoration of this august church, and he was especially anxious that a different system of patronage might be brought about. When the parishioners acquired the church, they had been subjected to an obligation to maintain two chaplains. The salaries of the chaplains were provided for by an annual rate, and the chaplains were elected by the votes of the ratepayers. In 1868 the offices of the two chaplains, who were independent of each other, had been united, and henceforward there was only one: but the old method of election and payment still continued, and it was neither advantageous to the church nor popular with the parishioners. At length, in 1883, an Act of Parliament was procured by which the patronage of St. Saviour's was vested in the See of Rochester, the parishioners being willing enough to surrender their right of election in consideration of being relieved from the chaplain's rate. An endowment for the rector was supplied by the Ecclesiastical Commissioners. In July, 1889, the Bishop set on foot a scheme for the restoration of the church, and on November 3 ensuing he preached in St. Saviour's an inaugural sermon for the fund. In the same month Sir Arthur Blomfield was selected as architect; the feeble and incongruous structure of 1839 was then swept away; and on July 24, 1890, the foundation stone of a new nave was laid by the Prince of Wales. A few months later, Bishop Thorold was transferred to Winchester, and in the summer of 1895 he passed from us, not permitted to witness the completion of the great work which mainly owed its origin to his zeal and energy.

The new nave having been erected, and other restorative work accomplished, at a cost of over £40,000, St. Saviour's was re-opened as a collegiate church on February 16, 1897, in the presence of the Prince of Wales, the Lord Mayor and Sheriffs likewise attending. The Archbishop of Canterbury took part in the service, and the sermon was preached by the Bishop of Winchester, Dr. Randall T. Davidson, who, as Bishop Thorold's successor in the See of Rochester, had taken a deep interest in the work. The church has been placed under the government of a Chapter, in which laymen as well as clergy are included. The Bishop of Rochester acts as dean, and the Bishop of Southwark as sub-dean, while the rector, Dr. Thompson, is chancellor. Thus equipped, St. Saviour's will be, in a manner, as a cathedral for South London. Perhaps it may one day become really a cathedral.

St. Saviour's is cruciform: it measures in length almost 300 feet, and in breadth about 130 feet; the tower, which possesses twelve bells, attains a height of 163 feet to the top of the pinnacles. The church is composed of the lady chapel, the choir, the transepts, and the nave. The lady chapel is considered one of the most beautiful specimens of the Early English style now in existence. It is also interesting historically, as having been the scene of the examination of some of the martyrs of Queen Mary's time by Gardiner, Bonner, and the other commissioners. On windows of the chapel are recorded the names of seven martyrs— John Hooper, Bishop of Gloucester; Robert Ferrar, Bishop of St. David's; John Philpot, John Bradford, John Rogers, Rowland Taylor, and Lawrence Saunders. In this chapel now stands the tomb of the illustrious Lancelot Andrewes, Bishop successively of Chichester, Ely, and Winchester. He died, aged seventy-one, on September 25, 1626, and was buried in the easternmost chapel, which hence became called the "Bishop's Chapel." In 1676, in consequence of a fire, the canopy over the tomb was broken, and a lengthy Latin epitaph, by Matthew Wren, Bishop of Ely, Sir Christopher's uncle, was destroyed, but the fine recumbent effigy of the great prelate fortunately escaped injury. When the "Bishop's Chapel" was demolished in 1830, the monument was transferred to its present position on the west side of the lady chapel. The Bishop's coffin is within the monument. His brother, Nicholas Andrewes, who died about six weeks before him, was also buried at St. Saviour's. Not far from the Bishop's tomb, against the west wall of the chapel, is a granite tablet, in shape like a heart, to the memory of the architect, George Gwilt, who "was buried on the south side of St. Saviour's Ladye Chapel, the complete restoration of which he gratuitously superintended." He died in 1856, at the age of eighty-one; his tomb is in the churchyard close under the south wall of the choir.

The choir, which possesses a triforium and clerestory, and is covered by a groined stone roof, is also a beautiful example of Early English work. The noble altar-screen was, as already noticed, presented by Bishop Fox, and bears much resemblance to the screen which he erected in Winchester Cathedral. There are thirty-three niches, which it is now proposed to fill with suitable figures. Six canopied choir stalls, very handsomely executed, form a memorial by the diocese to Bishop Thorold. Within the easternmost arch on the north side of the choir is an imposing monument to Richard Humble, Alderman of London, who died in 1616; it displays, under a canopy, kneeling figures of the alderman and his two wives. His daughter Elizabeth, who was buried here on the same day with her father, was the wife of William Ward, a goldsmith of London. Their son, Humble Ward, married Frances, the grand-daughter and heiress of Edward Sutton, Lord Dudley, and in 1644 he was raised to the peerage as Baron Ward, of Birmingham. From him the present Earl of Dudley is descended.

In the north aisle of the choir, in an arched recess which may have originally belonged to the tomb of one of the priors, is a recumbent figure of a knight, carved in oak; he is represented in chain armour, a helmet covers the head, and the feet rest on a lion; the legs are crossed, which, according to the traditional, though not unquestioned, explanation, would signify that the effigy was that of a Crusader. The character of the armour is judged to point to the time of Edward I., and this knight may therefore have been one of those who accompanied Edward on the last crusade. It has been thought not unlikely that he was one of the De Warrens, Earls of Surrey, who owned much property in this neighbourhood. Strype's description of this figure, as it appeared in his time, is rather comical :—

"Here, against the north wall, is placed an ancient figure of a

Knight Templar, cross-legged in armour, with his dagger drawn in one hand, and holding the sheath in the other. It is new painted and flourished up, and looks somewhat dreadful. It has been thrown up and down in the church before; and here they have placed it against the wall upright, whereas it ought to have been laid along, as the effigies of dead men on their tombs usually are."

With regard to the stained glass in the window above the recess which contains the knight's effigy, an inscription tells us that "this tribute is raised by the subscriptions of 670 parishioners of the working-class, in grateful memory of the late George Wood, of this parish, surgeon." Just west of this window is a tablet to John Symons, "Citizen and White Baker of London," "a good benefactor unto this parish," who died in 1625.

Under the next window, going westward, in an arched recess which, also, is probably the remnant of a prior's tomb, is a tablet in memory of Thomas Cure, who died in 1588. He was master of the saddle-horses to Edward VI., Mary and Elizabeth, as is set forth in his epitaph, which is in Latin verse, and includes some laborious puns on his name. Adjoining Cure's is an elaborate monument to John Trehearne, described as "Gentleman Porter to King James I." It displays large half-length effigies of Trehearne and his wife, while beneath are small kneeling figures of their two sons and four daughters. The epitaph is quaint.

> "Had Kings a power to lend their subjects' breath,
> Trehearne, thou shouldst not be cast down by death:
> Thy royal master still would keep thee then,
> But length of days is beyond reach of men.
> Nor wealth, nor strength, nor great men's love can ease
> The wounds death's arrows make, for thou hast these.
> In thy King's court good place to thee is given,
> Whence thou shalt go to the King's court in heaven."

In the wall of the south aisle of the choir is a not very pleasing window in memory of Gwilt. Farther west is a plain tablet to Abraham Newland, for twenty-five years chief cashier to the Bank of England, who died in 1807, aged seventy-seven. Against a pillar at the entrance to this aisle is a brass tablet, which bears the following curious inscription :—

"Susanna Barford departed this life the 20th of August, 1652, aged 10 years 13 weekes, the Non such of the world for piety and vertue in soe tender yeares.

"And death and envye both must say 'twas fitt
Her memory should thus in brasse bee writt.
Here lyes interr'd within this bed of dust
A virgin pure not stain'd by carnall lust :
Such grace the King of Kings bestow'd upon her
That now shee lives with him a maid of honour :
Her stage was short, her thread was quickly spunn,
Drawne out and cutt, gott Heaven, her worke was done,
This world to her was but a traged play,
Shee came and saw't, dislik't and pass'd away."

The organ, by Lewis, the gift of Mrs. Courage, is placed in a chamber at the junction of the south choir aisle and the south transept. This transept, it will be remembered, was restored, after having been damaged by fire, by Cardinal Beaufort. His arms, surmounted by his cardinal's hat, are fixed to a pillar on the east side near the entrance door. The great window at the south end of this transept has been recently filled with stained glass, in memory of his daughter, by Sir Frederick Wigan, the treasurer of the restoration fund : the subject is the Transfiguration. Sir Frederick also caused the tracery of the window to be restored. On the west wall is a monument, noticeable for the representation of a corpse which appears on it, to William Emerson, "who lived and died an honest man ; he departed out of this life the 27th of June Anno 1575 in the year of his age 92."

Above this is a monument, with half-length effigy, to John Bingham, "Saddler to Queene Elizabeth and King James, who was a good benefactor to this parish and free schole, he departed this life in September 1625 in the 75th year of his age." Bingham was one of the nineteen "bargainers," as they were styled, who procured the purchase of the church from James I. on behalf of the parishioners. On the same wall farther north is a monument, with bust, to Richard Benefield, a member of Gray's Inn. It bears a high-flown Latin inscription, but no date; it seems to be of about the same period as that of Bingham. Beneath it is a tablet to Elizabeth Newcomen, who died in 1675. She was the widow of a mercer and a very charitable woman, and was related to the Lant family, who have given their name to a street familiar to all readers of *Pickwick*. Still lower on the wall is a tablet to "Mistris Margrit Maynard, daughter of Master John Maynard, Minister of Mayfield in Susex." She died on March 14, 1653, "being aged," records the scrupulously exact writer of her epitaph, "13 yeares, 10 monthes, and 14 dayes." On the south wall of this transept, beneath the window, is a monument, with bust, to the Rev. Thomas Jones. He was one of the Chaplains of St. Saviour's from 1753 to 1762, in which year he died, aged thirty-three. "This monument," states the inscription, "is erected by John and Joseph Street, Gent., as a memorial of the edification they received from his faithfull labours in the ministry." His funeral sermon was preached by the celebrated William Romaine, who afterwards published a collection of his sermons, with "a short account of his life" prefixed. Jones "was always studying and contriving," says Romaine, "something that might be useful to their" (his parishioners') "*best* interest."

The window of the north transept is a memorial to the late Prince Consort. The most remarkable monument is that of the

Austins. To describe this elaborate memorial one cannot do better than quote the quaint words of good old John Strype:—

"It is emblematical of Christ and of the Resurrection, according to the pious fancy of the devout Mr. Austin, who set it up at first. First, there is the representation of a rock, upon which is writ 'Petra erat X.T.S,' *i.e.*, the Rock was Christ. Down this rock runs a stream of water, and through this same rock is creeping a serpent; whereby he strips his old skin, which hangs on that part which is not yet got through. At the foot of this rock, and out of it, grows up standing corn, on which is a label with these words, 'Si non moriatur, non reviviscit,' *i.e.*, if it dieth not, it liveth not again. Underneath this corn, upon the basis, is this significant motto, 'Nos sevit, fovit, lavit, coget, renovabit,' *i.e.*, He hath sown, cherished, washed us, and He shall gather us together, and renew us. Upon the top of this rock standeth an angel; in his left hand a sickle, his right hand pointing up towards the sun shining in his glory, with a label upon the lower rays of it, 'Sol Justitiae,' *i.e.*, the sun of righteousness. On the right and left sides of this monument are instruments of husbandry hanging by a ribband out of a death's head, as ploughs, whips, yokes, rakes, spades, flails, harrows, shepherds' crooks, scythes, etc., over this is writ, 'Vos estis Dei Agricultura'! *i.e.*, Ye are God's husbandry. On the outside of these, on the right and left, are two harvestmen with wings, the one with a fork, the other with a rake behind him. They are in light garments, sitting, and leaning their heads upon their hands, their elbows resting upon their knees, as weary and tired, and resting after their harvest work: and having straw hats on, very comely: underneath them these words—'Messores congregabunt'; *i.e.*, the reapers shall gather. Under all this is a winnowing-fan; within which is the representation of a sheet of parchment, as it were, stretched upon it. On which is writ the inscription."

The inscription, which is in Latin, and is written in figurative language, corresponding with the allegorical character of the monument, sets forth that this tomb for his mother, Lady Clarke, his wife, and himself, was made in his lifetime by William Austin; that Anne, his wife, was buried here in 1623; his mother, Lady Clarke, whose second husband had been Sir Robert Clarke, a Baron of the Exchequer, in 1626; and lastly, he himself, in 1633. Beneath the monument is another Latin inscription in praise of Austin's virtues and accomplishments. Austin was a barrister of Lincoln's Inn, a good scholar, and a very religious man. He composed a number of devotional pieces in prose and verse, which his second wife, who survived him, published in 1635, under the following title: "*Devotionis Augustinianae Flamma; or Certayne Devout, Godly, and Learned Meditations*—written by the excellently accomplisht Gentleman, William Austin, of Lincolne's Inne, Esquier—Set forth, after his decease, by his deare wife and executrix, Mrs. Anne Austin; as a surviving monument of some part of the great worth of her everhonoured husband, who changed his life Jan: 16th, 1633." On the title page is a portrait of this pious author. He left a son, also named William, who was a barrister of Gray's Inn. The younger Austin was a very learned man, and endeavoured to shine as a poet; but he overwhelmed his poetry with the cumbrous mass of his erudition. He too lies buried in St. Saviour's.

Another conspicuous monument in this transept is that of Lionel Lockyer, a notorious quack-doctor, who died in 1672. It is adorned with a reclining effigy of the man of art, and the epitaph is devoted to puffing his miraculous pills:—

> "Here Lockyer lies interr'd: enough, his name
> Speaks one hath few competitors in fame,
> A name so great, so gen'ral, it may scorn
> Inscriptions which do vulgar tombs adorn.

> A diminution 'tis to write in verse
> His eulogies, which most men's mouths rehearse.
> His virtues and his pills are so well known
> That envy can't confine them under stone,
> But they'll survive his dust and not expire
> Till all things else at th' universal fire.
> This verse is lost, his pills embalm him safe
> To future times without an epitaph."

As an advertisement this was certainly bold and ingenious; but, as a prophecy, it has turned out false. The verse has remained, but fresh multitudes of pill-mongers have arisen, and Lockyer's infallible remedy has been driven out by crowds of other equally infallible nostrums. There is also here a monument, with a well-executed bust, in memory of Richard Blisse, who died in 1703. Under this monument may be noticed an interesting relic of ancient times, which has been brought to light during the restoration. It is an aumbry—that is to say, a sort of cupboard in the wall for the reception of books, vestments, etc. Its presence here is accounted for from this transept having been used as the chapel of St. Peter. In the same transept are to be seen the remains of an ancient stone coffin, supposed to date from the latter part of the twelfth century and to have been that of a Prior, or else of a Crusader; possibly a Knight Templar. Another striking object is a stone figure representing a corpse, which was, most probably, originally fixed as a moral emblem on a Prior's tomb. Here also are piled up a number of carved oak bosses, ornaments of the fifteenth-century roof of the nave, fortunately preserved at its demolition. Conspicuous among the quaint devices of these bosses is the burr and tun, the rebus of Henry Burton, prior from 1462 to 1486, under whom the roof was erected. It is intended to make use of some of them for the decoration of the new oak ceiling to be placed under the tower. The roof of the north transept, which continued till about 1830, had similar bosses; the roof of the south transept had a shorter existence, and its appearance is not recorded. Affixed to a pillar beneath the tower on the south side is a monument to Susannah, wife of Frederick Perkins, who died in 1851. It is the work of Samuel Manning, and excites admiration by reason of the singularly graceful carving of two figures, a vase, and a floral wreath. An ornament worthy of the church is the magnificent chandelier. It is over 200 years old, having been presented in 1680 by Dorothy Applebee, who two years afterwards was interred within the choir.

The new nave has been built in the thirteenth-century style of architecture, so as to reproduce as far as possible the nave of Peter de Rupibus. The design, ably planned by Sir Arthur Blomfield, has been skilfully carried out, and the result is a noble one. The beautiful manner in which this new portion harmonizes with the rest of the church is specially noteworthy. An old Norman doorway and recess—relics of the original nave—still exist, preserved in the north wall: and there also remains, at the west end, a fragment of Early English arcading. In the nave stands the tomb of the poet John Gower. He was buried in the chapel of St. John the Baptist, which stood in the fifth bay from the west of the north aisle of the nave, and in which, as already related, he had founded a chantry. His tomb was removed in 1832, and set up in the south transept; but it has now been brought back to its original position above the vault where his body was laid. Upon the tomb, beneath a gorgeous canopy, is a recumbent effigy of the poet, the head resting on three volumes, representing his *Vox Clamantis*, *Speculum Meditantis*, and *Confessio Amantis*.

The great west window contains an elaborate and finely executed picture in stained glass of the Creation. It was presented in 1893 by Mr. Henry Thomas Withers, in memory of his parents and his brother. The window to the south of it commemorates St. Swithin, and the westernmost window in the south wall is in honour of Paulinus, one of the earliest bishops of Rochester. It is intended to utilize the remaining windows of the nave as memorials of famous men connected with the parish. Four in the south wall have already been accomplished: the easternmost commemorates Shakespeare; the next, Massinger; the third, John Fletcher; and the fourth, Fletcher's fellow-worker, Francis Beaumont. Shakespeare is thought to have written some of his greatest works in St. Saviour's parish, and the site of the theatre in which he was interested—the Globe, on the Bankside—is close to the church. His brother Edmund, "a player," was buried in the church on the last day of the year 1607. Fletcher died of the plague, on the Bankside, and was interred in the church on August 29, 1625. Massinger was carried to his last resting-place here on March 18, 1639. Beaumont lived for some time on the Bankside with Fletcher; he was not buried here, but in Westminster Abbey. The window next to Beaumont's is to be devoted to Edward Alleyn; the window at the north-west to Goldsmith; and in the north wall are to be memorials to Dr. Johnson, Alexander Cruden, Dr. Sacheverell, Bunyan, Baxter, and Chaucer.

Alleyn, the founder of Dulwich College, was a member of the Corporation of Wardens of the Parish. Philip Henslowe, his partner and the step-father of his wife, was a very influential parishioner, and one of the "bargainers" for the purchase of the church and rectory. Alleyn sleeps in his chapel at Dulwich, but Henslowe was buried here, "in the Channcell," on January 10, 1615. Goldsmith for a short time practised medicine on the Bankside. Johnson's connection with St. Saviour's was due to his intercourse with the Thrales, Henry Thrale being the owner of the neighbouring brewery which after his death became that of Barclay & Perkins. Alexander Cruden, the compiler of the renowned *Concordance*, was interred in 1770 in the burying-ground in Deadman's Place, Bankside, now covered by the premises of the brewery. Sacheverell, the most celebrated person who ever held that office, was elected Chaplain of St. Saviour's in 1705. Bunyan and Baxter both preached in the parish. Chaucer is, of course, selected because of the Tabard in Southwark, whence he and his fellow-pilgrims set forth for Canterbury.

Among those buried at St. Saviour's, of whom there is now no memorial, are Thomas, the third Duke of Norfolk of the Howard family, son of the victor of Flodden, and father of the poetical Earl of Surrey; he died in 1554; William Wickham, Bishop of Winchester, who died in 1595; Sir Edward Dyer, the friend of Sir Philip Sidney, a diplomatist and a poet, chiefly remembered from those exquisite verses of his on the blessings of a contented spirit, beginning,—

"My mynde to me a Kyngdome is";

he died in 1607: and Robert Harvard, one of the "bargainers," who, like Fletcher, fell a victim to the plague in 1625; he was the father of John Harvard, the founder of the famous college in New England, which has since developed into a university, and which still bears his name. John Harvard was baptized at St. Saviour's on November 29, 1607. Here also rest three chief magistrates of the city of London: Sir Edward Bromfield, Lord Mayor, 1636, who died in 1658; Sir George Waterman, Lord Mayor, 1671, who died in 1682; and Sir John Shorter, who died in 1688 during his Mayoralty. Catherine Shorter, Sir John's grand-daughter, was the first wife of Sir Robert Walpole.

Such are the history and associations of this venerable church. It is rich in memories of great names of old. It has now embarked on a new career of usefulness. May its future prove worthy of its grand past!

ST GEORGE THE MARTYR SOUTHWARK

THE church of St. George the Martyr, Southwark, stands on the east side of Borough High Street, at the corner of Long Lane. The date of its original foundation is unknown, but Stow mentions it as "sometime pertaining to the Priory of Bermondsey," by the gift of Thomas Arderne and Thomas, his son, in the year 1122.

The Marshalsea and King's Bench prisons were in close proximity to the church, and consequently prisoners who died in them were interred in St. George's. Bishop Bonner, who died in the Marshalsea on September 5, 1569, "was," says Stow, "at midnight buried among other prisoners in St. George's churchyard." Patrick Ruthven, youngest son of the first Earl of Gowrie, and brother of John, the third earl, and Alexander Ruthven, the conspirators, died in the King's Bench prison, and was buried at St. George's on May 24, 1652. After his release from the Tower, where he had been for many years imprisoned, he received a pension from the Crown, and when this ceased, owing to the Civil Wars, he endeavoured to support himself by practising the art of physic, in which he was well skilled, and which he had formerly exercised gratuitously. But his fate seems to indicate that his efforts met with but little success. His daughter was the wife of Vandyck. John Rushworth, Clerk of the House of Commons, during the Long Parliament, and author of the valuable *Historical Collections*,

ST GEORGE THE MARTYR, SOUTHWARK

closed his long life (he was about eighty-three years old) in the King's Bench prison, in 1690; he was buried behind the pulpit in St. George's Church. In the churchyard were also buried Nahum Tate, the poet laureate, and joint author with Brady

ST GEORGE'S CHURCH, SOUTHWARK (FROM THE NORTH-EAST)

of the celebrated metrical version of the Psalms, who died in the Mint, the Southwark sanctuary for debtors, "where," says Johnson, "he was forced to seek shelter by extreme poverty," on August 12, 1715; and Thomas Woolston, the deistical writer, who had been committed to the King's Bench prison for his *Discourses on the Miracles of Christ*, and died on January 27, 1733.

Edward Cocker, the famous arithmetician, who died in 1675, was buried in St. George's Church at the west end. He left his arithmetical works in manuscript, and they were published by John Hawkins, who kept a school which was situated close to the church, and had probably been established by Cocker. Hawkins, who is said by Hatton to have been not only an "ingenious mathematician and writing-master," but also "very pleasant and facetious in his conversation," died in 1695, and his remains were laid near those of Cocker.

At St. George's, in September, 1627, the astrologer, William Lilly, married his first wife, Grace Wright, his master's widow; and on January 23, 1653, General Monk married Anne Clarges, the farrier's daughter.

The church having become ruinous, the parishioners in 1733 obtained an Act of Parliament to have it rebuilt out of the funds for the erection of fifty new churches in and about London. The first stone of the present edifice was laid on April 23, St. George's Day, 1734, by Dr. Nathaniel Hough, the rector, acting as deputy for King George II. The architect was John Price, and the church was finished in 1736. Price died in November of the same year. It is built of red brick, with a stone steeple at the west. The steeple consists of a square tower, three octagonal stages, and an obelisk surmounted by a ball and vane; its height is 98 feet. There are eight bells. The north and south walls are each pierced with two rows of windows, six in each row. At the east is a Venetian window. The interior is not striking. There are no aisles, and the ceiling of the body of the church is flat; at the east end is a coved projection for the altar. The east window is filled with stained glass: the rest are plain. There are galleries on the north, south, and west, in the last of which is placed the organ. The pulpit, which stands on the north side, is of oak, and rests on four pedestals. On the walls are several monumental tablets, but none of any special interest.

The churchyard, which is open to the public, lies on the north and east of the church. In it may be observed a tomb of considerable size, on which are inscribed these four lines from Pope's *Elegy to the Memory of an Unfortunate Lady*:—

" How Lov'd, how Valued Once, avails thee not !
To whom related or by whom begot !
A heap of Dust alone remains of thee ;
'Tis all thou art, and all the proud shall be."

This church is probably best known to the general reader by Dickens' references to it in *Little Dorrit*, where he describes her as baptized and married within its walls. The north boundary wall of

ST GEORGE, SOUTHWARK
(VIEW FROM BOROUGH HIGH STREET)

the eastern portion of the churchyard is the wall of the old Marshalsea prison, though lowered from its former height. The block of buildings seen over the wall—now a factory—

ST GEORGE, SOUTHWARK (THE GREAT TOMB)

formed part of the old prison where Little Dorrit, the child of the Marshalsea, was born. Dickens himself, in early life, had experience of this place, and often passed in and out, as his father was, for a short time, imprisoned in it for debt, and the boy

ST GEORGE THE MARTYR, SOUTHWARK

Dickens had a room in the neighbouring Lant Street, a thoroughfare in which he afterwards placed Bob Sawyer's apartments.

The Rectory of St. George the Martyr, Southwark, has been hitherto in the sole patronage of the Lord Chancellor; but it has been recently arranged that, in future, one presentation out of every three shall be assigned to the Corporation of London, in consideration of their having undertaken, on the next avoidance of the united benefice of St. Margaret Pattens and St. Gabriel, Fenchurch, of which they and the Lord Chancellor are joint patrons, to transfer the sum of £300 per annum from the income of the united benefice to that of the living of St. George's. By this scheme, the stipend of the rector of this important parish will be exactly doubled.

ST. OLAVE SOUTHWARK

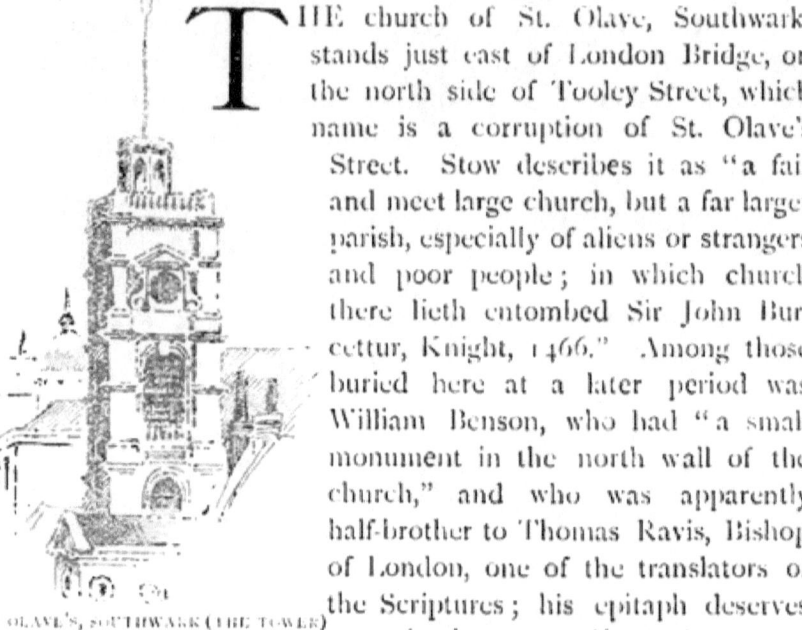

ST. OLAVE'S, SOUTHWARK (THE TOWER)

THE church of St. Olave, Southwark, stands just east of London Bridge, on the north side of Tooley Street, which name is a corruption of St. Olave's Street. Stow describes it as "a fair and meet large church, but a far larger parish, especially of aliens or strangers and poor people; in which church there lieth entombed Sir John Burcettur, Knight, 1466." Among those buried here at a later period was William Benson, who had "a small monument in the north wall of the church," and who was apparently half-brother to Thomas Ravis, Bishop of London, one of the translators of the Scriptures; his epitaph deserves quotation by reason of its quaintness:—

" Here th' earthly part of William Benson lies,
Whom Robert Benson had by Mary Lyle,
Hee heavenly mounted is above the skies,
With wings of faith, dissolved but for a while;
The linen which he sold was ne'er so white,
As is the robe wherein the soul is dight:
Yet Thomas mourns in black, his onely son,
And Richard (of whole blood) his eldest brother:

ST. OLAVE, SOUTHWARK

> But London's Reverend Bishop this hath done,
> Which was by Ravis born of the same mother:
> And William Lyle, first cousin to them all,
> (Long live his verse) penned this memorial.
> He departed in the 56 year of his age, An. Dom. 1603."

William Lyle's "verse" has "lived," for Anthony Munday transcribed it; but Benson's and all other monuments perished when the old church was pulled down.

ST. OLAVE'S CHURCH.

In 1733 the eastern portion of the ancient parish was severed from St. Olave's, and formed into a separate parish under the name of St. John's, Horselydown. In 1736 part of St. Olave's Church fell down, and, as the remainder was in a very dilapidated condition, the parishioners obtained powers from Parliament to raise, by a rate, £5,000 to rebuild it. They selected as their architect Henry Flitcroft, who had shortly before rebuilt St. Giles's-in-the-Fields, and under his direction the new church was completed in 1739. It was chiefly built of Portland stone. It was a good specimen of the architecture of that period, and is said to have borne a considerable resemblance to Wren's church of St. Dionis, Backchurch, demolished in 1878, though the latter was shorter and broader than St. Olave's. The greater part of the church was destroyed by fire in August, 1843, and it was reconstructed as we now see it, in the following year.

St. Olave's is so hemmed in by the crowd of adjacent buildings that only the south side of the church is visible; the upper part of the tower is, however, a prominent object seen from London Bridge. The tower rises at the north-west; it is completed with a balustrade, and has, on the centre, a small turret which supports a flagstaff. The westernmost division of the south front contains a doorway, and above it a circular window; then succeed two rows of windows, five in each row, the upper ones being circular; at the eastern end is a corresponding doorway with window above. The interior includes two aisles, each of which is separated from the main body by four Ionic columns, standing on bases of the same height as the pews. The ceilings are handsomely ornamented; those of the nave and chancel are arched, those of the aisles are flat. The east window and those in the north and south walls are filled with stained glass, but the windows of the clerestory are plain. Above the tables at the sides of the altar-piece, on which are inscribed the Lord's Prayer and the Creed, are niches which contain statues of Moses and Aaron. The pulpit is of oak, dignified and substantial in appearance; it stands on the north side. Over one of the pews, on the south side, is a remarkably fine sword rest, which bears the date 1674. There are galleries on the north, south, and west; the organ occupies the last of these; it has an extremely handsome case, and is, as will appear, an instrument of great interest technically.

In the vestry at the north-east of the church are numerous portraits of rectors and other clergy connected with St. Olave's. Noteworthy among them are those of Hugh Boulter, Archbishop of Armagh, who was rector from 1708 to 1722; William Romaine, the famous Evangelical preacher, who was curate here from 1756 to 1759; and the present Bishop of Aberdeen and Orkney, the Right Reverend the Honourable Arthur Gascoigne Douglas, who was appointed to the Rectory of St. Olave's in 1855, and resigned it in the following year. There is also a portrait of "Henry John Gauntlett, Mus. Doc., organist of St. Olave's church, Southwark, from 1827 to 1847, Pioneer in this country of the German plan of organ-building, and Designer of the grand thirty-two feet manual gamut instrument erected in the above named church 1844. Ob. 1876." In addition to these interesting portraits, there are engravings of London before the great fire; and of the original buildings of Queen Elizabeth's free Grammar School in Tooley Street. This school, which was incorporated in 1571, is now commonly called St. Olave's Grammar School. It was moved from Tooley Street in 1830, to make room for the approaches to New London Bridge, and it now occupies an imposing red-brick edifice, situated a little to the west of the Tower Bridge in Queen Elizabeth Street, which was formerly known as Back Street, but has been re-named in honour of the School.

The Rectory of St. Olave, Southwark, is in the patonage of the Crown.

ST MARY MAGDALENE, BERMONDSEY (SOUTH VIEW)

ST MARY MAGDALENE
BERMONDSEY

THE church of St. Mary Magdalene, Bermondsey, stands at the junction of Abbey Street and Bermondsey Street, in a large churchyard, which is now laid out as a recreation ground.

About the year 1094, William Rufus bestowed his manor of Bermondsey on a monastery of Cluniac monks founded by Aylwin Child, a citizen of London. The monks subsequently established near their monastery a parochial church, dedicated to St. Mary Magdalene. Part of the church having fallen down, and the remainder being very unsafe, it was entirely rebuilt in 1680. It is built of brick covered over with rough cast, consists of a nave, chancel, two aisles, and a south transept, and has a short tower and turret at the west. There are eight bells. The appearance of the tower and the west front has been much altered, but, as far as one can judge from views of the exterior in its original state, preserved in the vestry, by no means improved. The chancel was extended about thirteen years ago, and the pews were lowered, with the exception of the churchwardens' pew at the south-west. There are galleries on the north, south, and west walls; in the last of these the organ is placed. The altar-piece is of carved wood, and at its sides are painted figures of Moses and Aaron; above them are similar representations of St. James and St. Luke. The east window is filled with stained glass, showing St. Mary Magdalene at the feet of our Lord, erected, as an inscription states, in 1873, by Cyrus Legge, an inhabitant of the parish, and a member of the Metropolitan Board of Works. The font, which is in the transept, is handsome. It bears an inscription, recording that it, with its cover, was presented to the church by James Hardwidge, churchwarden, in 1808. The pulpit, which stands at the south-east of the nave, is of wood; it is not in any way remarkable. Over the north gallery are three hatchments.

On the north wall of the chancel, within the communion rails, is a large tablet to the memory of William Castle, who died in 1681. He was, we are informed by his Latin epitaph, a shipbuilder at Rotherhithe, a justice of the peace for the county of Surrey and a major in the militia. On account of the conscientious manner in which he performed all his duties, he was particularly beloved by Charles II. He was so pious, faithful, charitable, and affable, that he left few behind him equal to him in these virtues. "There is no need to say more," concludes the epitaph. "Go and imitate him." On the opposite wall of the chancel, outside the rails, is a monument to Sir William Steavens, who died in 1712.

Just outside the chancel is a large slab on the floor, thus inscribed:—

> "Where once the famous Elton did entrust
> The preservation of his sacred dust,
> Lies pious Whitaker, both justly twin'd,
> Both dead, one grave; both living had one mind:
> And by their dissolution have supply'd
> The hungry grave, and fame and heaven beside.
> This stone protects their bones, while fame enrolls
> Their deathless names, and heaven embrace their souls."

Edward Elton and Jeremiah Whitaker were both rectors of Bermondsey. They were both men of learning and both be-

ST MARY MAGDALENE, BERMONDSEY (WEST FRONT)

longed to the Puritan party. The former died in 1624, the latter in 1654.

A stone on the floor of the north aisle is inscribed to the memory of Elizabeth Tyers, who died in 1681 ; nine children of Nathaniel Roffey and Mary, his wife, who all died young ; Nathaniel Roffey himself, who died in 1733; and another Nathaniel, his son, who died in 1755. At the east end of the south aisle is a tablet in memory of a very charitable and benevolent lady, thus inscribed :—

"To the glory of God and in memory of Mary Eason, who living simply and humbly before God, found her chief pleasure in contributing towards the spiritual and temporal welfare of the people of this Parish and elsewhere. The gifts during her lifetime to Bermondsey and a munificent bequest to Middlesex Hospital remain as memorials of her. She was buried in Kensal Green Cemetery, near the members of the Eason family, of which she was the last survivor. Born 13th August 1807. Died 15th May 1889.

"'To do good and to communicate forget not : for with such sacrifices God is well pleased.' Hebrews XIII."

In the churchyard, at the south side of the tower, stands a ponderous tomb, on which is the epitaph of Richard Hawkins, of King's Lynn, Norfolk, merchant, who died in 1765. On the outside of the west wall of the south transept is a tablet with the following singular inscription : —

"Here lie the remains of Susanna Wood, wife of Mr. James Wood of the Kent Road, Mathematical Instrument Maker, who after a long and painful illness, which she bore with the greatest fortitude, departed this life the 16th of June 1810 in the 58th year of her age. She was tapped 97 times and had 461 gallons of water taken from her, without ever lamenting her case or fearing the operation

"Also the above Mr. James Wood, who departed this life the 10th of May 1837 aged 108 years. Much and devotedly lamented."

Since the surrender of the Abbey of Bermondsey to Henry VIII. the advowson of the rectory has passed through the hands of various private owners, and now it belongs to the Church Patronage Society.

ROTHERHITHE CHURCH

ST MARY ROTHERHITHE

TOMB OF CAPTAIN ANTHONY WOOD

ROTHERHITHE appears to have been originally a hamlet of Bermondsey. Edward III, gave the manor to the Abbey of Graces, which he had founded near Tower Hill, but in the reign of Richard II, the Abbot handed it over to the Monastery of Bermondsey, and it was retained by that religious house till its suppression by Henry VIII. Subsequently Rotherhithe, or, as it was commonly called, Redriff, became famous as an abode of sea-faring men, and hence Swift here fixed the residence of that adventurous voyager, Lemuel Gulliver.

RIVERSIDE CHURCHES

The church of St. Mary, Rotherhithe, stands not far from the water-side, in a street named after it, St. Mary Church Street. At the opening of the eighteenth century the foundations of the old church had become sapped by the inundations of the river, and it "was," says Strype, "in such danger of falling down that the inhabitants could not without danger of their lives assemble to hear Divine Service therein." It being thus imperatively necessary to rebuild the church without delay, the parishioners petitioned Parliament for assistance out of the duty on coals. They represented the dangerous state of the church, and the desirability of rebuilding it on a much larger scale, owing to the great increase of the inhabitants; explained that they were unable themselves to defray the cost of the work, owing to the immense augmentation of their poor-rate, consequent upon the loss of so many seamen, of whom the inhabitants mostly consisted, during the war with France; and finally, urged the plea of "the parishioners being chiefly seamen and watermen, who venture their lives in fetching those coals from Newcastle, which pay for the re-building the churches in London and parts adjacent." Their petition was not acceded to, but they raised a considerable sum by means of a brief and subscriptions, and were able to open their new church in the summer of 1715. The steeple, which contains eight bells, was not finished till 1738. It consists of a brick tower, completed by a stone cornice and pierced parapet, and a stone spire, resting on Corinthian columns and culminating in a ball and vane. The church is of brick with stone dressings, and includes a nave, chancel, and two aisles, which are separated from the main body by Ionic columns. The bases of these columns are wainscotted, as are also the lower parts of the walls. The ceilings are divided into compartments; those of the nave and chancel are arched, but those of the aisles are flat. The organ is placed in the west gallery; the north and south galleries have

ROTHERHITHE CHURCHYARD

been removed, and the pulpit has been lowered, and the pews cut down. There is an oak altar-piece, and in the window above it is a representation in painted glass of the Virgin Mary.

The monument which most attracts attention is in the churchyard. It is a brick tomb near the western extremity of the ground, enclosed by railings and surmounted by a flat slab of stone, thus inscribed :—

> "To the Memory
> of Prince Lee Boo,
> A native of the Pelew or Palos Islands;
> and Son to Abba Thulle, Rupack or King
> of the Island Cooroora;
> who departed this life on the 27th of December 1784,
> aged 20 years;
> This stone is inscribed
> by the Honourable United East India Company,
> as a testimony of esteem for the humane and kind treatment
> afforded by his father to the crew of their ship
> the Antelope, Captain Wilson,
> which was wrecked off that Island
> in the night of the 6th of August 1783.
> Stop, Reader, stop! let Nature claim a tear,
> A Prince of Mine, Lee Boo, lies bury'd here."

When Captain Wilson left Cooroora, Lee Boo was entrusted to his care by Abba Thulle, who hoped that his son might acquire in a civilized country much valuable knowledge which he would be able, on his return, to impart to his fellow countrymen. But, unfortunately, the prince, who is described as a most amiable and intelligent youth, did not live to re-visit his native island. He arrived safely in England with Captain Wilson, and remained with him in his house in Paradise Row, Rotherhithe, but he was soon attacked by small-pox, from which disease he died at the early age recorded in his epitaph. A full account of Captain Wilson's adventures and of Lee Boo's voyage to England

and his mode of life at Rotherhithe was published in 1788 by George Keate, who was well acquainted both with the captain and with the Prince; a portrait of the latter by Miss Keate, the author's daughter, is included in the book.

At the west of the tomb, within the rails, is an upright stone, on which is recorded the burial here of Christiana, the wife of Captain Wilson, who died in 1802, and of two other members of his family. "The body of the above-named Captain Henry Wilson," it is added, "who died the 10th day of May 1810, aged 70 years, was interred at Colyton near Axminster in Devonshire. He commanded the Honourable East India Company's Packet, the *Antelope*, which was wrecked on the Pelew Islands in the month of August, 1783, and was wonderfully preserved together with all the ship's company amongst strangers in a land unfrequented and unknown."

An additional memorial of these interesting events has been recently placed within the church, where on the north wall is a marble tablet with this inscription:—

"In the adjacent churchyard lies the body of
Prince Lee Boo,
Son of Abba Thulle, Rupack or King of the Island
Coorooraa, one of the Pelew or Palos Islands,
who departed this life at the house of
Captain Henry Wilson in Paradise Row in this Parish
on the 27. day of December 1784, aged 20 years.
This tablet is erected
By the Secretary of State for India in Council
to keep alive the memory of the humane treatment
shewn by the natives to the crew of the Honourable
East India Company's ship "Antelope," which was wrecked
off the Island of Coorooraa on the 9th of August 1783.
'The barbarous people shewed us no little kindness.'
Acts XXVIII. 2.
1802."

RIVERSIDE CHURCHES

On the north wall, to the west of this tablet, are brass plates, formerly on the floor of the middle aisle, with figures, much defaced, of a man and two wives, and an inscription to Peter Hills, mariner, one of the Elder Brethren of the Trinity House, who died, over eighty years old, in 1614. "This was made at the charge of Robert Bell." Hills and Bell founded a free school at Rotherhithe for eight sons of poor seamen. It was subsequently, by means of various donations, much enlarged and made to include girls as well as boys. The school-house stands opposite the church on the south side, and is ornamented with figures of a boy and girl, below which is an inscription recording that the school was founded by Hills and Bell, and was removed to its present position in 1797.

At the west of Hills' monument, the Royal Arms are affixed to the north wall: on the same wall, east of the tablet to Prince Lee Boo, is one to the memory of Captain Roger Tweedy, with the following inscription : —

"Roger Tweedy Esq. was interred in the middle ile of this church, in the year 1655. He gave by will two shillings every Lord's Day for ever, to be distributed among 12 poor seamen or seamen's widows in bread : the officers of this church to take care to distribute it : and those nearest of kin to him to enquire of its disposal ; and if not performed according to the will, to take it into their hands.

In commemoration of Mr. Roger Tweedy,
Who living was Landmen's Counsellor, Seamen's Glory
  Sch'sm's Scourge, and Truth's living Story.

His soul a Ship, with Graces fully laded.
Through surges deep did plow, and safely waded.
With Principles of Faith his ballane'd Mind
Did steddy sail 'gainst Blasts of boist'rous wind

ST MARY, ROTHERHITHE

> Of doctrine falce, which furiously did blow
> Like rowling waves, to toss him to and fro.
> This sayling Ship did precious wares distribute
> In every Port, as the acknowledg'd tribute
> Of Christ his King, Love's Crane did weigh
> The Council. Contribution he did pay.
> At Rotherheath hee did at length arrive,
> And to their poore his Tribute fully give ;
> And in this Port he doth at Anchor stay.
> Hopefully expecting Resurrection's Day,"

Against the wall, at the east end of the north aisle, near the vestry door, is a picture of Charles I. in his robes, kneeling in prayer at a table.

On the south wall is a tablet, which bears the following inscription :—

> "Next without this wall are buried Brian, Richard and Marke, Alize and Elizabeth, the three sonnes and two daughters of Nicholas Reynolds, Citizen and Goldsmithe of London, and of Elizabeth his Wife. The said Elizabeth, theyr younger Daughter, was married to Robert Wheatley, Salter, the XX. Day of August 1593, and she died the XVIII. Day of September the same yeare.

> These Blossoms yonge and tender, loe blowne downe by deadly winde,
> May urge the riper sort to knowe, like blaste shall them oute finde ;
> For Fleshe, as Grasse, away doth wither, no Age can yt eschewe,
> Yonge and olde decay together, when Death shall them pursue.
> No Parents, Friends, or Advocate, can him intreate to spare
> The Fayre, the Fyne, or Delicate, for threats he doth not care.
> Let that most certain Statue made, by God our myghty Kinge,
> All Men assure and eke perswade, Death shall them equal Fringe."

On the outside of the church are two monuments to sea captains. The older of these is on the west wall of the north aisle, and displays the representation of a ship under sail : it commemorates Captain Anthony Wood, who died in 1625. The other is on the north wall, and bears this inscription :—

> "As the Earth the Earth does cover,
> So under this Stone lies another.

Here lyes interred in this Vault the Body of Capt. Thomas Stone, Junior, of this Parish. He departed this Life the 9th of August 1666, and had to wife Agnes, which surviveth :

> To you that live possess'd, great Troubles do befal,
> Where we that sleep by Death do feel no Harm at all,
> An honest Life does bring a joyful Death at last,
> And Life again begins when Death is overpast.
> Death is the Path to Life, and Way to endless Wealth,
> The Door whereby we pass to everlasting Health.
> These forty years and two have passed here my Life,
> And eighteen years thereof thou, Agnes, wert my wife.
> My loving wife, farewel, God guide thee with His Grace,
> Prepare thyself to come, and I will give thee Place.
> Acquaintance all farewel, and be assur'd of this,
> You shall be brought to Dust as Tho. Stone here is.

The most distinguished name among the rectors of Rotherhithe is that of Thomas Gataker, who was presented in 1612, having previously been Preacher at Lincoln's Inn. He was an excellent scholar, and in his views a Presbyterian. Prior to the commencement of the Civil Wars, he suffered imprisonment for the sake of his opinions; afterwards he became one of the Assembly of Divines, and sometimes acted as Chairman of that body. He died in 1654, having been rector of Rotherhithe for forty-two years, and was here buried. In the churchyard, to the south of the church, is a large monument to the late rector, the Rev. Edward Blick, "formerly Fellow of Clare College, Cambridge," who died in his seventy-sixth year, in 1867, after holding the living for thirty-two years. The font, as an inscription upon it notifies, was given as a memorial of Mr. Blick, and a portrait of him hangs in the vestry.

The Rectory of Rotherhithe is in the gift of Clare College, Cambridge.

ST. GEORGE-IN-THE-EAST, WEST FRONT

ST GEORGE-IN-THE-EAST

ST. GEORGE'S-IN-THE-EAST, or St. George, Middlesex, was one of the churches built under Queen Anne's Act, and its parish was taken out of Stepney. It received its title in compliment to George I., and was consecrated in 1729. It stands on the east side of Cannon Street Road, south of Cable Street. It is built of Portland stone, and was designed by Nicholas Hawksmoor.

St. George's is a large church, measuring about ninety-one feet by sixty-five, and has a tower, at the west, about 160 feet high. This tower, which contains eight bells, is terminated by eight strange-looking columns, capped by large urns, and a balustrade; and a lofty flagstaff rises in the centre. Though there is something grand in its massiveness, it is, on the whole, more singular than beautiful. Beneath the tower is the main entrance, which is approached by a flight of steps, and on each side of which are two Ionic pilasters. The north and south walls each contain three side doors. There are two small towers, crowned with domes, on each of these walls, above the two easternmost of the doors. In the space between these towers the wall recedes. An apse projects at the east, and this end of the church is crowned with a pediment. The exterior is too heavy to be pleasing.

The principal doorway gives access to a vestibule; over the entrance from the vestibule to the church are affixed the Royal Arms. The interior presents the appearance of an oblong, with two shallow transepts, one at the west, and the other at the east, beyond the latter of which projects an apse, containing the altar.

The body of the church is divided into nave and aisles by two Doric piers and two Doric columns, rising from lofty bases, on each side of the nave. The piers are placed at the junction of the transepts with the main building, and the columns within it; and the columns are so arranged that the centre space between them forms a square, with a groined ceiling. The ceilings over the other portions of the building are arched, except in the squares formed in the angles of the main building by the piers and columns, and the walls, which have flat ceilings between entablatures carried by the piers and columns, and extended to pilasters and consoles on the walls. Above the altar are mosaics in five panels, and above these are five stained-glass windows. The windows were inserted about 1820; the mosaics, as is recorded by three brass tablets, in 1880. The three central panels, the middle one of which is about nine feet high, and has for its subject the Crucifixion, are in memory of John and Phœbe Knight, and were presented by their three sons: the north panel was given by T. M. Fairclough, in memory of his uncle, John Benton, who died in 1841; and that on the south was erected by Richard Foster, to commemorate the marriage of his parents in St. George's in 1805. The woodwork is of oak. The pulpit, which stands on the north side, is very large, and is overshadowed by an ample sounding-board. It is finely carved, and is said to have cost about £700. There are galleries on the north, west, and south. The west gallery contains the organ. The lower parts of the walls are panelled. The church possesses two fonts. The original one stands in the baptistery at the north-west; the other, which is quaint and ancient, is placed on the north side of the church, not far from the pulpit. It belonged to one of the demolished City churches, and, on account of the great number of baptisms here, was procured for St. George's by the late rector, the Rev. Harry Jones. The baptistery, which is

also used as a side-chapel for daily prayers, contains a memorial window to members of the Knight family, mentioned above, representing Our Lord and little children, and bearing date 1869.

The churchyard, which lies to the east and north of the church, is one of the prettiest in London. It was, we are informed by an inscription at the entrance, "put in order and laid out as a public garden at the sole expense of Augustus George Crowder, J.P." in 1886. In the centre of the ground is a large obelisk, surmounted by a flaming urn; on the west side of the pedestal is an inscription to Henry Raine, "of this Parish, Brewer," who died, aged fifty-nine, in 1738; on the east side, to Elizabeth Raine, "Relict of Rowland Raine, Brewer, of this Parish," who died, at the age of eighty-seven, in 1732; on the north side, to Sarah, wife of Henry Raine, who died in 1725, aged thirty-two. Below her epitaph is a female figure, leaning on the left elbow, with the hand on a book, and pointing with the right hand towards heaven. On the south side are the arms of the family. Henry Raine founded, during his lifetime, in 1719, Raine's Schools, which are now "administered by the Board of Governors, according to the provisions of a scheme made under the Endowed Schools Acts, and approved by Her Majesty in Council on the 11th day of July, 1877." Both schools are situated in Cannon Street Road; that of the boys on the west, and that of the girls and infants on the east side.

On the south side of the churchyard, to the west of the Raine monument, is an upright stone, "sacred to the memory of Mr. Timothy Marr, aged 24 years. Also Mrs. Celia Marr, his Wife, aged 24 years; and their Son, Timothy Marr, aged 3 months. All of whom were most inhumanly murdered in their dwelling-house, No. 29, Ratcliff Highway, December 8th, 1811." A long series of verses follows.

ST GEORGE-IN-THE-EAST

The story of the murder of the Marrs by John Williams is graphically told by De Quincey. Twelve days afterwards, Williams murdered a publican in the same neighbourhood, Williamson by name, and his wife and servant. He was arrested the following day, and, having been committed for trial, contrived to hang himself in his cell. His body was buried at the north end of Cannon Street Road at the junction of four ways.

In St. George's Churchyard was also interred Joseph Ames, Fellow of the Royal Society and of the Society of Antiquaries, to the latter of which he acted for many years as secretary; author of *Typographical Antiquities, An Historical Account of Printing in England*, published in 1749; and editor of *Parentalia, or Memoirs of the Family of the Wrens*, which Christopher Wren, the great architect's son, had compiled, and which Stephen Wren, his grandson, published in 1750. It stands recorded on the title-page that he did so, "with the care of Joseph Ames." Ames died on October 7, 1759, at the age of seventy-one. He lived in Wapping Street, where he followed the occupation of a ship-chandler and ironmonger, devoting all his leisure to antiquarian studies.

The Rectory of St. George's-in-the-East is in the gift of the Bishop of London.

In the years 1859 and 1860, St. George's acquired an unenviable notoriety owing to the unseemly "Riots," which, arising out of the unadvised action of the then rector, the Rev. Bryan King, a pronounced High Churchman, in introducing, with more zeal than discretion, changes in ritual which were highly distasteful to the parishioners, took place in the church Sunday after Sunday. The church was in consequence closed for several weeks in the autumn of 1859, and after it was re-opened, the services of a considerable body of police were procured to maintain order. But still the disturbances went on. At length, in

July, 1860, as there appeared no possible prospect of a reconciliation between the Rector and the parishioners, Mr. King was persuaded to leave the parish, and in a few months, the observances which had caused so much exasperation having been abandoned, peace was restored.

ST DUNSTAN
STEPNEY

STEPNEY, called in Domesday Stibenhede, and afterwards written Stebinhith, Stebunhith, Stebunheath, and other variations, was anciently a vast parish, comprising almost the whole of the eastern suburbs on the Middlesex side of the Thames. First, Whitechapel was severed from it, and then, in the reign of Charles II., Shadwell; in the eighteenth century, Stratford, Spitalfields, St. George's-in-the-East, Limehouse, and Bethnal Green were taken out of it; and early in the present century it lost Poplar and Blackwall. The manor of Stepney was an ancient appurtenance of the See of London; but, in 1550, Bishop Ridley gave it up to Edward VI., by whom it was immediately granted to Lord Wentworth, the Lord Chamberlain of his household, and it remained in the possession of that family till the beginning of the eighteenth century.

Stepney Church is dedicated to St. Dunstan, and it is also sometimes spoken of as the church of " St. Dunstan and All Saints," the latter of which titles seems to have belonged to it at a period anterior to its dedication to the great Saxon Archbishop. There was both a rectory and a vicarage of Stepney, the former of which was a sinecure. The rectory was in the gift of the Bishop of London, and afterwards in that of the Wentworths; and the Rector appointed the Vicar. In 1710, shortly after the the rectory and advowson had been acquired by Brasenose College, Oxford, the two offices were united, John Wright, who had been over thirty years Vicar of Stepney, becoming Rector also.

Some of the Vicars of Stepney were very distinguished men. Richard Fox was presented in 1485, but did not hold the vicarage long. He was greatly esteemed by Henry VII., who, as soon as he obtained the throne, made him his secretary and a Privy Councillor, and shortly afterwards Keeper of the Privy Seal. In 1486 he was raised to the See of Exeter, and was translated in 1491 to Bath and Wells, in 1494 to Durham, and finally in 1502 to Winchester. While Bishop of Winchester he founded Corpus Christi College, Oxford. He died in 1528, and was buried in his cathedral.

John Colet, the illustrious founder of St. Paul's School, was for a short time Vicar of Stepney; he resigned in 1505, on being promoted to the Deanery of St. Paul's. Colet died in 1519, and was succeeded at St. Paul's by Richard Pace, who had a few months before been appointed Vicar of Stepney. Pace was reckoned a skilful diplomatist, and was employed in foreign negotiations by Henry VIII. and Wolsey: but in 1529, having fallen into disgrace, he was imprisoned in the Tower, where he remained for two years: during his confinement his intellect became impaired. On being released, he retired to Stepney, and died there in 1532. He had resigned the vicarage in 1527, and his successor was Richard Sampson, Dean of Windsor. The Deanery of St. Paul's he retained till his death, but, owing to his incapacity to perform its duties, Sampson was appointed his deputy; and at length Sampson succeeded him in the deanery as well as in the vicarage. When he became Dean of St. Paul's, Sampson resigned the Deanery of Windsor. The vicarage of Stepney he had resigned about two years before. He was made Bishop of Chichester in 1536, and in 1543 translated to Lichfield and created President of Wales. He died in 1554, having had

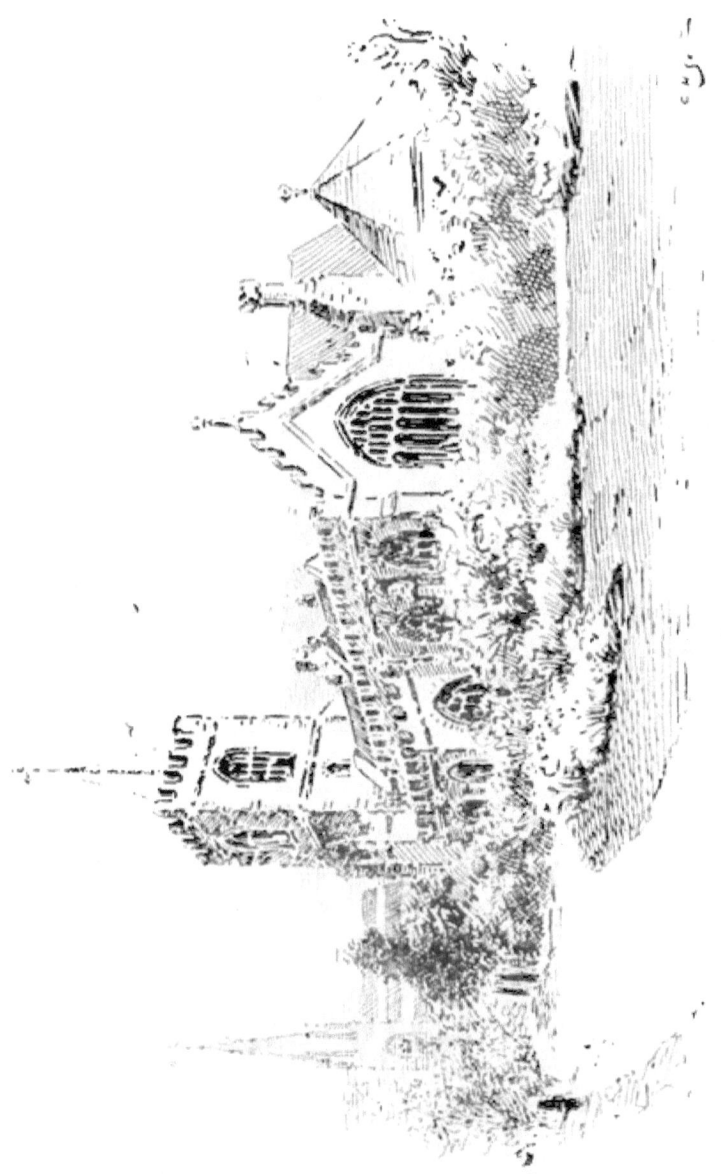

VEEDON CHURCH, SURREY.

a good deal of trouble in his later years owing to his attachment to Romanism. William Jerome, however, who became Vicar of Stepney in 1537, endured far greater sufferings for the reformed faith than Sampson underwent for Popery. He was burnt in Smithfield in 1541.

Dr. William Clarke, who was Vicar of Stepney from 1661 to 1679, and was also Dean of Winchester, deserves to be held in remembrance for his kindness towards his poorer clerical brethren. He left an estate in Essex to augment, by the annual sum of £30 each, ten small benefices situated in populous places. Four of these—the vicarage of Buckingham, the rectory of the Abbey in St. Alban's, Malden in Essex, and Stony Stratford—he named himself. He requested the Bishop of London and the Dean and Chapter of St. Paul's to select the rest. They fixed upon the vicarages of St. Giles, Northampton; St. Paul's, Bedford; Cirencester; Holy Trinity and St. Mary, Guildford; and Hatfield Regis and Deadham, Essex. Clarke's successor was John Wright, in whose person, as already noticed, the rectory and vicarage were first united.

St. Dunstan's Church is situated to the east of Stepney High Street, in a very large churchyard, which is tastefully laid out as a recreation-ground and forms an oasis which is doubtless much appreciated in that crowded locality. The church is an old Gothic edifice, containing a chancel, nave and two aisles, separated from the main body by clustered columns and pointed arches, apparently of the Perpendicular period. It measures 114 feet in length by 54 feet in breadth, and the height to the ceiling of the nave is 31 feet. At the west end is a square, battlemented tower about 90 feet high, in which are hung ten bells. The turret in the wall of the south aisle, containing remains of the stairs to the rood loft, indicates that the chancel formerly extended further westward than we now see it, and the easternmost bays of the aisles were chapels, within the screen, but not extending so far east as the main chancel; and an oblique opening known as a squint, through the walls of what

ST. DUNSTAN, STEPNEY. SOUTH PORCH.

was the north chapel, to enable persons therein to view the high altar, may still be observed. The internal roofs are of a plain character, containing woodwork of various periods, the most interesting, perhaps, being that over the south aisle, which in the carvings of the supports rising from stone corbels in the wall displays shallow ornamental work of the late sixteenth or early seventeenth century. The windows are all of Perpendicular character, but have, together with the external stonework, been repaired and restored. There are galleries on the north and south. The organ is placed to the north of the chancel.

On the north side of the chancel, within the communion rails, is the elaborate altar-tomb of Sir Henry Colet, twice Lord Mayor of London—in 1486 and 1495—the father of Dean Colet. He resided in a large mansion near the church, and died in 1510. He was a mercer, and the Mercers' Company have always kept his tomb in repair. On the south wall of the chancel, at a considerable height from the ground, is a monument to Sir Thomas Spert, the founder of the Corporation of the Trinity House. His epitaph is as follows:—

"D — O — M — Hereunder was laid up the Body of Sir Thomas Spert, Knight, sometime Comptroller of the Navy to King Henry VIII, and both the first Founder and Master of the Society or Corporation of the Trinity House. He lived innobled by his own Worth: and dyed the 8th of September, in the year 1541. To whose pious Memory the said Corporation hath gratefully erected this Memorial

> Not that he needed Monument of Stone,
> For his well-gotten Fame to rest upon:
> But this was reared to testify that he
> Lives in their Loves, that yet surviving be.
> For unto Virtue, which first raised his Name,
> He left the Preservation of the same,
> And to Posterity remain it shall
> When Brass and Marble Monuments do fall.
> Learn for to die while thou hast Breath
> So shalt thou live after thy Death."

Lower down is inscribed:—

"Anno 1622, by the Company of the Trinity House, this monument was erected 81 years after the decease of their Founder—1725."

There is a representation of a lightship, and at the bottom:—

"This monument was again repaired and beautified by the Corporation of the Trinity House in commemoration of their Founder in the year 1806. Earl Spencer, Master, Capt. Jos. Cotton, Dep. Mas^r."

On the north side, west of Colet's tomb, is a monument to Robert Clarke, son of Roger Clarke, Alderman of London, who died in 1610, aged thirty-six years. It is ornamented with kneeling figures of the deceased and his wife, Margaretta, by whom it was erected. She describes him, in the inscription, as "a man humble in prosperity, and a liberal distributor to the poore, courteous and affable to all; an upright and just dealer in this world, and a most religious seeker of the world to come."

On the opposite side is a tablet to William Dawtrey, of Lincoln's Inn, who died in 1589, with an inscription highly praising his abilities and legal learning; and another in memory of Thomasine, wife of John Brewster, who died in 1596. In the south-east corner is a large monument to Benjamin Kenton, who died in 1800, at the age of eighty-two. He was a native of Stepney, and having amassed considerable wealth in commercial pursuits, distinguished himself by his liberality towards hospitals and other charitable institutions. In allusion to his active benevolence, his monument is decorated with sculpture representing the departure of the good Samaritan from the inn, with the explanatory verse,—

"And on the morrow when he departed, he took out two pence, and gave them to the host, and said unto him, 'Take care of him; and whatsoever thou spendest more, when I come again, I will repay thee' (St. Luke x. 35)."

RIVERSIDE CHURCHES

In the north east corner, beyond Colet's tomb, is a memorial to the Rev. Thomas Dod, Rector of Stepney, who died in 1727. Also on the north side, farther west, is a tablet to another rector, Henry Leche, who died in 1742.

On the north of the nave, high up, is a monument, with kneeling figures, to Elizabeth, widow of Richard Startute, fishmonger of London, who died in 1620; it was erected, as the inscription sets forth, by her daughter, Clare, and her son-in-law, Michael Merrial. On the same side, more to the east, is a monument, with bust, to Sir John Berry, a gallant naval officer, who died, aged fifty-four, in 1689. Against the west wall is a monument to his widow, Dame Rebecca, who married for her second husband Thomas Elton of Stratford Bow, and died in 1696. Upon it are inscribed the following quaint lines in her honour:—

> "Come ladies, ye that would appear
> Like angels fine, come dress you here;
> Come dress you at this marble stone,
> And make this humble grave your own
> Which once adorn'd as fair a mind,
> As ere yet lodged in womankind.
> So she was dress'd, whose humble life
> Was free from pride, was free from strife
> Free from all envious brawls and jars,
> Of human life the civil wars;
> These ne'er disturbed her peaceful mind,
> Which still was gentle, still was kind.
> Her very looks, her garb, her mien,
> Disclos'd the humble soul within.
> Trace her through every scene of life,
> View her as widow, virgin, wife;
> Still the same humble she appears,
> The same in youth, the same in years:
> The same in low and high estate,
> Ne'er vex'd with this, ne'er moved with that.
> Go, ladies, now, and if you'd be
> As fair, as great, and good as she,
> Go learn of her humility."

ST DUNSTAN, STEPNEY

This memorial is commonly called the "Fish and Ring" monument, because a fish and ring appear in the arms with which it is emblazoned. Their appearance occasioned a tradition that Dame Rebecca was the heroine of the ballad entitled *The Cruel Knight: or, Fortunate Farmer's Daughter*, the story of which is to this effect. A knight, well skilled in magic, discovers that a child has been newly born who is destined to be his wife; but as she is a maiden of low degree, he endeavours to avoid his fate, and with this object seeks to destroy her. When she is grown to womanhood he leads her to the seashore with the intention of drowning her, but finally agrees to spare her life on condition that she shall never come into his presence again, unless she brings with her a certain ring, which he forthwith casts into the sea. She afterwards finds the ring in a fish she is cooking, and she and the knight are married. The "Fish and Ring" monument was originally placed on the outside of the church against the east wall, but has been removed to its present position for its better preservation.

Over the staircase leading to the north gallery is a tablet to Abraham Rallings, mariner, who died in 1644. On the south wall, towards the east end, is a tablet with a long Latin inscription to James Augustus Blondel, M.D., who died in 1734. Against the north wall is one to Hugh James, son of Hugh James, Rector of Upwell, who died in 1728.

Beneath the south east window is an inscription stating that this and the adjoining windows were presented by friends of the family in memory of Lieutenant Harold Charrington, R.A., son of Spencer Charrington of this parish, who was killed by Arabs in the desert of Mount Sinai on August 11, 1882. There are also some monuments in the church to members of the Charrington family.

At the west end, just within the church, is placed an ancient stone coffin, which was unearthed during the restoration of the church. In the west porch, on the north side, over a table of benefactors, there has been let into the wall a stone thus inscribed:—

> "Of Carthage wall I was a Stone.
> Oh Mortals! Read with pity:
> Time consumes all, it spareth none,
> Man, Mountain, Town nor City.
> Therefore, Oh Mortals! now bethink
> You whereunto you must,
> Since now such stately Buildings
> Lie buried in the dust.
> Thomas Hughes — 1663."

This seems to indicate that Thomas Hughes brought the stone from the ruins of Carthage, and planted it at Stepney; but who he was is unknown. It was originally fixed in the wall at the north-east; but, for fear of its becoming defaced, it has been transferred to this more sheltered situation.

In the south porch is a rudely carved sculpture of the Crucifixion, and in the north porch is another rude carving showing a figure adoring the Virgin and the infant Saviour. There are several monumental tablets on the outside of the church; among them may be noticed those of "Honest Abraham Zouch, of Wappin, Rope Maker," who died in 1648, and Captain Lawrence Browning, who died in 1675. In the vestry, which is situated at the north of the chancel, are several objects of interest, among them being a map of the parish, dated 1703, and exterior and interior views of the church, the former bearing date 1755, and the latter 1818; a copy of the figure of Bishop Fox in the east window of Winchester Cathedral; a print of Dean Colet; and engravings of the monuments of Sir Henry Colet and Sir Thomas Spert.

Weever mentions some notable tombs in Stepney Church, which have long vanished; those of Henry Stewart, Lord Darnley, son of the Earl of Lennox, who died in infancy in 1545, and whose younger brother, also named Henry, became the husband of Mary, Queen of Scots, and the father of James I. Dean Pace, who was buried in the church close to the high altar; John Kyte, who was, like Pace, a diplomatist, and was sent as ambassador to Spain, was made Archbishop of Armagh in 1513, Bishop of Carlisle in 1522, and died in 1537; and Nicholas Gibson, who was Sheriff of London in 1538, and founded a free school at Ratcliffe "for the instruction of threescore poore men's children by a schoolmaster and an usher; with an almeshouse for fourteene poore aged persons." He died in 1540. One cannot but regret that his monument has perished, for the truly poetical epitaph, which Weever has recorded, breathes a noble spirit of faith, charity, and resignation:—

"Here was I borne, and here I make myne end.
Though I was Citizen and Grocer of London,
And to the office of Schrevalty did ascend:
But things transitorie passe and vanische sone;
To God be geeven the thanks if that I have ought done,
  That to His honowre, and to the bringing up of youth,
  And to the succowre of the age; for surely this is soth.

By Avise my wyff children were left me non,
Which we both did take as God had it sent:
And fixed our myndes that joyntly in on,
To releve the poore by mutuall consent.
Now, mercifull Jesu, which hast assystyd owre intent,
  Have mercy on owre sowles, and as for the residew
  If it be Thy will, Thou mayst owre Act continew."

John Strype, that good old historian and antiquary, to whose untiring industry we owe so much valuable information, mentions the burial here of his father and two brothers.

"North ile, above the stone step . . . Just about this place lies buried John Van Stryp, Citizen, Silk-thrower, and Merchant of London, who deceased Jan 1647.

Near the same place lye interred by him two of his sons, John and Daniel, who dyed young."

In the churchyard are a vast number of tombs, but the older ones which stood close to the church walls have been removed during alterations, and some have fallen to pieces, so that it is not easy to find anything of historical interest in this wide-spreading place of sepulture. Prominent among the nearest to the church on the south side is the tomb of Matthew Mead. He was a Puritan divine, and ministered at Shadwell till he was ejected under the Act of Uniformity in 1662. He was afterwards minister to the Nonconformists at Stepney. In 1683 he was in danger from his alleged complicity in the Rye-House Plot, and took refuge in Holland, but returned to England when safety was restored. His Latin epitaph tells us that he died, in his seventieth year, in 1699, having laboured unremittingly and gloriously, with an undaunted spirit, for country, faith, and freedom. He was the father of Dr. Richard Mead, for many years the most eminent physician of his time, but for whose skill and care the *Night Thoughts* would never have been written, as Young himself has gratefully put on record:—

> "How late I shuddered on the brink! How late
> Life called for her last refuge in despair!
> That time is mine, O Mead! to thee I owe;
> Fain would I pay thee with eternity,
> But ill my genius answers my desire;
> My sickly song is mortal past thy cure,
> Accept the will; that dies not with my strain!"

And again he remarks that he is

> "Alive by miracle; or what is next,
> Alive by Mead!"

To Mead also, his fellow-physician, the poetical John Armstrong addressed, in language of reverence, the *Art of Preserving Health*:—

ST DUNSTAN, STEPNEY

> "Nor should I wander doubtful of my way,
> Had I the lights of that sagacious mind,
> Which taught to check the pestilental fire
> And quell the deadly Python of the Nile.
> O thou beloved of all the graceful arts
> Thou long the favourite of the healing Powers;
> Indulge, O Mead! a well-designed essay,
> Howe'er imperfect, and permit that I
> My little knowledge with my country share,
> Till you the rich Asclepian stores unlock
> And with new graces dignify the theme."

Dr. Mead, who was born at Stepney, and here commenced his professional career, died in 1754, in his eighty-first year, and was buried in the Temple Church. His son, also named Richard, was interred in Stepney Churchyard in 1762.

Near Mead's tomb is one which attracts attention from the oddity of its inscription:—

> "To the memory of Betsey Harris, who died suddenly while contemplating the beauties of the Moon the 24th of April 1831 in her 23rd year."

In Stepney Churchyard was buried a very gallant man, Sir John Leake, whose deeds were thus recorded in his epitaph:—

> "To the memory of the Honourable Sir John Leake, Knt., Rear Admiral of Great Britain, Admiral and Commander in Chief of her late Majesty Queen Anne's Fleet, and one of the Lords Commissioners of the Admiralty: departed this life the 21st of August, 1720, aetat. 64 years, one month, seventeen days: who, anno 1689, in the Dartmouth, by engaging Kilmore Castle, relieved the city of Londonderry in Ireland; also, anno 1702, with a squadron at Newfoundland, he took and destroyed fifty-one sail of French, together with all their settlements. Anno 1704, he forced the van of the French fleet at the Malaga engagement; relieved Gibraltar twice, burning and taking

thirteen sail of French men of war; likewise, anno 1706, relieved Barcelona, the present Emperor of Germany besieged therein by Philip of Spain, and took ninety sail of corn ships; the same year taking the cities of Carthagena and Alicant, with the islands of Ivica, Majorca, Sardinia, and Minorca."

On the accession of George I., Leake, who was suspected of not regarding the Hanoverian dynasty with any particular favour, was superseded in his command by Lord Aylmer. The rival Admirals both died at Greenwich in the same year and the same month, Leake surviving Aylmer three days. Here also was interred, in 1680, a very singular personage, by name Roger Crab. A pamphlet, mostly of his own composition, published in 1655, describes his opinions and mode of life, of which a summary is given in the title, which is as follows:—

"The English Hermite, or Wonder of this Age. Being a relation of the life of Roger Crab, living neer Uxbridg, taken from his own mouth, shewing his strange reserved and unparallel'd kind of life, who counteth it a sin against his body and soule to eate any sort of flesh, fish, or living creature, or to drinke any wine, ale, or beere. He can live with three farthings a week. His constant food is roots and hearbs, as cabbage, turneps, carrots, dock-leaves, and grasse: also bread and bran, without butter or cheese. His cloathing is sack-cloath. He left the Army, and kept a shop at Chesham, and hath now left off that, and sold a considerable Estate to give to the Poore, shewing his reasons from the Scripture."

He observes in his book:—

"Had my parents been so innocent as to have taught me this Doctrine in the time of my youth, I had saved my skull from being cloven to the braine in the late War for the Parliament against the King, and also saved my selfe from the Parliament's two years Imprisonment, which they gave me for my paines, and from my sentence to Death in the Field by my Lord Protector."

What he had done to bring upon himself the anger of the Lord Protector and the Parliament, he does not inform us; but we may reasonably conclude that the stroke which cleft his skull "to the braine" somewhat unsettled his intellect. He confesses that at the time of writing his narrative his vegetable diet by no means agreed with him, but, as he lived another five-and-twenty years his constitution apparently got inured to it. He had a long rhyming epitaph, in which he was styled "a temple undefiled with blood."

Among the entries in the parish register are recorded the baptism, on March 11, 1685, of William King, who was for forty-four years (1719-1763), Principal of St. Mary Hall, Oxford, and made himself celebrated by the extreme toryism of his sentiments; the marriage, on December 12, 1594, of Edward, third Earl of Bedford, and Lucy Harrington, who, as Countess of Bedford, was honourably known as the generous patroness of poetic merit; and that on July 27, 1669, of Sir John Cutler and Alicia Tipping; the burial, on August 26, 1596, of a man-servant of Sir Walter Raleigh; also that, on May 28, 1773, of the Rev. John Entinck, a voluminous miscellaneous writer, amongst whose numerous works were *A Naval History*; a *History of London, Westminster, and Southwark*; a *Present State of the British Empire*; a *Spelling Dictionary*, and a *Latin and English Dictionary*; of which the two last seem to have had the largest circulation.

The Rectory of St. Dunstan, Stepney, is now again, as it was in the days of old, in the patronage of the Bishop of London.

INTERIOR OF ST. ANN'S CHURCH

ST ANNE
LIMEHOUSE

THE church of St. Anne, Limehouse, was one of the fifty new churches appointed to be built under Queen Anne's Act, and its patron saint was selected in compliment to that sovereign. It was consecrated in 1730, and Limehouse, which had hitherto been a hamlet to Stepney, was made a distinct parish. The church stands on the south side of Commercial Road East, between Church Row on the west and Three Colt Street on the east, in a churchyard, which, though curtailed on the north at the beginning of this century, in consequence of the construction of the Commercial Road, is still extensive, and is laid out as a recreation-ground.

Nicholas Hawksmoor was the architect of St. Anne's, which is built of Portland stone. The exterior is striking and dignified; but the description of the different effects produced by it, which is given by Strype's continuator, John Mottley, who wrote under the name of Robert Seymour, can only be ascribed to the exuberant imagination of the "ingenious" person from whom he derived it.

"This church," says an ingenious architect, "is a most surprising, beautiful structure, which at a great distance shows a solemn solidity; yet, when nearly viewed, opposite to an angle, is one of the most airy, light, elegant, and magnificent buildings in this kingdom. The church itself consists of such simple beauty, that there is hardly anywhere to be produced its parallel; and its east or chancel end (which is of the Doric order, strictly executed after the ancient manner, without any other base to the pilasters than the square basement of the building) is certainly in the most august taste. The tower is a most magnificent pile, exhibiting the most solemn reverend aspect when viewed in front; and when at an angle the most gay and airy. This different appearance, upon changing the point of view, is surprisingly beautiful."

The appearance of the tower also suggested an odd conceit to Malcolm, the author of *Londinium Redivivum*, who "assures" his readers "that a sailor might be deceived by a distant view, in supposing it a very large ship coming towards him under an easy sail, with a flag flying at her maintop."

The tower, which is placed at the west end, is a very conspicuous object. It concludes with an octagonal lantern, with prominent Tuscan columns, surmounted by urns, and upon it is placed a tall flagstaff. Beneath it is the main entrance door, which is reached by ascending fifteen steps. The east front displays a central round-headed window, on each side of which are two pilasters, and beyond the pilasters two windows, one of them very small, on each side. The extremities of the eastern wall are dominated by two little towers. There are also towers at the west ends of the north and south walls, above the side doorways, which, like the chief entrance, stand at the top of a flight of steps.

The general plan of the interior is very similar to that of Hawksmoor's church of St. George's-in-the-East, already described, but without the transepts. The details, however, differ. The altar-recess is rectangular instead of apsidal, having an arched ceiling. The other compartments of the ceiling are flat with enrichments in plaster work. The church is more lofty than St. George's, and the order here used is composite. The

ST. ANNE, LIMEHOUSE (THE TOWER)

two aisles are each divided from the nave by two columns and one pier, there being corresponding pilasters on the east and west walls. The original fittings are said to have been handsome, but were mostly destroyed by fire in 1850. There are galleries on the north, south, and west, in the last of which the organ is placed. The pulpit, which stands on the north side, is of oak, and very fairly carved. It is mounted by means of a long flight of stairs, which commence a considerable distance off in the chancel. The font, which is situated at the west, is a handsome one. The window above the altar is filled with stained glass, representing the Crucifixion. The north and south walls each present two rows of plain windows. The north and south sides of the eastern recess have each four small windows. The light is freely admitted, the walls are coloured a pale green, and the church has a generally cheerful appearance.

The memorials of the dead are not particularly interesting, nor are there many of them in the church itself, though the tombs in the churchyard are numerous. In the vestibule, at the west end, through which entrance is gained to the church, is a monument surmounted by a female figure with the right hand pointing upwards, in memory of Maria Amelia Charlesworth, wife of the Rev. Samuel Beddome Charlesworth, twelve years Rector of Limehouse, and previously Rector of Limpsfield, Surrey. She died, aged fifty-five, in 1881, and was buried in Limpsfield Churchyard. "Her whole life from early childhood," says her epitaph, "was consecrated to the service of God, as the friend and loving instructor of the poor and their children, and in seeking to lead sinners to the Lord Jesus Christ as God their Saviour."

Also, in the vestibule, is a tablet to James Rollinson, "a man greatly beloved," who died, in his fifty-sixth year, in 1884. William Curling, "an eminent shipbuilder of this parish," who died in 1853, in his eightieth year, is commemorated by a tablet, with a highly laudatory inscription, at the east end of the north wall. A small slab in the chancel floor bears the name of "William George Yabsley, Organist of this Church 1882–1894. Died Easter Day, 1894."

The Rectory of St. Anne, Limehouse, is in the patronage of Brasenose College, Oxford.

ALL SAINTS', POPLAR

POPLAR

IN 1817, Poplar, which had hitherto continued a hamlet to Stepney, was created a distinct parish, and a parish church was built and dedicated to All Saints. Of greater interest, however, is the old chapel, which was made into a distinct church in 1867, and is now called the church of St. Matthias.

The history of the chapel is as follows :—In 1642 the inhabitants petitioned the East India Company to give them a piece of ground on which to erect a chapel and a house for the chaplain. The Company acceeded to this request, and gave the ground which was behind their alms-houses, and, in addition, sixty loads of stones that were lying there. The chapel appears to have been commenced at least as early as 1650, but as funds were not plentiful, the inhabitants again invoked the assistance of the Company, who granted them £200, and in the following year a further sum of £50. In 1654 the building was finished, and Thomas Walton was appointed the first chaplain by the Vicar of Stepney. The total cost exceeded £2,000, towards which Gilbert Dethick, a member of the famous family of heralds, contributed £100. Other particular benefactors mentioned are; Sir Henry Johnson, Thomas Tomlins, and Maurice Thompson. Dr. Josiah Woodward, who was chaplain in Strype's time, and from whom that historian obtained his information about the chapel, very quaintly narrates a story illustrating the piety of Mr. Thompson, "from whom," he says, "the present Lord Haversham is descended."

"And at the preaching of the first sermon in this chapel, our aforesaid benefactor, Mr. Thompson, gave an uncommon instance of his great humility and piety, in that he condescended to go into the clerk's desk, and there named and set the first Psalm that was sung in this chapel. And though some, perhaps, thought that he did a thing too mean for his quality; as the dancing of King David before the Ark was censured of old; yet the great honour, whereby God has since distinguished his posterity, may serve to demonstrate the sure accomplishment of God's promises of exalting the humble, and honouring those that honour Him."

After the appointment of the first chaplain, the Vicar of Stepney did not again exercise the patronage. The inhabitants in 1656 offered the right of nomination to the East India Company, as a token of gratitude for the munificence which the Company had shown towards them. Subsequently they endeavoured on several occasions to deprive the Company of this privilege, but the matter was finally settled in 1721, when the inhabitants, having besought the Company to repair the chapel, consented to a proposition on their part to keep it in constant repair, on the understanding that the Company's right to appoint the chaplain should be no longer disputed. The Company originally allowed the chaplain £20 a year, with lodgings and a garden and field. This they afterwards increased to £50, and towards the close of the eighteenth century further augmented it to £100. Two attempts were made in the seventeenth century, and another at the time of Queen Anne's Act for building new churches, to get Poplar formed into an independent parish. But they were unsuccessful, owing to the refusal of the Company to make a fixed endowment, and their insisting on treating the chaplain's stipend merely as a voluntary subscription, revocable at their pleasure. In 1776 the chapel was almost rebuilt by the Company.

ALL SAINTS', POPLAR, EAST END AND PULPIT.

The chapel, or, to speak more correctly, St. Matthias' Church, stands to the south of the East India Dock Road at the further end of an open space which is arranged as a recreation-ground. It is an insignificant building, with a small turret at the west end, and as the recreation-ground is rather large, it may easily be overlooked by those who are not familiar with the locality. A new chancel was made in 1875, and the church has been much altered, considerably to the detriment of its appearance. Some of the original fittings are said to have been constructed out of pieces of ships. The four columns on each side, which separate the aisles from the nave, were originally masts. The aspect presented by them is somewhat strange, but decidedly pleasing. The wooden eagle of the lectern is excellently carved, and is the work of a ship's carpenter. Each support of the communion table comprises a cluster of four legs all well carved. The top of the table is, however, modern and plain. On the ceiling are the arms of the East India Company.

On the south wall is a monument to Robert Ainsworth, the compiler of the famous Latin Dictionary used by so many generations of schoolboys. Ainsworth, who was a native of Lancashire, kept a school for many years in the eastern suburbs of London. He died in 1743, at the age of eighty-three, and a Latin epitaph written by himself is inscribed on his monument. On the north wall is a bas-relief by Flaxman, with an epitaph by Hayley, to the memory of George Steevens, the Shakespearean commentator. Steevens was born at Poplar, was baptized here in May, 1736, and buried here in January, 1800. He was the son of George Steevens, a sea-faring man, who died in 1763, and was interred in the chapel. There are several other monuments on the walls, but none of any remarkable interest. The most imposing is one—at the east end of the south aisle—to Philip Worth, a captain in the East India Company's service, who died in 1743.

The tombs in the churchyard are numerous. One of the

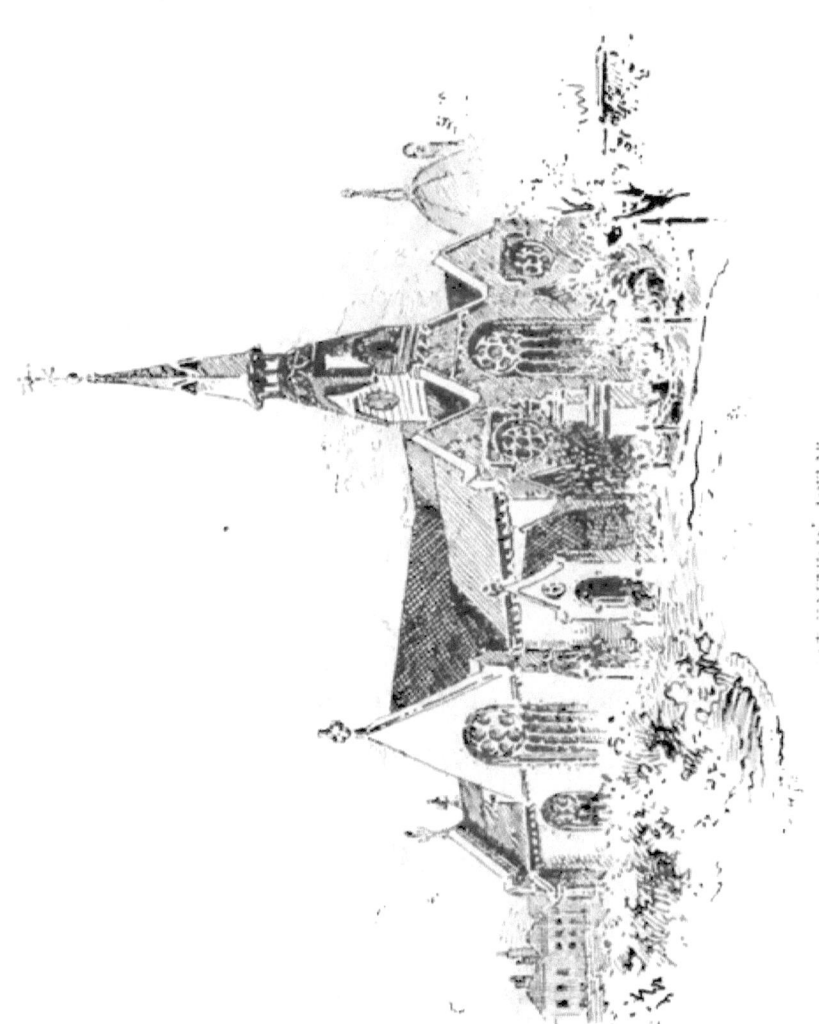

ST. MATTHEW'S, DOLLAR.

oldest is that of William Curtis, a commander in the East India Company's service, who died in 1669. The inscription records that: "he left by his will sixty pounds per annum for ever to apprentice poor children of Poplar, Mile End, Limehouse, Shadwell and Ratcliff, and for other charitable purposes. Also for an Annual Sermon to the Trustees in April or May." This inscription is evidently of comparatively recent date. The quaint lines, which Strype mentions as being on his tomb, have not been re-cut. They were as follows :—

"William Curtis of this Parish, Gent., warns you to Repentance.

> Whiles you can, before this Bed on you have Power,
> Make your Calling and Election sure.
> Fix your Mind on the Day of Doom,
> Be always waiting till your change do come.
> That so through Christ you rais'd may be,
> To heavenly Joys and blest Eternitie.

Deceased this Life the 27th of September 1669.

> Who in this Life fifty years did stand,
> And to East India sometime did bear command ;
> Who in his Life-time kept not fast his Door,
> And afterwards provided for the Poor,
>   Sixty Pound per Annum, for ever."

The most prominent tomb in the churchyard is that of Samuel Jones, a captain in the Navy, who died in 1734. "He engaged a superior force of the French off Cape Revella in 1706, and off Beachy Head in 1707 ; and with signal bravery and conduct put them to flight." His tomb, which is very large, is surmounted by an urn, and is ornamented with a bas-relief representing a ship. In the north corner of the churchyard is a great obelisk, standing on four balls, which are placed at the angles of a pedestal, in memory of Daniel Coppendale, who died in 1722. Dr. Gloster Ridley, chaplain of Poplar from 1729 to 1774, the

ST. MATTHIAS', POPLAR, INTERIOR

most distinguished man who ever held that office, was buried in the churchyard. He was born at sea in 1702 on board the

Gloucester East Indiaman, after which vessel he was named. He was a poet, a dramatist, and a controversial writer in defence of the Church of England; his most celebrated work was a Life of Bishop Ridley, the Martyr, who belonged to the same family as himself. In 1768 a prebend of Salisbury was bestowed on him by Archbishop Secker. Dr. Ridley was a benefactor to Poplar, for he revived the united Charity School for Poplar and Limehouse, which had for some years been discontinued, and secured the proper performance of the charitable wishes of Sir Henry Johnson, expressed in his will dated 1683, but neglected by his heirs. He was also Lecturer at Limehouse. His epitaph was written by Bishop Lowth.

All Saints, Poplar, is situated to the east of St. Matthias', and is also on the south side of the East India Dock Road. It stands in a good-sized churchyard. It is a stone, classical building—one of the best of its time, was designed by Charles Hollis, and consecrated on July 3, 1823, by Dr. William Howley, then Bishop of London, and subsequently Archbishop of Canterbury. At the west end is a portico, behind which rises a very graceful steeple, which attains the height of 161 feet. There are ten bells. A tall flagstaff is planted on the roof at the east end— an uncommon position. The interior would certainly be handsome, if the woodwork were not unfortunately of a mediocre character. A gallery runs all round the north, south, and west walls. The north and south walls each possess two rows of windows, six in each row. They are all filled with stained glass, except the easternmost and westernmost of the upper row on the south side, and the westernmost of the upper row on the north side. A recess at the east contains the altar. The entrance to it is formed by two lofty pilasters, between which are two detached colums, the entablature of which is continued to the pilasters. Over the entrance are the Royal Arms. The organ is at the west in the gallery; the font is at the same end beneath the gallery; the pulpit is on the south side close to the entrance to the eastern recess. The ceiling is unornamented; it is flat in the centre, but coved at the sides.

The Rectory of All Saints, Poplar, is in the gift of Brasenose College, Oxford; the Vicarage of St. Matthias is in that of the Bishop of London.

GREENWICH, ST. ALFEGE

ST ALFEGE
GREENWICH

IN the year 1011, the Danes, having sacked the city of Canterbury, carried Alfege, the Archbishop, a prisoner to their camp at Greenwich, and there, on his firmly refusing to pay them the large ransom which they demanded, they slew that brave patriot on April 19, 1012. Alfege was canonized, and the church of Greenwich, said to have been built on the spot where he died in his country's cause, was dedicated to him.

Greenwich had a long and intimate connection with English kings and princes. Edward I. sometimes resided here, and so did Henry IV.; Henry V. granted his possessions here to his brother Humphrey, Duke of Gloucester, the "good Duke Humphrey" of Shakespeare. Greenwich Park owes its origin to Duke Humphrey, by whom it was enclosed in 1433. A portrait of him in stained glass was in the old church of St. Alfege. After his death the house or palace, which he had rebuilt, came back to the Crown. It was enlarged by Edward IV, and again by Henry VII. Henry VIII. was born at Greenwich on June 28, 1491, and was baptized in the church of St. Alfege. He had a strong affection for his native place, and greatly augmented and ornamented the palace. Here he married Katherine of Arragon, on June 11, 1509, and here on February 18, 1516, their daughter Mary, afterwards Queen of England, was born. On May 13, 1515, the marriage of the King's sister Mary, widow of Louis XII. of France, with Charles Brandon, Duke of Suffolk, was publicly solemnized at Greenwich Church, they having already been privately married in France. On September 7, 1533, was born, at Greenwich, the daughter of Henry VIII. and Anne Bullen, afterwards the great Queen Elizabeth. Johnson remembered this when he wrote *London* :—

> "On Thames's banks in silent thought we stood,
> Where Greenwich smiles upon the silver flood;
> Struck with the seat that gave Eliza birth,
> We kneel, and kiss the consecrated earth."

At Greenwich too, at the beginning of 1540, was celebrated that fourth marriage, with Anne of Cleves, which caused Henry so much disappointment.

Charles II. commenced to rebuild the palace, and John Webb, Inigo Jones's pupil and executor, was employed as architect, and probably made use of some of the designs of his illustrious master; but the work was left unfinished. William and Mary assigned the palace for a hospital for aged and disabled seamen, and the new buildings were gratuitously designed by Sir Christopher Wren. It was not, however, opened till the reign of Queen Anne. Its subsequent history, and the transference of the premises, some five-and-twenty years ago, to the uses of the Royal Naval College, are well known.

In the old church of St. Alfege were several interesting monuments; amongst them those of Clement Adams, Master of the Children of the Chapel, who died in 1516; Richard Bower, Gentleman of the Chapel, and Master of the Children to Henry VIII., Edward VI., Queen Mary, and Queen Elizabeth, who died in 1561: and the illustrious composer, Thomas Tallis, Musician in the Chapel under the same four sovereigns, who died in 1585. His epitaph, a quaint one, has been preserved for us by Strype :—

ST ALFEGE, GREENWICH

> "Enterred here doth ly a worthy wyght,
> Who for long tyme in musick bore the bell,
> His name to shew was Thomas Tallys hyght,
> In honest vertuous life he did excell.
> He served long tyme in chappell with grete prayse,
> Fower sovereynes' reygnes (a thing not often seen)
> I mean Kyng Henry and Prynce Edward's dayes,
> Quene Mary, and Elizabeth our Quene.
> He maryed was, though children he had none,
> And lyved in love full thre and thirty yeres
> Wyth loyal spouse, whos name yclypt was Jone,
> Who here entombd him company now bears.
> As he did lyve, so also did he dy.
> In myld and quyet sort (O! happy man)
> To God ful oft for mercy did he cry,
> Wherefore he lyves, let death do what he can."

Tallis is better known to the ordinary Churchman than any musician of his day, since he was the author of the festival setting of the responses which is still in universal use in the Church of England.

Robert Adams, Surveyor of the Queen's Works, described as an architect of great skill, and a man most religious and virtuous, who died in 1595, was commemorated by a monument, erected in 1601, by Simon Basil, the Queen's Clerk of the Works. Here also was a monument to a more celebrated man, William Lambard.

William Lambard, who was born in 1536, was the son of John Lambard, Alderman of London, and Sheriff in 1551. He studied law at Lincoln's Inn, of which learned society he subsequently became a Bencher, and was a most indefatigable antiquary. In 1592 he was made a Master in Chancery, and in 1597 he was appointed Keeper of the Records at the Rolls Chapel. At the beginning of 1601 he became Keeper of the Records in the Tower; and on August 19 of the same year he died at West

Combe in the parish of Greenwich, the manor of which he had inherited from his father. Lambard was the author of several interesting and valuable works, the most celebrated of which is the *Perambulation of Kent*, the earliest of our county histories, which was published in 1576. He also composed "Αρχαιονομια," a translation of a collection of Anglo-Saxon laws, which appeared in 1568; treatises on the office of justice of the peace and the duties of constables and other local officers; and *Pandecta Rotulorum*, an account of the Records in the Tower, which he presented to Queen Elizabeth only fifteen days before his death. Besides these, he left behind him in manuscript, *Archeion; or a Commentary upon the High Courts of Justice in England*, which was published by his grandson in 1635; and materials for a general account of England on the lines of the *Perambulation of Kent*; these were at length given to the world in 1730, under the title of *Dictionarium Anglie Topographicum et Historicum*. Lambard was a charitable as well as a learned man. He established at Greenwich, in 1576, an almshouse or hospital for twenty poor persons, which he called "the College of the Poor of Queen Elizabeth," and which is said to have been the first institution of this kind founded by a Protestant. He drew up some very elaborate regulations as to the selection of the inmates, and placed his charity under the control of the Master of the Rolls and of the Drapers' Company, of which his father had been a member. One of the first bequests to Lambard's College was the sum of ten shillings per annum, left in 1587 by Joan Tallis, the widow of the musician. Since then it has received considerable benefactions. It was rebuilt in 1819, and is situated exactly opposite the South Eastern Railway Station.

The roof of the old church of St. Alfege collapsed in 1710, and a new church took its place. The fine collection of monuments of the distinguished dead was annihilated. Lambard's alone

ST ALFEGE, GREENWICH

survived. It was removed by his descendant, Thomas Lambard, and re-erected in Sevenoaks Church, where it remains to this day. Among the monuments which thus perished were those of Ralph Dallans, the organ builder, who died in 1672, while constructing an organ in Greenwich Church; and Sir William Hooker

GREENWICH, ST ALFEGE (INTERIOR)

Sheriff of London in 1665, and Lord Mayor in 1673, who died in 1697.

At Greenwich—with no memorial to mark the site of their graves—were buried, March 21, 1661, Lady Stayner, and, November 28, 1662, her husband, Sir Richard Stayner, a very gallant sailor. He served under Admiral Blake, and greatly distinguished himself against the Spaniards in 1656. In the following year he was with the heroic admiral in his last and grandest achievement, when he sailed into the bay of Santa Cruz, where lay sixteen Spanish galleons, and, protected though they were by the guns of a strong castle on the shore and six or seven smaller forts, burned every one of them, without the loss of a single English ship. In this splendid victory Stayner bore no inconsiderable part. When Blake, perceiving that it was impossible to carry off the galleons from their strongly guarded position, resolved to burn them, he "sent," says Clarendon, "Captain Stayner with a squadron of the best ships to fall upon the galleons, which he did very resolutely." On his return home, Stayner was knighted by Cromwell, and made a vice-admiral; and at the Restoration he was again knighted by Charles II., and made rear-admiral of the fleet.

The church of St. Alfege stands on the west side of Church Street, out of which Nelson Street branches off eastward about opposite to the north-eastern extremity of the church, and Stockwell Street about opposite to the south-eastern. After the fall of the old building, the parishioners succeeded in getting their new church included amongst the fifty to be built under Queen Anne's Act. It was consecrated by Bishop Atterbury in September, 1718. The body of the church was designed by Nicholas Hawksmoor; the steeple, which was not completed till 1730, is generally attributed to John James. The church is of Portland stone. The steeple rises at the west; it consists of a tower, a cupola resting on Corinthian columns, and a short spire, culminating in a ball and vane. There are ten bells. The east front is crowned with a pediment, and displays a large window in the centre, and smaller windows, each separated from it by a pilaster, at the sides. The north and south walls each present two rows of windows and a projecting entrance at the centre. The exterior is, on the whole, very imposing, and the interior is undeniably a fine one. There are no aisles, and the plan of the building is rendered cruciform by the projections already noticed on the north and south. The ceiling is flat and unornamented, except for a large circle, formed by mouldings, which encloses the greater part of it. The woodwork is of dark oak, solid and handsome. There are three galleries : the west gallery holds the organ ; the north and south galleries are continued along the east wall to the sides of the recess which contains the altar. The lower parts of the walls are panelled. The pulpit, which stands on the south side, is lofty and majestic, and is covered by a magnificent sounding-board. The altar-piece is of oak, and is flanked by Corinthian columns ; the decorations around it are said to have been executed by Sir James Thornhill. The window above is filled with stained glass representing the Crucifixion. On the east wall, beneath the extension of the north gallery, is a brass tablet in memory of Tallis, erected in 1876.

The easternmost window of the north wall over the gallery is in memory of General Wolfe. It displays a figure of St. George, at the sides of which are inscribed the names of the battles in which Wolfe was engaged : on the left side, Dettingen, Fontenoy, Falkirk ; on the right side, Culloden, Maestricht, Rochefort. Below the figure of St. George is a line from Gray's *Elegy* :—

"The paths of glory lead but to the grave,"

very appropriately placed here, since Wolfe was a great admirer of that poem, and repeated it to his officers the evening before his famous victory, saying that he would rather have been the author of it than take Quebec. Beneath are the figures of two cherubs holding a tablet, on which is depicted the scene of the General's death, copied from the picture by West. Above the tablet, "Quebec"; below it, "I thank God, and die contented," Wolfe's last words. At the bottom is this inscription, "James

Wolfe, General, born at Westerham 2 Jan. 1727. Died at the moment of victory, on the Heights of Abraham, Quebec, 13 Sep. 1759. Buried in the vaults of this church—November 1759."

Wolfe's body was brought to England, and, on November 20, 1759, it was laid beside that of his father, Lieutenant-General Edward Wolfe, who had been buried at Greenwich on April 2 of the same year. The elder Wolfe lived in a house at Blackheath. Except this window, which has only been quite recently erected, there is no memorial to the conqueror of Quebec in the place of his interment; but cenotaphs were erected in his honour at Westerham in Kent, his birthplace, by his fellow-townsmen, and in Westminster Abbey, at the public expense.

In the window on the south side, corresponding with that of General Wolfe, is a representation of a baptismal scene, beneath which appear the Royal Arms. Below is the following inscription:—"This window is placed here in memory of Isabella Elizabeth Hemmant, and to commemorate the baptism of H.M. King Henry VIII. in Greenwich Parish Church, A.D. 1491."

On the east wall over the north gallery is a bas-relief, on which appears the figure of an officer falling from his horse into a soldier's arms, with figures of other soldiers behind. This is the monument of Colonel Edward Sanders, a distinguished Indian officer, who fell in action, 1841.

Over the staircase leading to the south gallery is a grand oak frame, surmounted by the Royal Arms; on it are set forth the particulars of benefactions. Among the charitable deeds recorded is the following :—

"1694.—The Royal Hospital founded by King William and Queen Mary; confirmed by Queen Anne in 1702. Opened for Maimed Seamen in 1704, by order of His Royal Highness Prince George of Denmark, Lord High Admiral of England."

There were formerly in the church pictures of Queen

Elizabeth's tomb, Charles I., Anne and George I.; but these, sad to relate, were sold by some tasteless churchwardens.

In the churchyard, close to the tower, on the south side, enclosed by railings, is the large tomb, surmounted by a sarcophagus, of Sir John Lethieullier, who was a son-in-law of Sir William Hooker, was Sheriff of London in 1674, and died at an advanced age in 1718. Against the north side of the tower is a marble monument, crowned with an urn, to Sir James Creed, who died in 1762, and several members of his family. Near the south wall of the church is the gravestone of Lieutenant-General William Skinner, for twenty-one years chief engineer of Great Britain, who died in 1780.

At Greenwich were interred, without memorials: February 26, 1716, Richard Newcourt, for nearly twenty-seven years Principal Registrar of the Diocese of London, and subsequently a Procurator General of the Court of Arches, and author of that most valuable work, *Repertorium Ecclesiasticum Parochiale Londoniense: an Ecclesiastical Parochial History of the Diocese of London*; August 23, 1720, Mathew, Lord Aylmer, a distinguished seaman, who in 1709 was appointed Admiral and Commander-in-Chief of the Fleet, was re-appointed to that office, in the place of Sir John Leake, at the accession of George I., and was in the same year, 1714, made Governor of Greenwich Hospital, during his tenure of which position he originated the Royal Hospital School for the Sons of Seamen; and, February 3, 1760, Lavinia, Duchess of Bolton, who, as Miss Fenton, was the original Polly Peachum, and by her charming singing contributed in no small degree to the unparalleled success of the *Beggar's Opera*.

The patronage of the benefice of Greenwich was given in the thirteenth century to the Abbot and Convent of Ghent, but when Henry V. suppressed the priories alien, it was granted to the Carthusian monastery at Shene. Henry VIII. procured it from the prior and convent in 1530 by means of an exchange, and the vicarage has from that time remained constantly in the gift of the Crown.

Dr. Samuel Squire, with whose name Gray concluded the lines in which he sketched his own character—

> " A post or a pension he did not desire,
> But left Church and State to Charles Townshend and Squire "

—was Vicar of Greenwich from 1751 till his death in 1766. He was made Dean of Bristol in 1760, and Bishop of St. David's in the following year, but continued to hold his vicarage. He was succeeded at Greenwich by Dr. John Hinchliffe, who resigned the living in 1769, on being appointed to the Bishopric of Peterborough.

ST PAUL
DEPTFORD

IN consequence of the great increase of the population of Deptford, an additional church was built here under the provisions of the Act of Queen Anne for erecting fifty new churches in and about London. The edifice was consecrated on June 30, 1730, by Bishop Gibson, and dedicated to St. Paul.

St. Paul's Church, Deptford, stands in the midst of a large churchyard, extending from High Street on the west to Church Street on the east. It is of Portland stone, and is a strikingly handsome building. Thomas Archer was the architect. At the west is a flight of steps leading to the principal entrance. In front of the entrance is a dignified portico, above which rises a tapering spire. The north and south sides are each ornamented with Doric pilasters, supporting entablature and pediment, and have each at the centre a doorway to which access is gained by means of steps and a terrace. The east front displays a Venetian window and two subsidiary windows. The church measures 89 feet in length by 77 feet in breadth. It possesses two aisles, which are separated from the main body by Corinthian columns. The chancel terminates in a circular recess, wherein the altar is placed. The ceilings of the nave and aisles are flat, and are embellished with cornices and other ornaments. There are galleries on the north and south, and also one on the west, at a higher level, constructed to contain the organ—a fine instrument, originally built by Bridge, in 1730, and presented to the church by Benjamin Ffinch. All the wood-work is of dark Dutch oak, solid and majestic in appearance. The pews have been recently lowered, and it is intended to utilize some of the old wood for choir stalls. Prior to the late alterations the junction of nave and chancel was marked by a dwarf screen of carved woodwork, rising from the top of the pews, and extending across the church—a practice of which many examples formerly existed in the City churches. The pulpit originally occupied a central position in front of the altar-recess; it was moved in 1873, and deprived of its sounding-board. It has since been again moved, and is now on the north side; it has been reared on a four-legged platform, provided with a ladder-like flight of steps, and the result is rather odd than dignified. The sounding-board, which is large and very handsome, has been ignominiously cast out into the churchyard, where it is made to serve as the roof of a shelter for the gardener. The font, a recent acquisition, was brought from Rochester Cathedral; it is of a square shape, resting on four pillars, one at each angle, and further supported at the centre by a thick pedestal. To the south and west walls are affixed tablets commemorating benefactors. In the vestry may be seen a view of the interior of the church in its original state, and a view of the exterior, showing the old rectory, a quaint red-brick building pulled down in 1882.

On the north side of the chancel is a monument, by Nollekens, to Admiral Sayer, whose epitaph is as follows:—

> "In memory of James Sayer Esq, Vice Admiral of the White, son of John Sayer Esq and Katherine his wife, one of the daughters and coheirs of Rear Admiral Robert Hughes and Lydia his wife, who all lie buried in the old church of this town, with many of their issue. He was a man of the strictest honour and integrity; an active and

DEPTFORD, ST PAUL

diligent officer. In the war of 1739, he had the thanks of the Assembly of Barbadoes for his disinterested conduct in the protection of their trade; and he first planted the British standard in the island of Tobago. In the war of 1756, he led the attacks, both at the taking of Senegal and Goree: and was Commander in chief off the French coast at Belle Isle, at the time of making the peace, in 1763. As his life was most exemplary, he met death with a becoming fortitude, after a tedious and most painful illness, on the 29th of October 1776, aged 56 years."

On the same side is a monument to Mary, daughter of Benjamin Ffinch, and wife of Richard Hanwell, of Oxford. She died in 1754.

On the opposite side of the chancel is a very large monument, consisting of a tomb, sarcophagus, and urn, in memory of Matthew Ffinch, who died in 1745, and other members of that family. There is also a monument, with medallion bust, to Dr. Charles Burney, the eminent classical scholar, son of the Historian of Music and brother of Madame D'Arblay. He was Rector of St. Paul's, Deptford, and died here, at the age of sixty, on December 28, 1817. "The Parishioners of St Pauls Deptford," says the inscription, "erected this monument as a record of their affection for their revered pastor, monitor, and friend; of their gratitude for his services, and their unspeakable regret for his loss." The figure of St. Paul, the work of W. Collins, in the east window, was presented by Dr. Burney and six leading parishioners in 1813. After Burney's death his valuable library was purchased for the nation for the sum of £13,500, and deposited in the British Museum. His widow, a daughter of Dr. William Rose, the famous Chiswick schoolmaster, whose assistant Burney had been, survived him less than four years. A bust of Dr. Burney stands in the vestry.

ST PAUL, DEPTFORD

The churchyard contains a large number of tombs, but none of any extraordinary interest. Margaret Hawtree was buried here in 1734, with an inscription stating that—

> "She was an indulgent Mother, and the best of wives,
> She brought into this world more than three thousand lives."

She was a celebrated midwife, and presented both this parish and that of St. Nicholas with a silver basin for christenings.

On the south side of the churchyard is a tombstone, erected by the officers and men of the R Division, Metropolitan Police, as a token of their esteem for the memory of James Hastie, a constable of that division, who, on February 20, 1846, in this parish, while in the execution of his duty, received injuries from which he died fourteen days later.

By the Act of Parliament establishing the rectory of St. Paul's, Deptford, the advowson was, after a first presentation by the Crown, assigned to the Wickham family, then patrons of St. Nicholas. The patronage now appertains to the See of Rochester.

Dr. Richard Conyers was Rector from 1775 till his death in April, 1786. He is praised by Cowper in *Truth*:—

> "'Tis open, and ye cannot enter—why?
> Because ye will not, Conyers would reply—
> And he says much that many may dispute
> And cavil at with ease, but none refute."

John Newton preached his funeral sermon. He lies buried in the churchyard.

The Rev. Benjamin Sanderson Ffinch, a great grandson of the donor of the organ, was Rector from 1834 to 1874.

DEPTFORD, ST NICHOLAS

ST NICHOLAS DEPTFORD

DEPTFORD, ST. NICHOLAS—ONE OF THE GATEPOSTS

THE church of St. Nicholas is the original parish church of Deptford. It stands at the end of the Green, close to the Stowage. At the west rises an ancient weather-worn tower of flint and stone, which may perhaps date from the fourteenth century. It is 67 feet in height, and contains eight bells; but these are not now rung, as it has been declared dangerous to do so, having regard to the dilapidated condition of the upper portion of the tower. The total dimensions of the church are 86 feet in length and 62 feet in breadth. It consists of a nave, chancel, and two aisles, and is built of red brick, which contrasts oddly with the old flint and stone tower. It is of a much more recent date, having been rebuilt on a larger scale to accommodate the greatly increased number of inhabitants in 1697. Isaac

Loader, a wealthy parishioner, then High Sheriff of Kent, contributed over £900 to the rebuilding; but the work was so ill-performed that extensive repairs, which cost the parish about £400, were obliged to be executed before twenty years had elapsed.

There is a gallery at the west, which contains the organ, built originally by Father Smith; but the north and south galleries were taken down some years ago, and the oak sittings, which are said to have been very handsome, were sold, and deal substituted. The pulpit, which stands on the north side, is of oak, and is very finely carved. Above the entrance to the recess at the east in which the altar is placed, are affixed the Royal Arms. There is a very handsome oak altar-piece, surmounted by the Royal Arms; near the top some glass is inserted, on which are depicted the Virgin with the Infant Saviour, and Joseph, and the shepherds adoring. Against the east wall at the end of the south aisle hangs a picture of Queen Anne, by Kneller. It was intended for St. Paul's, Deptford; but as it was sent before that church was in a fit state to receive it, it was placed in St. Nicholas, where it has ever since remained. Beside it, protected by glass, is an elaborate piece of wood-carving, representing the prophet Ezekiel in the valley of the dry bones. The workmanship is splendid, and it is said that this carving was executed by Grinling Gibbons. It was at Deptford that Gibbons was discovered by John Evelyn, who brought his great artistic abilities before the notice of Charles II. The carving was formerly placed over the entrance to the mortuary at the south side of the churchyard.

Deptford, having been the seat of the Royal Dockyard and the Trinity House, is of course full of naval associations. In the church and churchyard are numerous memorials to seamen and shipbuilders. On the north side of the chancel is a monument of alabaster, with kneeling effigy, to Edward Fenton, who sailed with Sir Martin Frobisher, attempted to discover the north-west passage, and commanded the admiral's ship in the fight against the Spanish Armada. He died in August, 1603. The monu-

DEPTFORD, ST NICHOLAS—THE TOWER

ment was erected by the Earl of Cork, who married the daughter of Fenton's brother, Sir Geoffrey. There is also an inscription to Roger Boyle, the Earl's eldest son, who died in boyhood at Deptford in 1615. At Deptford reposes another of the Armada heroes, William Hawkins, who died in 1589. His monument, which was in the chancel of the old church, has perished. It was erected by his brother, the famous Sir John, who recorded upon it that he was "a worshipper of the true religion, an especial benefactor of poor sailors, a most just arbiter in most difficult causes, and of a singular faith, piety and prudence." "That, and the fact that he got creditably through some sharp work at Porto Rico," says Charles Kingsley, in *Westward Ho!* "is all I know of William Hawkins; but if you or I, reader, can have as much or half as much said of us when we have to follow him, we shall have no reason to complain."

On the east wall, at the end of the north aisle, is a monument to Peter Pett, a member of the great shipbuilding family of that name, and the inventor of the frigate, a representation of which species of ship adorns his memorial. He died in 1652, in the sixtieth year of his age, and his quaint Latin epitaph tells us that "he was a most just man and the Noah of his age, who, after he had walked with God and brought to light an invention even greater than that recorded of his prototype (for it was as an ark by which our mastery of the sea and our rights were saved from shipwreck), was called away from the tempests of this world, God being his pilot, and his soul resting in the bosom of his Saviour as in an ark of glory." On the same wall is a monument to Jonas Shish, Charles II.'s master shipwright, who died in 1680; and his sons, John, master shipwright of the King's Yard at Deptford, and Thomas, master shipwright of the King's Yard at Woolwich, who died in 1686 and 1685 respectively. Two of this family—Jonas Shish, who gave £16, and Charles Shish, who gave £5—appear in the list of subscribers to the rebuilding of Rotherhithe Church.

High on the south wall, above where the gallery formerly was, is a tablet to John Turner, captain of the *York* man-of-war, who, after having fought bravely against the Dutch and the Algerine pirates, died, aged twenty-seven, in 1672. On the north of the chancel, close to Fenton's monument, is that of George Shelvocke, F.R.S., Secretary of the General Post Office, "who," says his epitaph, "at a very early period of life, attended his father in a voyage round the world; during the course of which he remarkably experienced the protection of Divine Providence, and ever retained a most grateful remembrance thereof." He died in 1760, at the age of fifty-eight. His father, whose voyage is here referred to, was Captain George Shelvocke, whose tomb is in the churchyard, close to the east wall of the church; the inscription is as follows:—

> "Here lyeth the body of Captain George Shelvocke, descended of an ancient family in Shropshire; but long an inhabitant of this town. He was bred to the sea-service, under Admiral Benbow, and served on board of the Royal Navy in the wars of King William and Queen Anne. In the years of our Lord 1719, 20, 21, and 22, he performed a voyage round the globe of the world, which he most wonderfully, and to the great loss of the Spaniards, compleated, though in the midst of it he had the misfortune to suffer shipwreck upon the Island of Juan Fernandez on the coast of the kingdom of Chili. He was a gentleman of great abilities in his profession, and allowed to have been one of the bravest and most accomplished seamen of his time. He departed this life in London, Nov. 30, 1742, in the 67 year of his age."

His wife, Susanna, daughter of Captain Richard Strutton, is commemorated by a tablet on the outside of the east wall, just above her husband's tomb. She died long before him—in 1711.

On the outside of the north wall, towards the west end, is a tablet to John Addey, a master shipwright to James I., who died in 1606. The inscription states that it was set up at the expense of the parish in 1788, his original monument having perished. Beneath this is a second tablet, declaring that John Addey bequeathed £200 "to procure a perpetuale annuity towards the reliefe of the poor people of Deptford to last for ever"; that a piece of ground on the east side of Church Street was purchased with this money, and that in the year of the erection of the tablet—1862—the annual income of the charity had increased to over £650, out of which 40s. each was annually given to 100 poor parishioners of Deptford, and large schools for the poor children of the town were maintained. "This tablet," concludes the inscription, "is erected by the Trustees of the Charity to commemorate this good deed of a good Man." Below, at the foot of the wall, is a grave-stone marked with John Addey's name. Addey's School is in Church Street, on the estate purchased with his bequest. An inscription in the front states that it was built in 1821, and enlarged in 1862.

Within the church, on the floor of the north aisle, is the grave-stone of John Benbow, son of Admiral Benbow. In 1702, being the mate of an East Indiaman, he was shipwrecked on the coast of Madagascar, where he met with many adventures amongst the natives. He finally got back to England on board a Dutch vessel, and died in 1708. On the east wall, at the end of the south aisle, is a tablet to Robert Castell, "who lived beloved and died lamented by all good men." The year of his death was 1698. When the church was rebuilt, he had the organ gilded at his sole expense.

On the same wall is a monument to Sir Richard Browne, "of Sayes Court in Deptford," and Dame Joanna, his wife,—their son Christopher, and Thomasine, his wife, and Sir Richard, Christopher's son, and his wife, Elizabeth. The elder Sir Richard, states the inscription, "was younger son of an ancient family of

Hitchin in Suffolk; seated afterwards at Horsley in Essex; who being student in the Temple was, by Robert Dudley the great Earl of Leicester, taken into the service of the Crown, when he was Governour of the United Netherlands. And was afterwards by Queen Elizabeth made Clerk of the Green Cloth; in which honourable office he also continued under King James, until the time of his death, in May, 1604. Aged 65 years." The younger Sir Richard, his grandson, "was," we are informed, "Gentleman of the Privy Chamber to King Charles I. and Clerk of the Privy Council to his Majesty, and to King Charles II. And, after several foreign and honourable employments, continued Resident in the Court of France from King Charles I. and from King Charles II. to the French kings, Lewis XIII. and Lewis XIV., from the year 1641 until the happy Restoration of King Charles II, Anno 1660. He deceased 12 February 168¾. Aged 78 years.

"This table was erected by John Evelyn of Sayes Court, Esq., who married Mary sole Daughter and Heir of Sir Richard."

John Evelyn, who thus acquired Sayes Court, which by his skill and taste in gardening he rendered famous, retired in his later years to his paternal seat at Wotton, in Surrey, and there he was buried. There are tablets, in St. Nicholas, close to Sir Richard Browne's monument, in memory of two of his children, who died young. His name is commemorated in Deptford by Evelyn Street, and that of his troublesome visitor, Peter the Great, by Czar Street. The house at Sayes Court was used as a workhouse from 1759 to 1848, and during this period it was rebuilt. It was afterwards used as an emigration depot. In 1881 it was made into almshouses by Mr. W. J. Evelyn, and is still thus used. The park has been converted by Mr. Evelyn into a recreation ground for the inhabitants, and the hall, which stands in it, is employed for the purposes of an Institute, under the management of the Goldsmiths' Company. A tablet on the north wall of the church records the benefaction of Sir John Evelyn, who in 1750 gave some land for the benefit of the poor of the parish.

The posts of one of the churchyard gates are decorated with antique carvings of a skull and cross-bones.

The parish register notes the burial of Christopher Marlowe, "slaine by ffrancis Archer, the 1 of June 1593."

The patronage of the living of St. Nicholas, Deptford, belonged until the dissolution of monasteries to the Abbot and Convent of Begham in Sussex. After that event the advowson of the vicarage was retained by the Crown till the reign of Charles I. Since then it has been always in the hands of private patrons. Among them was Sir John Cutler. Dr. George Stanhope was Vicar of St. Nicholas from 1700 till his death in 1728. He was made Dean of Canterbury in 1703, and gained a considerable reputation by his theological works. He exerted himself greatly in the establishment of a school at Deptford, towards which he himself contributed £150. He was buried at Lewisham, of which place also he was vicar. His school is no longer in existence, but the endowment is used for the granting of exhibitions to boys and girls of the parishes of St. Nicholas and St. Paul, Deptford. The living was held from 1737 to 1762 by a clergyman with the sad-sounding name of Thomas Anguish. A monument was erected to his memory in the churchyard.

INDEX

Alleyn, Edward. Memorial window to, in St. Saviour's, Southwark, 222.

Andrewes, Lancelot, Bishop of Winchester, Tomb of, in St. Saviour's, Southwark, 213.

Anne, Queen, Picture of, by Kneller, in St. Nicholas, Deptford, 306.

Archer, Thomas, Architect of St. John's, Westminster, 151; of St. Paul's, Deptford, 299.

Arnold, Sir Edwin, Lines by, in St. Margaret's, Westminster, 177.

Ashmole, Elias, Tomb of, at Lambeth, 145.

Austin, William, Monument to, in St. Saviour's, Southwark, 218, 219.

Bacon, Francis, lived at Twickenham Park, 32; baptized at St. Martin's-in-the-Fields, 186.

Barnard, Sir John, buried at Mortlake, 60, 61.

Baxter, Richard, Memorial window to, in St. Saviour's, Southwark, 222, 223.

Beaufort, Cardinal, South transept of St. Saviour's, Southwark, restored by, 208; his arms affixed to a pillar, 216.

Beaumont, Francis, Memorial window to, in St. Saviour's, Southwark, 222.

Benson, E. W., Archbishop of Canterbury, Lines by, in St. Margaret's, Westminster, 167.

Berkeley of Stratton, John, Lord, Monument to, at Twickenham, 30, 32.

Blake, Admiral Robert, Memorial window to, in St. Margaret's, Westminster, 177, 178.

Blake, William, married at Battersea, 121.

Bligh, Vice-Admiral William, Tomb of, at Lambeth, 149, 150.

Blomfield, Sir Arthur, Fulham Church rebuilt by, 88; new nave of St. Saviour's, Southwark, built by, 212, 221.

Blomfield, Charles James, Bishop of London, Memorial window to, at Fulham, 95; tomb of, 98.

Blood, Colonel Thomas, buried at St. Margaret's, Westminster, 179.

Bolingbroke, Henry St. John, Viscount, Monument to, by Roubiliac, at Battersea, 116, 117.

Bonner, Edmund, Bishop of London, buried at St. George's, Southwark, 224.

Bourchier, Thomas, Archbishop of Canterbury, Arms of, on the Font at Mortlake, 57.

INDEX

Bourne, Vincent, buried at Fulham, 97.

Brooks, Bishop Phillips, Memorial window to, in St. Margaret's, Westminster, 167.

Bunyan, John, Memorial window to, in St. Saviour's, Southwark, 222, 223.

Burney, Dr. Charles, Rector of St. Paul's, Deptford, 302.

Butts, Sir William, Monument to, at Fulham, 89, 90.

Byron, Admiral John, buried at Twickenham, 39.

Byron, Lord, Lines of, on Sir Peter Parker, 171, 172.

Cambridge, Duke and Duchess of, buried at Kew, 52, 53.

Campbell, Thomas, married at St. Margaret's, Westminster, 180.

Caroline, Queen, Death of, at Hammersmith, 82, 83.

Catherine of Arragon, Queen, Portrait of, in stained glass, at St. Margaret's, Westminster, 162.

Cavendish, Lord Frederick Charles, Memorial window to, in St. Margaret's, Westminster, 169, 170.

Caxton, William, Memorial window to, in St. Margaret's, Westminster, 166, 167.

Charles I., King, Picture of, in Rotherhithe Church, 247.

Chaucer, Geoffrey, Memorial window to, in St. Saviour's, Southwark, 222, 223.

Cheyne, Lady Jane, Monument to, by Bernini, at Chelsea, 131, 132.

Churchill, Charles, Account of, 154-156.

Clive, Catherine, Monument to, at Twickenham, 36, 37.

Colet, Sir Henry, father of Dean Colet, Tomb of, at Stepney, 262.

Compton, Henry, Bishop of London, Tomb of, at Fulham, 95; views of, about burials, 96.

Cowper, William, Adventure of, in St. Margaret's Churchyard, 180.

Crab, Roger, Strange history of, 270, 271.

Crispe, Sir Nicholas, Loyalty of, 80, 81; bust of Charles I., placed in Hammersmith Church by, 82, 85.

Cruden, Alexander, Memorial window to, in St. Saviour's, Southwark, 222, 223.

Dacre, Gregory, Lord, Monument to, at Chelsea, 130.

Danvers, Dame Magdalen, mother of George Herbert, buried at Chelsea, 136, 137.

Dickens, Charles, his "Little Dorrit," 227, 228; his room in Lant Street, 229.

Disraeli, Benjamin, Earl of Beaconsfield, his description of St. John's Church and Rectory, Westminster, 152, 154.

Dryden, John, Epitaph by, at Twickenham, 33.

Dudley, Mary, Lady, Monument to, in St. Margaret's, Westminster, 168.

Elizabeth, Queen, Portrait of, in stained glass, at Battersea, 114; born at Greenwich, 290.

INDEX

Evelyn, John, his residence, Sayes Court, Deptford, 311, 312.

Eversley, Charles Shaw Lefevre, Viscount, Memorial to, in St. Margaret's, Westminster, 169.

Farnborough, Sir Thomas Erskine May, Baron, Memorial window to, in St. Margaret's, Westminster, 169.

Fauconberg, Countess of, daughter of Oliver Cromwell, buried at Chiswick, 72.

Fenton, Captain Edward, Monument to, in St. Nicholas, Deptford, 306, 307.

Fitzwilliam, Richard, Viscount, Monument to, at Richmond, 24, 25.

Flaxman, John, Monuments by, at Richmond, 24; at Poplar, 282.

Fletcher, John, Memorial window to, in St. Saviour's, Southwark, 222.

Flitcroft, Henry, Architect of St. Olave's, Southwark, 232.

Foscolo, Ugo, Monument to, at Chiswick, 70, 71.

Francis, Sir Philip, Monument to, at Mortlake, 59, 60.

Gainsborough, Thomas, Tomb of, at Kew, 54, 55.

Garrick, David, Epitaphs by, at Chiswick, 66, 68.

Gibbon, Edward, baptized at Putney, 105.

Gibbons, Grinling, Monument by, at Fulham, 93; carving in St. Nicholas, Deptford, said to be his, 306.

Gibbs, James, architect of St. Martin's-in-the-Fields, 182-185; bust of, in the church, 186; portrait of, in St. Martin's Town Hall, 188; architect of St. Mary-le-Strand, 190-194; steeple of St. Clement Danes built by, 199, 200.

Gibson, Edmund, Bishop of London, Tomb of, at Fulham, 94, 96; rector of Lambeth, 150.

Goldsmith, Oliver, Memorial window to, in St. Saviour's, Southwark, 222.

Gorges, Sir Arthur, Monument to, at Chelsea, 129, 130.

Gower, John, Benefactor to St. Mary Overy, 208; tomb of, 221.

Grandison, Oliver St. John, Viscount, Monument to, at Battersea, 115, 116.

Hamey, Dr. Baldwin, Monument to, at Chelsea, 127, 128.

Harvard, John, baptized at St. Saviour's, Southwark, 223.

Hatherley, William Page, Baron, Memorial window to, in St. Margaret's, Westminster, 168.

Hawksmoor, Nicholas, Architect of St. George's-in-the-East, 251, 252; of Limehouse Church, 273-276; of Greenwich Church, 294, 295.

Henry VII., King, Portrait of, in stained glass, at Battersea, 114.

Henry VIII., King, baptized in Greenwich Church, 289; memorial window to, 296.

Hogarth, William, Tomb of, at Chiswick, 67-69.

Hook, Theodore Edward, Tomb of, at Fulham, 97.

Hunter, John, buried at St. Martin's-in-the-Fields — subsequently removed to Westminster Abbey, 187.

INDEX

Impey, Sir Elijah, Monument to, at Hammersmith, 84, 85.

Jackson, John, Bishop of London, Fulham Church consecrated by, 88; memorial window to, at Fulham, 95; tomb of, 98.
James I., King of Scotland, married at St. Mary Overy, 208.
James, John, Architect of Twickenham Church, 29; of Greenwich steeple, 294.
Johnson, Hester, Swift's "Stella," baptized at Richmond, 26, 27.
Johnson, Dr. Samuel, his account of Sir Nicholas Crispe, 81; his remarks on Pope's epitaph on Elizabeth Corbett, 174, 175; his seat at St. Clement Danes, 201; memorial window to, in St. Saviour's, Southwark, 222; his "London," 290.

Kean, Edmund, Monument to, at Richmond, 25.
Kneller, Sir Godfrey, buried at Twickenham, 37, 38.

Lambard, William, Account of, 291-293.
Laud, William, Archbishop of Canterbury, chapel of Hammersmith consecrated by, 79.
Lawrence, Thomas, and family, Monuments to, at Chelsea, 132.
Leake, Admiral Sir John, buried at Stepney, 269, 270.
Lee Boo, Prince, Tomb of, at Rotherhithe, 244, 245.
Liverpool, Louisa Theodosia, Countess of, Monument to, by Chantrey, at Kingston, 6.
Longley, Charles Thomas, Archbishop of Canterbury, Memorial window placed in Putney Church by, 100.
Lowth, Robert, Bishop of London, Tomb of, at Fulham, 96.

Marlowe, Christopher, buried at Deptford, 312.
Mary of Modena, Queen, sought shelter at Lambeth, 141.
Massinger, Philip, Memorial window to, in St. Saviour's, Southwark, 222.
Milton, John, Memorial window to, in St. Margaret's, Westminster, 171; his house in Westminster, 179.
Moore, Thomas, married at St. Martin's-in-the-Fields, 186.
Mordaunt, John, Viscount, Monument to, at Fulham, 92.
More, Sir Thomas, chapel added to Chelsea Church by, 123, 128-130, 133; monument of, 125, 126.
Morris, Sir Lewis, Lines by, in St. Margaret's, Westminster, 178.

Newcourt, Richard, buried at Greenwich, 297.
Nollekens, Joseph, Monument by, at Isleworth, 45; in St. Paul's, Deptford, 300.
Northumberland, Jane, Duchess of, Monument to, at Chelsea, 128, 129.

Otway, Thomas, buried at St. Clement Danes, 205.

Pearson, J. L., R.A., Chiswick Church rebuilt by, 63.

INDEX

Pepys, Samuel, married at St. Margaret's, Westminster, 180.

Pope, Alexander, Monuments to himself and parents at Twickenham, 33, 35; his epitaph on Kneller, 38; his house at Chiswick, 73; epitaph by, in St. Margaret's, Westminster, 174, 175.

Raleigh, Sir Walter, Tablet to, in St. Margaret's, Westminster, 166; memorial window to, 170.

Rich, Mrs., daughter of Oliver Cromwell, buried at Chiswick, 72; married at St. Martin's-in-the-Fields, 186.

Robinson, John, Bishop of London, Tomb of, at Fulham, 96.

Sacheverell, Dr. Henry, Memorial window to, in St. Saviour's, Southwark, 222, 223.

Salisbury, Robert Cecil, Earl of, baptized at St. Clement Danes, 204.

Sayer, Vice-Admiral James, Monument to, in St. Paul's, Deptford, 300, 302.

Shakespeare, William, Memorial window to, in St. Saviour's, Southwark, 222.

Sharp, Granville, Monument to, at Fulham, 95.

Shelvocke, Captain George, Tomb of, at St. Nicholas, Deptford, 309.

Sherbrooke, Robert Lowe, Viscount. Memorial to, at St. Margaret's, Westminster, 165.

Sherlock, Thomas, Bishop of London, Tomb of, at Fulham, 96.

Sidmouth, Henry Addington, Viscount. Monument to, at Mortlake, 59.

Sloane, Sir Hans, Monument to, at Chelsea, 135, 136.

Smart, Admiral Sir Robert, Monument to, at Chiswick, 74.

Smith, Alderman Henry, Monument to, at Wandsworth, 110.

Smith, William Henry, Memorial windows to, in St. Martin's-in-the-Fields, 186.

Spert, Sir Thomas, Founder of the Trinity House, Monument to, at Stepney, 262, 263.

Stayner, Admiral Sir Richard, buried at Greenwich, 293, 294.

Steevens, George, Monument to, at Poplar, 282.

Stuart, Arabella, Memorial window to, in St. Margaret's, Westminster, 167.

Suckling, Sir John, baptized at Twickenham, 39; his "Ballad upon a Wedding," 46.

Sunderland, Dorothy, Countess of, Waller's "Sacharissa," baptized at Isleworth, 46.

Tait, Archibald Campbell, Archbishop of Canterbury, Memorial window to, at Fulham, 95.

Tallis, Thomas, buried at Greenwich, 290, 291; memorial to, 295.

Tenison, Thomas, Archbishop of Canterbury, Tomb of, at Lambeth, 144; Vicar of St. Martin's-in-the-Fields, 188.

Thomson, James, Monument to, at Richmond, 20, 21.

Thorold, A. W., Bishop of Winchester,

INDEX

restoration of St. Saviour's, Southwark, originated by, 211, 212.

Tradescant, John, Monument to, at Lambeth, 148, 149.

Vancouver, Captain George, Monument to, at Petersham, 13.

Wakefield, Gilbert, Monument to, at Richmond, 23.

Walpole, Horace, Epitaph at Putney by, 104.

West, Nicholas, Bishop of Ely, Chapel at Putney built by, 100, 101.

Wolfe, General James, Anecdote of, 24; memorial window to, at Greenwich, 295, 296.

Woodfall, Henry Sampson, Monument to, at Chelsea, 135.

Wren, Sir Christopher, Isleworth Church partially designed by, 41; St. Clement Danes rebuilt by, 199, 200, 202; Greenwich Hospital designed by, 290.

Wynter, Sir Edward, Monument to, at Battersea, 117, 118.

Young, Edward, His "Night Thoughts," 179, 268.

Zoffany, Johan, Monument to, at Kew, 55.

BY

A. E. DANIELL

WITH NUMEROUS ILLUSTRATIONS BY

LEONARD MARTIN

WITH A MAP SHOWING THE POSITION OF EACH CHURCH

Imperial 16mo, 6s.

The intention of this book is to present to the public a concise account of each of the churches of the City of London. If any reader should be induced to explore for himself these very interesting, but little known buildings, wherein he cannot fail to find ample to reward him for his pains, the object of the writer will have been attained.

This volume is profusely illustrated from drawings specially made by Mr. Leonard Martin, and from photographs which have been prepared expressly for this work.

"The author of this book knows the City churches one and all, and has studied their monuments and archives with the patient reverence of the true antiquary, and, armed with the pen instead of the chisel, he has done his best to give permanent record to their claims on the nation, as well as on the man in the street."—*Leeds Mercury.*

"His interesting text is accompanied by numerous illustrations, many of them full-page, and altogether his book is one which has every claim to a warm welcome from those who have a taste for ecclesiastical archæology."—*Glasgow Herald.*

"This is an interesting and descriptive account of the various churches still extant in London, and is illustrated by several excellent photographs. . . . His work will be of value to the antiquarian, and of interest to the casual observer."—*Western Morning News.*

"Mr. Daniell's work will prove very interesting reading, as he has evidently taken great care in obtaining all the facts concerning the City churches, their history and associations."—*London.*

"The illustrations to this book are good, and it deserves to be widely read."—*Morning Post.*

ARCHIBALD CONSTABLE & CO
2 WHITEHALL GARDENS WESTMINSTER

Boswell's Life of Johnson

Edited by AUGUSTINE BIRRELL.

With Frontispieces by ALEX ANSTED, a reproduction of Sir JOSHUA REYNOLDS' Portrait.

Six Volumes. Foolscap 8vo. Cloth, paper label, or gilt extra, 2s. net per Volume. Also half morocco, 3s. net per Volume. Sold in Sets only.

"Far and away the best Boswell, I should say, for the ordinary book-lover now on the market." — *Illustrated London News.*

". . . We have good reason to be thankful for an edition of a very useful and attractive kind." — *Spectator.*

"The volumes, which are light, and so well bound that they open easily anywhere, are exceedingly pleasant to handle and read." — *St. James's Budget.*

"This undertaking of the publishers ought to be certain of success." — *The Bookseller.*

"Read him at once if you have hitherto refrained from that exhilarating and most varied entertainment; or, have you read him? — then read him again." — *The Speaker.*

"Constable's edition will long remain the best both for the general reader and the scholar." — *Review of Reviews.*

In 48 Volumes

CONSTABLE'S REPRINT
OF
The Waverley Novels

THE FAVOURITE EDITION OF
SIR WALTER SCOTT.

With all the original Plates and Vignettes (Re-engraved). In 48 Vols.

Foolscap 8vo. Cloth, paper label title, 1s. 6d. net per Volume, or £3 12s. the Set. Also cloth gilt, gilt top, 2s. net per Volume, or £4 16s. the Set; and half leather gilt, 2s. 6d. net per Volume, or £6 the Set.

"A delightful reprint. The price is lower than that of many inferior editions." — *Athenæum.*

"The excellence of the print, and the convenient size of the volumes, and the association of this edition with Sir Walter Scott himself, should combine with so moderate a price to secure for this reprint a popularity as great as that which the original editions long and fully enjoyed with former generations of readers." — *The Times.*

"This is one of the most charming editions of the Waverley Novels that we know, as well as one of the cheapest in the market." — *Glasgow Herald.*

"Very attractive reprints." — *The Speaker.*

". . . Messrs. Constable & Co. have done good service to the reading world in reprinting them." — *Daily Chronicle.*

"The set presents a magnificent appearance on the bookshelf." — *Black and White.*

ARCHIBALD CONSTABLE & CO
2 WHITEHALL GARDENS WESTMINSTER

1422–1509

EDITED BY JAMES GAIRDNER

OF THE PUBLIC RECORD OFFICE

3 Vols. Fcap. 8vo. With 3 Photogravure Frontispieces, cloth gilt extra, or paper label uncut, 16s. net.

These letters are the genuine correspondence of a family in Norfolk during the Wars of the Roses. As such, they are altogether unique in character; yet the language is not so antiquated as to present any serious difficulty to the modern reader. The topics of the letters relate partly to the private affairs of the family, and partly to the stirring events of the time: and the correspondence includes State papers, love letters, bailiff's accounts, sentimental poems, jocular epistles, etc.

"This edition, which was first published some twenty years ago, is the standard edition of these remarkable historical documents, and contains upward of four hundred letters in addition to those published by Frere in 1823. The reprint is in three small and compact volumes, and should be welcome to students of history as giving an important work in a convenient form."—*Scotsman.*

"Unquestionably the standard edition of these curious literary relics of an age so long ago that the writers speak of the battles between the contending forces of York and Lancaster as occurrences of the moment."—*Daily News.*

"One of the monuments of English historical scholarship that needs no commendation."—*Manchester Guardian.*

ARCHIBALD CONSTABLE & CO
2 WHITEHALL GARDENS WESTMINSTER

NOW BEING PUBLISHED

The New Popular Edition

OF THE

Works of George Meredith

Crown 8vo, 6s. each.

With Frontispieces by BERNARD PARTRIDGE, HARRISON MILLER, and others.

THE ORDEAL OF RICHARD FEVEREL
EVAN HARRINGTON
SANDRA BELLONI
VITTORIA
RHODA FLEMING
THE ADVENTURES OF HARRY RICHMOND
BEAUCHAMP'S CAREER
THE EGOIST
DIANA OF THE CROSSWAYS
ONE OF OUR CONQUERORS
LORD ORMONT AND HIS AMINTA
THE AMAZING MARRIAGE
THE SHAVING OF SHAGPAT
THE TRAGIC COMEDIANS
SHORT STORIES
SELECTED POEMS

ARCHIBALD CONSTABLE & CO
2 WHITEHALL GARDENS WESTMINSTER

"One has grown accustomed to the association of Mrs. Steel's name with novels which deal exclusively with Indians and Anglo-Indians. Such powerful and remarkable books as 'The Potter's Thumb' and 'On the Face of the Waters,' point to a specialism which is becoming one of the salient features of modern fiction; but 'In the Tideway,' although dealing entirely with England and Scotland, presents the same keen and unerring grasp of character, the same faculty of conveying local atmosphere and colour, the same talent for creating strong and dramatic situations, and the same originality of thought and expression. . . . It is too late in the day to speak of Mrs. Steel's position. This is assured, but <u>this book adds greatly to an established position. It is profoundly impressive.</u>"—*St. James's Budget*.

"Wonderfully bright and lively; both in dialogue and incidents."—*Scotsman*.

"Admirably written."—*Glasgow Herald*.

"The story is beyond question powerful. The characters are life-like, and the dialogue is bright and natural."—*Manchester Guardian*.

"As it is, the book is a sheer triumph of skill, one degree perhaps less valuable than a fully conceived presentation of the actual, but none the less admirable within its limits. There is care shown in every character. . . . But the real art, perhaps, lies less in the sequence of events or the portrayal of character, than in just this subtle suggestion everywhere of the abiding causeless mystery of land and sea."—*Academy*.

ARCHIBALD CONSTABLE & CO

2 WHITEHALL GARDENS WESTMINSTER

The Folly of Pen Harrington

By JULIAN STURGIS. 6s.

"Decidedly to be recommended as light and lively reading."—*Manchester Guardian*.
"Very pleasant reading indeed."—*Glasgow Herald*.
"The tale throughout is fascinating."—*Dundee Advertiser*.
"A thoroughly entertaining story."—*Daily Telegraph*.
"Bright, piquant and thoroughly entertaining."—*The World*.
"A clever and brightly-written novel."—*Black and White*.
"Will hold its own with any work of the same class that has appeared during the last half-dozen years."—*The Speaker*.

Green Fire: A Story of the Western Islands

By FIONA MACLEOD,

Author of "The Sin Eater," "Pharais," "The Mountain Lovers," etc.

Crown 8vo, 6s.

"There are few in whose hands the pure threads have been so skilfully and delicately woven as they have in Fiona Macleod's."—*Pall Mall Gazette*.

The Laughter of Peterkin

A Re-telling of Old Stories of the Celtic Wonderworld.

By FIONA MACLEOD.

Crown 8vo, 6s. Illustrated.

A book for young and old.

Odd Stories

By FRANCES FORBES ROBERTSON.

Crown 8vo, 6s.

The Dark Way of Love

From the French of M. Charles le Goffic.

Translated by E. WINGATE RINDER.

Some Observations of a Foster Parent

By JOHN CHARLES TARVER.

Crown 8vo, 6s.

"If there were more schoolmasters of the class to which Mr. Tarver evidently belongs, schoolmasters would be held in greater honour by those who have suffered at their hands. His 'Observations of a Foster Parent' are excellent reading; we hope they will reach the British parent. He may be assured the book is never dull."—*Glasgow Herald*.
"A series of readable and discursive essays on Education. The book deserves to be read."—*Manchester Guardian*.
"The book is one which all parents should diligently read."—*Daily Mail*.

ARCHIBALD CONSTABLE & CO

2 WHITEHALL GARDENS WESTMINSTER

www.ingramcontent.com/pod-product-compliance
Lightning Source LLC
Chambersburg PA
CBHW021151230426
43667CB00006B/341